THE

NEW

SAVAGE

NUMBER

THE NEW SAVAGE NUMBER

HOW MUCH MONEY DO YOU *REALLY* NEED TO RETIRE?

TERRY SAVAGE

WILEY

John Wiley & Sons, Inc.

Published by John Wiley & Sons, Inc., Hoboken, New Jersey.
Published simultaneously in Canada.

For general information on our other products and services or for technical support, please contact our Customer Care Department within the United States at (800) 762-2974, outside the United States at (317) 572-3993 or fax (317) 572-4002.

Wiley also publishes its books in a variety of electronic formats. Some content that appears in print may not be available in electronic books. For more information about Wiley products, visit our web site at www.wiley.com.

ISBN 978-0-470-53876-0

Printed in the United States of America

10 9 8 7 6 5 4 3 2 1

Grow old along with me!
The best is yet to be,
The last of life, for which the first was made . . .
                                        —Robert Browning

CONTENTS

Part 3   Investing for Retirement

Part 5   Long-Term Care: The Greatest Risk of All

Part 6   Estate Planning: The Price of Success

PREFACE

Will we *ever* be able to retire? The answer remains the same as my message in the first edition of *The Savage Number*: Yes. You can and will retire—but you will have a different definition and time frame for that decision.

In the few short years since the first edition of *The Savage Number*, the question has changed from "How much do you need?" to "Is it possible?" The massive stock market crash, the swoon in real estate values, and a major recession have shaken Americans' faith in their financial future.

But, just as Americans were too optimistic about their retirement prospects a few years ago, I believe we have become far too pessimistic about the future.

As I prepare this updated edition of *The Savage Number*, I am pleased that my message remains the same: You *can* reach financial security, if you make a plan and stick to it—and if you have realistic goals.

My original purpose in writing this book was to give a reality call to all those who had been planning to retire early—and live on their inflated house values and stock market profits. The recent economic and market activity haven't changed my advice—but the world's financial woes have made more people open to the message.

Some of the writing seems prescient, as in my warning chapter about stock market valuations, or the danger of relying on residential real estate to fund your retirement. I had even written about the dangers of mortgage-backed securities and their impact on real estate values!

But it's not "game over" for America—or for your retirement plans.

I have not changed my fundamental belief in the future growth of the American economy, and with it the stock market. And the stock market is the one way you can have access to participate in all that growth, and build your own wealth.

I'm not a market timer, as you'll see from this book. But when the extremes of either pessimism or optimism sway the greatest number of people, it's time to stand back and rethink your position.

The pendulum always swings to extremes. In the past decade, we've moved from an extreme of optimism about having it all to an extreme of negativity about America's potential to survive and prosper. Now you see why it's so important to have a disciplined financial plan.

Let's agree on one thing: If the pessimists are correct, then it really doesn't matter how your investments are structured. If it's the end for America, then you don't need to worry about the value of your stock portfolio!

But before you give up on the future, take a closer look at history. America has been though tough times before—and we've always come back stronger and growing. It's not just the lessons of the Depression in the 1930s. That sounds like ancient history. We don't have to go back that far to learn that it's never wise to bet *against* America.

Those under age 50, who are shocked by the current economic recession, don't remember the recession of 1980–1982. That was an equally scary time—when the prime rate was 21 percent, mortgage rates were 15 percent, both unemployment and inflation had reached double digits, and the Dow Jones Industrial Average was under 800!

But America came through those tough times—and soared to a new era of economic growth based on productivity created by technology. In that dismal recession of 1981, few would have guessed that within 20 years the stock market would trade over 14,000 or that Internet technology would revolutionize the way we work, live, and learn.

History never repeats exactly—but it does teach us lessons. This has been a different kind of recession from any we've seen before—because it is fueled by an unprecedented level of debt. (That is something I have warned against in all my writings for the past 20 years!) So we'll need a different sort of resolution.

Remember Newton's law of physics that you learned in high school? *For every action there is an equal and opposite reaction.* Excesses of debt must unfortunately be wiped out, creating an excess of pain for those who overborrowed. If America can get through this process without losing the free markets that created such wealth throughout our history, then we will be setting the stage for the next period of real growth.

It is never possible to know the future. Forecasts, predictions, and prognostications are always impacted by current events. It is our job to plan for all of those eventualities—whether ongoing economic slowdown or the next boom that will be triggered by an invention yet unknown.

And we must also be prepared to survive mistakes made by well-meaning politicians and economists. No one political party or economic theory has a monopoly on good—or bad—ideas. But we know that economic growth requires a currency that retains its value, laws that protect the value of assets, and markets that can be trusted.

That's what *The New Savage Number* is all about—creating your own financial security that will help you ride through the tough times, even in retirement. Now it's more important than ever that you understand the risks—and potential rewards—of your investments, and your entire financial plan. So let's get *re*-started!

THE
NEW
SAVAGE
NUMBER

INTRODUCTION

Can You Retire?

In spite of—or perhaps as a result of—stock market reversals, declining home values, and job insecurity, you've decided to give some serious thought to the possibilities of retirement. You may be approaching the traditional retirement age and seeing your dreams recede. Or you may be just starting your career, and wondering about whether you should invest your hard-earned money in a seemingly capricious stock market.

If you believe in your future—and the future of America—then you must plan, save, and invest for that future. That's true no matter what your age or stage in life. Over the long run, that has always been a winning formula.

You've seen the scary headlines about the impact of the financial markets' collapse upon boomer retirement plans. Dreams of early retirement have given way to the nagging worry that you'll *never* be able to retire. Savings and retirement assets have melted away, before your eyes.

Now you can respond in one of two ways: (1) you can refuse to think about it, or (2) you can take time to figure out your options and get help. Plans may have to be revised, but that can't happen until you take an honest look at your situation—and get some disciplined, professional help. Believe me, getting good help with retirement planning is easier and less expensive than you think. The whole point of this book is to show you the way.

When it comes to retirement planning, you need both a goal and a plan to reach that goal. You want a simple answer to your most important financial question: *How much money do I need to retire?* And then as you enter retirement, you have one more question: *How much money can I spend every month and not run out of money before I run out of time?*

Well, let me ask *you* a few questions:

- At what age do you want to retire?
- How much money have you saved already?
- How much money do you think you'll need every month for living expenses?
- What's your estimate for the inflation rate during your retirement years?
- What's your risk tolerance for investments?
- And by the way, how long do you think you'll live?

If you knew those answers for sure, retirement planning would be easy. But life is filled with uncertainty. That's no excuse for avoiding the issue.

A quick search of the Internet on the subject of retirement calculators offers nearly one hundred web sites, mostly from financial services companies and financial planning firms. They will instantly calculate how much money you need to retire based on your answers to those basic questions. The amounts may be intimidating.

One of the best online calculators is the "Ballpark Estimate" worksheet at www.choosetosave.org. It will show you how much you *should* be saving every month. But you'll need more than these calculators to plan for a successful retirement. You need personalized advice about how to invest your money along the way. And you'll need a withdrawal plan that ensures you won't run out of money before you run out of time.

Now that kind of personalized advice is within reach of the average American, in a format that is not only understandable and practical, but individual. It's called Monte Carlo modeling, but it has nothing to do with gambling. Quite the contrary. It's a very exacting analysis of probabilities. And it's the basis for making informed decisions about our retirement finances.

The *Savage Number*—how much money you *really* need to retire—is a personal and unique number, but it is knowable. It comes with advice on getting *to* the number, as well as getting *through* your retirement years with enough money to cover foreseeable expenses. In fact, the Savage Number is readily available to you, at no cost but your willingness to think about it and accept help. It will take more than a few minutes and a few mouse clicks, but it will be well worth your time.

You may not have a lot of money saved. In fact, you may not have saved anything. You may be living with credit card debt. Time marches on, even if your investments don't. And at some point in the future, you're going to want to retire, or your job will retire from you.

What does the word *retire* mean? Each of us will have our own definition. You may have been thinking of retirement as a full-time vacation in a sunny spot near a golf course. For others retirement will mean a part-time job to maintain a reasonable standard of living. And for some, it will be dependence on programs like Social Security and Medicare.

Odds are we'll live longer than our parents will. And odds are they'll use up all their money living longer than they planned. So we won't have an inheritance to rescue us. And odds are our children—for those who have them—won't want to spend their scarce dollars taking care of us.

Should we be scared? Absolutely not. We're the generation that grew up in the shadow of the Cold War and the Soviet Union; nuclear fears and the Doomsday Clock; unprecedented inflation that spawned a 21 percent prime interest rate and 15 percent mortgage rates; the worst recession since the Great Depression; the biggest bear market since the crash of 1929; and the worst terrorist attack on our country since Pearl Harbor.

We've survived all that. Certainly we can survive retirement! And we can do it in style, if we start thinking about it now—thinking about the balance between living our lives to the fullest today and giving ourselves a chance at the lifestyle we want in the future.

Baby boomers have always changed America, and we're about to do it again as we age. Younger workers are learning from our mistakes—and starting earlier to save and invest—and plan for *their* retirement. Given wise leadership and sensible tax policies, America will grow into a new future, with new technologies. And that economic growth will support retirees *and* bring investment opportunities to the next generations. It will also provide the resources for you to reach your own Savage Number, and your own secure retirement.

PART 1

RETRO-RETIREMENT

CHAPTER 1

THE SAVAGE NUMBER

The subject of retirement both beckons and repels. If you didn't want to think about retirement before the recent stock market crash and the recession, is it any easier now?

The answer is a resounding *yes*. That's because now everyone is aware that retirement is going to be a problem—*if* we define it in the traditional way. But it's also easier because now there are more resources dedicated to helping you rethink the possibilities for your retirement—whether it's on the near horizon or many years down the road.

Today my original comments about redefining retirement make even more sense. I called this section "Retro-Retirement" to explain that the retirement in your future might look a lot more like your grandparents' situation than the one you were dreaming about. Generations before us worked longer, had fewer years of leisure, and cut back their lifestyles in retirement.

If you're a younger reader, Gen X or Gen Y, you can still remodel your retirement plan. Time is on your side, if you start to plan now. But for baby boomers, who always expected a different and better retirement lifestyle, it's time to face reality. Only if we agree to work longer, save more, and adjust our plans can we enjoy retirement security.

It's time to face an important Savage Truth: Time is money. Time can leverage money, if younger workers save regularly and invest wisely. And time can devastate our retirement resources though a longer life expectancy. That's why it's so important to rethink retirement now, while we still have some flexibility.

There's another fact to face: We must rely on ourselves, and not our government for support above the basic necessities of life. Boomer retirement is likely to be a Category 5 hurricane, sweeping onshore in the United States. Our government simply won't be able to create the resources to fund our retirement dreams, without creating a devastating inflation. No, our retirement lifestyle is definitely up to us. And what one generation demands will impact the next.

We may avoid thinking about retirement because we assume we can't make our dreams come true or because we're too busy surviving the present to worry about the future. Or maybe we fool ourselves into thinking that something will come along to save us. After all, it always has. But those aren't realistic approaches.

We all share that lingering worry: *Can I possibly retire?*

There's a simple answer to that question. We can, and will, retire at some point. Or the job will retire from us! The challenge is to make the most of those retirement years by making sensible decisions now.

Most retirees will need to continue to earn extra money, even during their "retirement" years. Leisure time and work time will require a different sort of balance. But we're living longer—and that leaves us more time to divide between work and play. And the sooner we start thinking about that new retirement reality, the easier it will be to shape it.

SHAPING RETIREMENT REALITY

Thinking about the Savage Number can be overwhelming. It includes not just the money you need in order to retire, but also the money you must continue earning—either on your investments or by other income—while you are *in* retirement. It involves deciding how much you can withdraw to spend and still make your money last as long as you do. And it carries the responsibility of investing to meet your goals amidst uncertainty about everything from inflation to health-care needs.

Retirement will take on an entirely different meaning for the baby boomer generation. We'll live longer, need more money, have less security from Social Security, pay more for medical expenses, and generally face more financial challenges than any other generation. Retirement no longer means whiling away a few years in a golfing community or enjoying the sun on a park bench, as it may have for our parents or grandparents. Longevity adds to uncertainty.

But don't fear. Just as the baby boomers redefined society from kindergarten to college to the job market, the power of this huge generation will redesign retirement. We will work longer, though probably at different jobs than our life careers. We will be flexible about our lifestyles and more concerned about our health than about our material possessions.

Boomers chose the Beatles and the Rolling Stones. Boomers were fueled by McDonald's and Coke. And, in turn, companies that catered to boomers became profitable investments. That will happen again, as retiring boomers demand new products and services. Because of its size, the boomer generation will always impact the economy. And the economy will find a way to accommodate us.

Boomers are reaching age 50 at a rate of more than 12,000 a day—one person every eight seconds. That statistic comes from AARP—the organization that sends you a birthday greeting and a membership application on the day you turn 50. They should know!

Over the next decade, the 76 million members of the baby boomer generation will start reaching the traditional retirement age of 65. Today, there are more than 35 million Americans over the age of 65. By 2025, that number will nearly double. (See Figure 1.1.) Seniors will comprise a voting pool with more clout than ever.

That power of the baby boomer generation will last a long time because people are living longer. Today, when a man reaches age 65, his life expectancy is another 16.3 years. A 65-year-old woman today can expect to live another 19.2 years. But those are just averages. That means half of us will live longer, and half won't make it that far. And we'll never know in advance which half we fall into. We worry when we hear of friends dying from cancer or suffering with infirmities. Suddenly we feel our mortality. But statistics show that the fastest-growing population cohort is people over age 100. You might be one of them!

Percent
Change

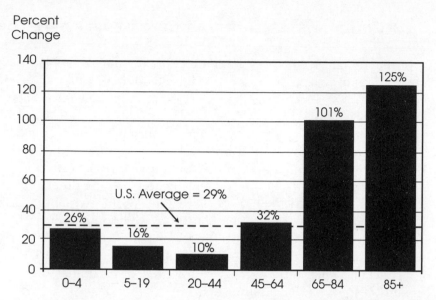

Figure 1.1 The United States Is Aging: Projected Change in Population by Age Group, 2000–2030
Source: Milken Institute. Reprinted with permission.

We can assume, on average, that we'll live longer than our parents because of advances in medical science that prolong life. And given our influence, we'll be heard in the halls of Congress when we demand more attention to our needs—from nursing homes to drug benefits.

Boomers will also be teaching their children a living lesson about saving and spending. If you're a member of Gen X or Y, you've seen firsthand the dangers of living on credit card debt and home equity. You've also seen unprecedented volatility in the stock market. But that shouldn't scare you out of investing in America—and the world. After all, once you've finished taking care of your aging parents, you're going to need investment growth to fund your *own* retirement.

This gap between the generations has the potential to cause great social stress. So we must be aware of how dependent we are on each other to solve the multigenerational retirement issue.

Avoiding Generation Warfare

Government can't take care of boomers if the younger generations refuse to be taxed to pay for our care. Unless boomers plan for our own secure future, we risk creating generation warfare in the United States. If your own children aren't willing to take care of you, how can you expect other people's children to do the job through their tax dollars?

It's not just a question of morality. Even in a growing economy, there simply won't be enough of the next generation to support us *and* educate their own children. During the baby boomers' peak working years, 1980 to 2000, there were almost four people of working age for each person over age 65. But as we boomers retire, that ratio will shift. By 2035, there will be fewer than three people working for each person over 65. And remember that those workers— our children—will be trying to care for their own families on what remains of their paychecks after taxes.

As you can see in Figure 1.2, unless cuts are made in government programs, retiree benefits will soon consume the majority

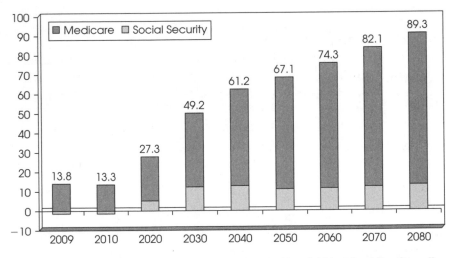

Figure 1.2   Percentage of Income Tax Revenues Needed to Meet the Payroll Tax Shortfall on Social Security and Medicare
Source: National Center for Policy Analysis (NCPA). Calculations based on data from the 2008 Medicare and Social Security Trustees Reports. Reprinted with permission.

of our tax revenues, leaving little for defense, education, or other national needs. According to the trustees of the Medicare program, by 2019, 24 percent of all income tax revenues will be needed for the Medicare program. The curve grows exponentially. By 2040, 51 percent of all income tax revenues will have to go to Medicare. Social Security trust funds are expected to have a negative outflow of cash by 2017—and to become insolvent by 2041.

Actually, Social Security has for many years been a system of transfer payments. Even as you get a statement from Social Security listing your contributions and promised benefits, you should realize that those benefits are being funded each year out of general tax revenues. There is no trust fund, no shoebox in Baltimore with your money inside it. The deduction from your paycheck this week will pay for a retiree's check next month.

According to the Congressional Budget Office, the $659 billion in benefits that Social Security paid out in the 2009 fiscal year exceeded payroll taxes collected ($653 billion) for the first time since 1984, when that huge Social Security tax increase was enacted to fix the system for the boomer generation.

Now they predict that there will be only an $83 billion surplus in the fund by 2018. And that prediction will be impacted by declining payroll taxes caused by prolonged unemployment. The bottom line: There simply isn't enough money coming in to pay for all those promised benefits.

Social Security is likely to undergo major changes before or during your retirement. The benefits you expect to receive will be postponed to a later retirement age—and could even be means-tested—to keep those payments from sinking the entire federal budget. Social Security is *not* your safety net. And no matter how much you've saved for your retirement, the biggest hole in your personal safety net is the rising cost of health care.

Medicare cannot continue to fund the current level of health benefits—including the newest treatments and prescription drug benefits—for this growing population of seniors. Don't look to your previous employer for help. Companies are cutting back on retiree health benefits at a time when costs for medical services are rising twice as fast as traditional measures of consumer price inflation.

Neither Medicare nor Social Security covers the cost of long-term custodial care, either in your own home or in a nursing home, except for a very limited number of days after a hospitalization. Government tries to provide custodial care for impoverished seniors through state-run Medicaid programs, but the facilities that offer that care will be sorely strained by the huge boomer generation.

Planning to become impoverished by gifting assets to your children so that Medicaid will cover your care is a recipe for disaster. You'll give up the freedom of choice you get when you purchase long-term care insurance to cover those costs.

Some people are hoping that the government will simply print enough money to fund the promised government retirement benefits. But creating more money through inflation destroys the value of everything you've saved. We learned that lesson in the 1970s, when the government tried to create enough new money to have both guns and butter. We certainly don't want our government to try to give us both bridges and benefits in 2030, just when both are wearing thin!

Government is not the solution. It will contribute, but not enough. Sometimes it's even part of the problem. State and municipal pension promises are under attack by taxpayers who refuse to authorize state income tax hikes. Even some corporate pension promises are being called into question. It's up to us to rearrange current lifestyles and expectations for the future. And we have to do it now, while we have flexibility.

HOPING FOR A MIRACLE?

There will be no miracle solutions to make your retirement dreams come true—not the government, the stock market, the family home, or a windfall inheritance.

For a while, it seemed like the stock market would bail out boomers' retirement dreams. Employees were admonished for decades to save and invest money in company retirement plans or individual retirement accounts, but many failed to do so. Those who did had unrealistic expectations. The stock market crash has destroyed their hopes that outsized investment returns would offset a lack of diligence in savings.

If history is a guide, stock market investments should outperform other alternatives over the long run—at least 20 years. But even the recent experience with stock market losses should not be an excuse to stay away from stocks. In fact, it's the reverse: You'll need even more exposure to equities in your retirement investment assets to rebuild your financial plans. It's a paradox, but just when people are most scared of the market, they should keep in mind that it has always offered the greatest opportunity to profit over the long run.

For some people, hopes for a financial miracle rested on residential real estate. But real estate is a market just like stocks—and far less liquid. By now, you should have learned that when any market's gains exceed historic trends, the bubble will burst. Housing prices in many areas collapsed by a greater percentage than stock prices. And it will take years for housing prices to recover—unless a major inflation psychology takes over. But don't give up on using your home equity: Reverse mortgages will still offer seniors a way to create tax-free retirement income, if they've paid down almost all of their mortgage balance, as explained in Chapter 14.

And forget about inheriting money from your parents. According to AARP, in recent years baby boomers who had received an inheritance received a median of just under $48,000. Those who received much more than that were wealthier to begin with. Almost two-thirds of inheritances went to families with a net worth of about $150,000. As parents live longer and spend more, inheritances will dwindle. In fact, many boomers will need to provide financial assistance to their aging parents.

You're Not Alone

Not surprisingly, the recession has brought a new sense of reality to the subject of retirement planning. Dreams of early retirement and relaxing leisure have given way to a new understanding of how costly retirement will be—and how ill-prepared most of us are for this reality.

The 2009 Employee Benefit Research Institute (EBRI) survey on retirement confidence hit its lowest level since the survey was started in 1993. Only 20 percent said they were "very confident" about their retirement prospects, compared to 40 percent in 2007!

People tend to underestimate savings requirements, life expectancy, and the rising cost of health care, while overestimating how much they can draw on their savings. Even small miscalculations of those numbers can result in huge errors. The EBRI study reveals that only 44 percent of workers report they and/or their spouse have tried to calculate how much money they will need to have saved by the time they retire. And an equal number simply guess at how much they will need for a comfortable retirement.

Worrying about retirement is fodder for cartoons. There are just so many uncertainties: how long you'll live, how much your money can earn, the rate at which inflation will eat away at your savings, and the rising costs of health care.

Pepper . . . and Salt

THE WALL STREET JOURNAL

LITZLER

"The financial strategy for my retirement should count on me still being alive."

Source: From the *Wall Street Journal*—permission, Cartoon Features Syndicate.

The challenge of planning for retirement may seem overwhelming, but you have to face reality. Will you ever be able to save enough to fund a secure retirement? If saving more isn't possible, and if extraordinary investment returns are unrealistic, then working longer—either longer *hours* now or longer *years* later—may be the only alternative. That will allow the money you currently have in savings and investments to grow for a few extra years while you set aside a few more years of retirement plan contributions.

Even a few years of additional contributions and delayed withdrawals can make a big difference. But that may not be enough. It's time to reexamine the entire concept of retirement.

THE LIKELY SOLUTION: RETRO-RETIREMENT

Have you noticed that what's old is new again? Vintage is in style—whether in fashion, home design, or even music. Retro-chic is happening everywhere. So what's wrong with a retro-retirement? It's time to take a new look at a vintage idea and give it our own modern twist.

Think about it. Your grandparents, and their parents, worked until they died. They didn't complain. That's just the way it was. Even the stock exchange was open on Saturday, until 1952. Their recreation took place on Sunday. It wasn't until the late twentieth century that the idea of retirement was built around the concept of working less, or not at all, while living on a pension—an unending stream of income that would subsidize a lifestyle. Suddenly, workers could buy recreational vehicles, mobile homes, and cottages at the lake. Our higher standards of living were extended into retirement years.

But in the new reality, we're living longer, and it's costing more. And the stock market crash has decimated IRA and 401(k) assets that might have supported this dream. It's time to recrunch the numbers and revise the plan—if you ever had one.

The first step is an attitude adjustment. Maybe it's sour grapes, but boomers who have worked all their lives might find it a bit boring to play golf or tennis, to sit on the beach, or to drive across the country. We're creating our own concept of retirement that will be every bit as defining of our generation as the Beatles and the Rolling Stones. We'll work, and we'll play on our own schedule. It will be retro-chic to do both—and to do them in style.

It's not impossible for boomers to retire, but we must redefine the term. Almost certainly, it will involve working longer. But then we'll be living longer. Health care may cost more, but we'll probably be healthier than our parents. We may have less money, but we'll have a better chance to enjoy what we have. It all starts with facing up to the choices.

THE STARTING POINT

These three questions require no specific knowledge to answer, but a lot of self-discipline and honesty. There are no right or wrong answers.

1. How old do I expect to be when I die? _____
2. How do I rank the following three retirement solutions?
   Working longer before retiring _____
   Lowering standard of living in retirement _____
   Saving more now _____
3. If I knew I could get trustworthy advice about how to save, invest, budget, and withdraw, I'd be willing to confront the financial issues of retirement. _____ (yes *or* no)

With so much uncertainty, how can anyone know the Savage Number? Well, here's a helpful thought: You don't have to hit the number right on the head. Getting close counts more in retirement than in horseshoes!

CHAPTER

2

TIME IS MONEY

There's never a perfect time to think about your financial future. I doubt that anyone gets in the mood to do financial planning, unlike being ready for food, or sex, or sleep! But procrastination is the enemy of success, especially when it comes to investing. So here's a little incentive to get you in the mood for money!

In recent years, we've all become more aware that both time *and* money are running out. That makes our use of time even more precious. Knowing that these precious resources are finite should be an incentive to take an immediate and realistic look at your financial plan.

There will never be enough time to do all the things you want to do, to make all the money you want to make, to enjoy all the things life has to offer. The secret is to make use of the time you have, starting right this minute.

Time is money. If you're like most people, you feel you don't have enough of either. And you're probably right. But if you were asked to choose between the two, your answer would be revealing. If you choose time, it means you've reached the point in life where realities change. You understand this simple truth: *Time can buy you money, but no amount of money can buy you time.*

And that understanding colors the way you look at your future. Time has become a finite commodity. The issue now is to make the most of time and to make sure you have the money to do that, even though you will never know how much time you have left. The challenge is not to count the minutes, but to make the minutes count.

CONSUMING TIME AND MONEY

It's not your imagination that time is flying faster than ever. The days of your childhood, when summer stretched on endlessly, are long behind you. Now the days, months, and years fly by quickly. You ask:

Where did all the time go and where did all the money go? Some of the money that slipped through your fingers is all around you. Your home, car, furniture, and clothing are all a reflection of how you spent your working time. Every acquisition has a price, and the price was the time you spent making the money to buy it.

Some of those acquisitions are long gone—clothing that went out of style and was given away, cars that depreciated in value and were sold. Other acquisitions have grown in value. Your education was costly, but it was valuable in creating the ability to earn more money. Your savings and investments, though battered by bear markets, continue to use the leverage of time to grow in value.

Overall, we grew up in a society that was based on consumption. Neither terrorist acts nor economic recessions have kept the U.S. consumer from shopping and adding to consumer debt. In a recent MetLife trends study, more than half of the respondents reported that they manage their finances by living paycheck to paycheck. (See Figure 2.1.) If that's how you're getting by, you're not alone. It's not surprising that younger employees, ages 21 to 30, have little savings or investments. But it is shocking to find that more than half of older employees, ages 61 to 69, are also waiting for the next paycheck to pay their bills.

If you think this lack of planning is a result of low incomes, think again. Fully one-third (34 percent) of higher-income workers earning $75,000 or more are also dependent on the next paycheck for survival. Thirty percent of those earning $100,000 or more say they're living month to month. All of the people in this survey worked for corporations and were receiving some level of benefits. Half of them said they were worried about outliving their retirement savings.

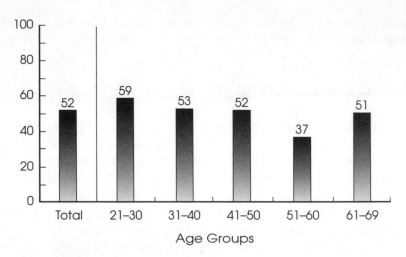

Figure 2.1   Percentage of Respondents Saying They Live Paycheck to Paycheck by Age
Source: Metropolitan Life Insurance Company. Reprinted with permission.

RUNNING OUT OF TIME

But worrying and doing something about it seem to be mutually exclusive. It's as if Americans were addicted to debt, even though they should have understood that interest payments limit their ability to plan for a secure future. In June 2005, the national savings rate went negative, as people lived on borrowed money to maintain their lifestyle. Then reality came crashing home as the burden of unwise mortgage debt and home equity loans loomed larger in a recessionary economy. Only belatedly did the savings rate turn higher.

Bankruptcy has become an epidemic, but the process wipes out equity as well as debt. It's unthinkable that as the baby boomer generation ages, many of its members will live at a subsistence level. A return to economic growth will solve many of the problems of supporting an aging population. But an economy can't grow if the government sucks up its resources through higher taxes.

Changing personal money habits to deal with retirement planning is filled with uncertainties: How much money is enough? How much time will you have? Is it too late to start? Actually, the answers are easier than you think. Although you can't buy time, you can make better use of your time to add to your retirement savings. It's never too late to start the process.

What's Your Time Worth?

It's critically important to evaluate your personal relationship to time and money—a valuation that will be different for every individual.

It's difficult to put a dollar value on a minute, a day, or a year of your time. You can divide your annual after-tax salary by the number of hours you worked. That will give you the dollar value of one hour of your time. But most of us would say we're worth far more than that mathematical calculation—because, of course, we're underpaid!

Still, give it a try. Figure out how many hours you work in an average week, and divide your weekly paycheck by that number. Remember to use the *after-tax* figure for your pay. It's a rough calculation; but you may find your work is worth $20 an hour, $50, $100, or more. Knowing how hard you work to earn your money gives you a new perspective when it comes to spending it.

When you make any purchase, it's worth computing how much of your work time the item would cost. If you take home $50 per hour, then a $250 winter coat will cost you almost one workday. But if your take-home pay is only $25 an hour, the coat will cost you nearly two days of work. Perhaps you could find something less expensive. That new flat-screen high-definition TV at $500 will cost you 20 hours of work. Is it worth it? This is not a lesson in budgeting; it's an exercise in valuation, and it will lead you to your own personal conclusions. There is no right or wrong.

The answer to the question "Is it worth it?" will depend not only on the per-hour cost of your time, but on how you will use the item you're buying. In fact, one of my favorite pastimes is computing a "wear quotient." Wearing that $250 winter coat for two years gives a wear quotient of $1 per day ($250 divided by about 250 cold-weather days over two years). But a $250 dress worn twice has a wear quotient of $125. Consider your own wardrobe. You may have a mutual fund full of style but no substance in your closet. Also think about sporting goods, car accessories, or electronics that didn't give you enough use to justify their costs in terms of your time.

Consider the potential impact of time on the money you *don't* spend today. What could have been done with the money instead? It's not always easy to compute the future value of current expenditures. You may go into debt to earn an advanced degree in business that will increase your value to prospective employers. These days, many students graduate from college with student loan debt well over $100,000. It will be up to them to prove the long-term value of their investment in education.

THE TIME VALUE OF MONEY

Another way to value time is to measure how it can make your money grow without any extra input from you. Investing $2,000 a year ($38.46 per week) in an individual retirement account (IRA), growing in a stock index mutual fund at the stock market's historic average rate of slightly over 10 percent, could build a huge retirement fund. Starting today, and based on those historic returns, a 20-year-old could make that annual $2,000 investment inside an IRA for 50 years and have an account worth $3.1 million at retirement! Funding an IRA at $5,000 a year could generate a nest egg worth more than $8 million in 50 years—if the stock market continues its average performance of the past 75 years. If it's too late for you, tell a young person!

Clearly, the power of compound interest—the impact of time on money—is a major force of nature. The problem is that when you're young, you have no idea that time is such a valuable commodity because you have so much of it. When you're young, money (not time) is the immediately scarce resource. You don't have the long-term perspective until you have hindsight.

Unfortunately, we learn the value of time only when we recognize it is a finite commodity. And it is not only finite, but indefinable. No one gives us a sneak peek at when it will run out. If we knew for sure, it would be easier to plan. Even so, it's never too late to vow to make the very best use of the time we have.

The greatest financial mistake we can make is to waste time. Following are some common time wasters and solutions to help you avoid them.

HOW TO AVOID WASTING TIME (AND MONEY)

Time *can* buy you money—if you stop wasting it. The real trick is to make your plan automatic, so you don't waste time deciding whether you have enough money to invest every month.

Time Waster: Worry

If you're nearing retirement and you haven't started saving, you might think it's hopeless. But worrying about money doesn't create more money. It just wastes time you could be using to change your financial situation.

Solution: It's never too late to start a regular program of automatic investing. Have money taken out of your paycheck or checking account before you spend it. Do it through the retirement plan at work. Or open an individual retirement account. Remember, it's quite possible you will live beyond age 85. That gives the money you invest today plenty of time to grow in the future. (See the section titled "Starting Small—No Excuses!" in Chapter 10 for information about the All-American Equity Fund, a diversified mutual fund that lets you start investing with as little as $100, plus $30 a month in an automatic contribution plan.)

Time Waster: Drudgery

Many people confuse the drudgery of money management with the idea that they're taking control of their finances. Paying bills is the perfect example. The time you spend writing and mailing checks each month could be better spent evaluating your retirement plan statement.

Solution: Start paying your bills online with just a click of your mouse. It's safe, it's free (or inexpensive), and it saves time. Go to your bank's web site to get started. For more information on using your computer to eliminate time-wasting money drudgery, see Chapter 6.

Time Waster: Complaining

Complaining about how underpaid, overworked, or unappreciated you are is a horrible waste of time.

Solution: Do something different with your time. Start your own small business on the side, or take a night school course to make yourself more valuable to your employer. If you've lost your job, along with millions of others, think creatively about your talents, and how you can earn extra money. Volunteering to help others can set you on the path to creating a business that builds on your talents. Invest the time you spend complaining into building your own future.

CHAPTER

3

THE 10 KEY QUESTIONS

L et's see where we are so far. Retirement is the goal. You're willing to face the challenge of finding the Savage Number. You tested yourself and realized you'll need some help getting there. You've bought into the principle that time is money. And you're worried about being able to retire.

So let's get specific about the 10 key questions you'll face in retirement planning. Ask yourself:

1. How long will I live?
2. What will inflation do to the value of my savings?
3. How can I save enough?
4. How should I invest the money I've saved for retirement?
5. How much will I spend to live in retirement?
6. How much can I withdraw each month without running out of money?
7. What's the biggest danger to my retirement plans?
8. How can I earn money during retirement?
9. How can I retain control of my financial life?
10. What if I have money left over when I die?

Let's take the questions one by one. But keep in mind that while it's easier to explain things in terms of averages, very few things in real life are actually average. It's not averages you need to deal with in retirement planning, but probabilities. They're much more likely to get you to your retirement goal. So the average numbers in this chapter are just designed to give perspective. Dealing with specific probabilities for your retirement plan comes in the next section.

How Long Will I Live?

This is truly the one unanswerable question. The life expectancy for the overall U.S. population was a record 76.9 years in 2000. But for today's healthy 50-year-olds, the life expectancy is 82 for women and 78 for men. And once you've reached age 75, the life expectancy is 87 years for women and 85 for men, according to Social Security. Table 3.1 shows the odds that the Society of Actuaries is projecting for today's 65-year-olds. But haven't you always considered yourself to be above average? Why stop thinking that way now? You may live far longer than average.

For a realistic, and very personal estimate of how long you're likely to live, there's a fascinating online calculator at www.livingto100 .com. You'll be asked to input everything from medical information (blood pressure, cholesterol) to dietary and exercise habits—down to whether you buckle your seatbelt and floss your teeth. That information, combined with demographic data, may give a surprising result when you click to calculate your life expectancy. (You'll probably start living a healthier lifestyle if you don't like the results!)

Confronting your own mortality is the first, and most difficult, issue in retirement planning. The earlier you start planning for retirement, the better. But you don't start taking the issue seriously

Table 3.1   Conditional Probability of Survival at Age 65

To Age	Female	Male
70	93.9%	92.2%
75	85.0	81.3
80	72.3	65.9
85	55.8	45.5
90	34.8	23.7
95	15.6	7.7
100	5.0	1.4

Source: Copyright 2009 by the Society of Actuaries, Schaumburg, Illinois. Reprinted with permission.

until your body betrays you, or until your friends begin having health problems and you realize you could be next. Then you see the miracles of modern science and realize that it is possible to cure those ailments and live a longer life than your parents ever dreamed. That's when you start thinking you'd better plan to live longer.

Why bet against the odds? The real issue is whether you'll feel worse if you run out of money because you live longer than you planned, or if you die before you have a chance to spend the money you saved!

WHAT WILL INFLATION DO TO THE VALUE OF MY SAVINGS?

Inflation is another force of nature—economic nature—that's unpredictable in the short term. Annual inflation has *averaged* about 3 percent over the past 80 years, but there have been brief periods when inflation was much higher or lower. In the early 1980s, consumer price inflation briefly hit a 13 percent annual rate. In 2007, there were worries that inflation would be replaced by deflation—falling consumer prices.

The definition of inflation is excess creation of money. Inflation shows up in the form of higher prices, and higher interest rates demanded by lenders to offset the declining buying power of their dollars. And when people really fear for the future buying power of their currency, they want to switch out of dollars, and into assets such as gold, commodities, or other currencies that may retain their value (more on that in Chapter 9).

In the wake of the 2008–2009 bailout of the economy, trillions of dollars of new money was created by the Federal Reserve. And the Treasury borrowed trillions more, to fund its rescue and bailout operations. That was done to offset the contrary forces of deflation—falling prices of assets ranging from stocks to real estate. Somewhere down the road, all that money creation has set the stage for future inflation.

Inflation destroys the value of the dollars you have saved, giving you less buying power. There's a simple formula for calculating the impact of inflation. It's called the "Rule of 72."

THE RULE OF 72

If you divide any number into 72, the resulting answer is the number of years it will take for your money to double—or for its buying power to be cut in half by inflation. For example, if you estimate that inflation will average 3 percent, dividing that number into 72 tells you that in roughly 25 years your buying power will be cut in half. That means you'll need twice the number of today's dollars to buy the same goods and services. Conversely, if you expect to earn 6 percent annually on your money, dividing that number into 72 tells you that your money will double in 12 years.

We plan for our retirement in dollars, wondering if we'll have enough of them. But when planning your retirement, you must consider not only how much money you need, but what your money will *buy*!

Obviously, even a little bit of inflation can do a lot of damage. The secret of retirement investing is to make sure your money is earning more than inflation is consuming. But to beat inflation, you'll have to take a little more risk. And that brings us to the next question.

HOW CAN I SAVE ENOUGH?

You probably can't save *enough*—depending on how you define that term—so stop stressing over the dollar amount. Unless you win the lottery or sell shares in your company to the public, it's unlikely that you'll ever have more money than you can spend. Most people can always manage to increase their lifestyle cost to accommodate a rising income. It's a lesson in how wants can easily become needs.

Retirement is simply the reversal of that process. Unless you've saved enough, you'll shed those parts of your lifestyle that are no longer needed, and you'll focus on issues that suddenly become important, such as health and health care. The definition of *enough* will change as you age, and it won't be as painful as you imagine. The true definition of *enough* is a combination of savings, spending, and continued earning that will give you a reasonable retirement lifestyle.

When you're in your peak earnings years, it's hard to deal with the concept of enough because there are so many competing demands for your cash. Just when you pay off the first car, you need a second. Just when you get your home furnished, you face college for your children. Just when your children are in college, you realize you might have to help your parents in their older years. And in the meantime, you have to live.

There are so many important uses for the money you're earning that it's hard to contemplate setting anything aside for savings. In fact, it won't happen, unless you do it automatically—before you see it and spend it. That's the advantage of the company retirement plan or automatic checking withdrawals for an individual retirement account (IRA).

But you've heard that speech before. You know it's pretax money, so you get to save cash that would have gone to the government. You know you might get a matching contribution from your company—free money. That message has been drilled into Americans over the past decade, yet the Employee Benefit Research Institute's latest national retirement confidence survey finds that key attitudes about retirement savings have hardly changed since the first survey in 1991. The survey concludes, "Many workers appear to have optimistic expectations about retirement and retirement income that might lead them to be complacent about their retirement savings needs."

You're not one of them because you took the time to pick up this book. I remember my mother crossing her arms in exasperation when kids raised a fuss: "Enough is enough!" she'd say. I never could define "enough" then, and I can't now. But I always know when I'm getting close.

How Should I Invest the Money I've Saved for Retirement?

If you've managed to save some money for retirement, the most important question you'll face is how to invest it. Your investment decisions will have a big impact on your retirement lifestyle. It's important that you understand your investment choices and the inherent risks involved in each, and that you get unbiased, professional advice about allocating your funds among those investments.

If you have multiple investments—401(k) plans, IRAs, after-tax savings— you'll need to coordinate them to make sure your overall portfolio is appropriate. And now that you've watched some of your hard-earned money simply disappear into the void of the stock market crash, you need to reassess your risk tolerance and goals.

Simply put, you need an investment plan, not a hodgepodge of accounts, funds, and stocks that might once have been appropriate but now need reevaluation. The financial services industry offers multiple possibilities for accessing that kind of planning, but you need to understand the basics to make sure you get *good* advice.

Start with a trusted adviser, chosen by more than a television commercial or a persuasive phone call. As you'll see in Chapter 7, you can access independent advice from fee-only financial planners. But you can also get excellent financial advice from brokers and salespeople who work on commissions if you know how to analyze their recommendations, and if you get references from their successful clients. If you're willing to do a little work, you can find all the advice you need just by using your computer. Do you need to become an expert investor? Absolutely not. But you do need to understand the long-term risk-and-reward characteristics of stocks, bonds, real estate, and alternative investments. That's a must, whether you're using an individual adviser or a technology-based planning service.

How Much Will I Spend to Live in Retirement?

Living in retirement will cost more than you think. Over the years, many financial planners have developed formulas involving a percentage of preretirement costs, typically around 75 percent to 80 percent, to maintain your lifestyle in retirement. They point out that you will no longer have expenses for commuting, business clothes, and dry cleaning those clothes. You can eat lunch more cheaply at home, and you can take vacations whenever you find a cheap airfare package instead of waiting for your authorized vacation dates.

On the other hand, you'll be spending more on health care and prescription drugs, the segment of the economy in which prices are increasing fastest. Hikes in property taxes and utility rates can increase your cost of living, even in a home where the mortgage is paid off. And the clothes in your closet won't last another 30 years!

The smart thing is to look backward before you look ahead. Don't try to budget. Instead, go back over your checking account for the past year or two, and see where all the money you currently earn has been going. Consider it a reality check on your current lifestyle. (This process is a lot easier if you bank online and track your spending in money management software like Quicken. See Chapter 6 for details.) How much went for housing, utilities, clothing, entertainment? Now, analyze each category, and ask yourself how much you'll really cut your spending in retirement.

If your reality check tells you that you don't want to alter your lifestyle, then all you need is the income to sustain it. It will be there if you start planning before you retire from your full-time job. Otherwise you'll have to consider a life without expensive restaurants, stylish clothes, and generous gifts to your children. The earlier you confront these issues, the more likely you are to achieve your most realistic retirement-lifestyle goals.

HOW MUCH CAN I WITHDRAW EACH MONTH WITHOUT RUNNING OUT OF MONEY?

Assuming you've done a reasonable job of saving money for retirement, and that you continue to save and invest in spite of the stock market crash, this is the most critical question you'll ask. And it's the one question that does not lend itself to an easy answer. There are so many variables—the growth of your investments, inflation, and longevity, for example—that it would take a sophisticated computer program to give you a reasonable answer.

Fortunately, the major financial services companies have designed programs to give you that answer—or a range of answers—so you can plan your retirement withdrawals. That's the subject of the next chapter. But first, you must confront a psychological barrier: invading principal, spending your savings.

Your parents or grandparents probably had a horror of invading their principal, of spending their savings instead of just living on the income from investments. They learned that lesson from their parents, the generation that lived through the Depression. Thanks to medical advances, your parents are living far longer than they expected. Because (hopefully) they have lived frugally during their retirement years, they can now dig into their principal (your hoped-for inheritance) to avoid depending on you. Good-bye inheritance.

But we baby boomers are likely to have no choice. We'll be trying to strike a balance between growing our retirement savings so we can withdraw the profits and earnings to live on, and using up our principal at a rate that will allow our savings to last as long as we do. The more money you take out, the less there is to earn interest or investment profits. It's a delicate balance because the most significant factor is unknowable: how long you'll live. And making predictions based on average investment returns or average longevity can be very dangerous.

There is a solution—besides a dartboard—to making these predictions. In Chapter 7, I'll introduce you to several inexpensive services that can bring order to your wishful thinking about retirement withdrawals. But first there are other issues to confront.

WHAT'S THE BIGGEST DANGER TO MY RETIREMENT PLANS?

Here's a clue: It's not a financial crash or another bear market. The big potential sinkhole for your planned retirement is health-care costs—more specifically, the need for long-term care.

The simple laws of supply and demand are bound to result in higher health-care costs as the huge baby boomer generation ages. You don't need a computer to predict that. Eventually, competition might bring prices down, but that hasn't happened yet. You must factor rising health-care costs into your retirement spending scenario.

If Medicare continues to fund expanded services for seniors, you can expect that there will eventually be some rationing of those benefits, whether by age or by income. Company-funded retirement health-care benefits are likely to cost more, if they are available at all. Current retirees have learned that those promises don't hold up under the threat of by rising costs that sink corporate profits. There's always a loophole in the fine print.

The most devastating cost of living longer won't be the expensive medical or pharmaceutical needs. It will be the cost of long-term *custodial* care, which is not covered under Medicare, Medicare supplements, or Social Security. State Medicaid programs for the impoverished do cover the cost of long-term care, but mostly in state-financed nursing homes. One visit will tell you that's not where you want to spend your retirement years. And the recession has forced sharp cutbacks in all state budgets, especially for nursing home care.

Because government appears to be offering free long-term care under Medicaid, many retirees are being advised to spend down or to transfer their assets so they can qualify for this needs-based program. That's a mistake that will mushroom in consequences as more baby boomers need care. Retirees who don't have private long-term care insurance policies will have few choices. They'll be placed in a Medicaid-funded nursing facility that will be overwhelmed by the duality of aging boomers and state budget cutbacks. And states will "look back" for many years to recapture assets that were transferred to family members.

It's wise to purchase long-term care insurance coverage while you are young and healthy so you'll have the option of remaining in your home and choosing the type of home health care or assisted-living facility you want. If you start early, it's simple and inexpensive. I'll show you how to avoid this looming crisis in Part 5.

How Can I Earn Money during Retirement?

Now is the time to start thinking about your ability to earn money during retirement. If you've worked at a job for years, figure out creative ways for the company to keep you on part time. Or use your corporate experience to start a new career as a self-employed consultant. This is the time to do an assessment. Abilities that you take for granted—using a computer, sales or management skills, leadership talents—might be in demand at nonprofit organizations that can pay you a salary. Or you might find fulfillment, as well as money, in teaching your skills to others, or in caring for children or the elderly.

As the recession made the job market more competitive, the difficulty of continuing to earn an income has become more apparent. Seniors are doing jobs they never considered: driving limos or taxis, waiting tables, selling products. This is one of the byproducts of the combined economic slowdown and growing cost of senior living.

The worst time to confront this issue is the month before you retire, when you're emotional and facing disruption in your everyday life. If you start to volunteer or to build a business on the side while you're still on the job, your transition to part-time work or self-employment will be a lot easier. Of course, you'll have to consider the impact of earnings on other benefits, such as Social Security, which we'll do in Chapter 12.

How Can I Retain Control of My Financial Life?

Managing your money in retirement is more complicated than it was when you were working full time because you'll have to confront issues that were handled automatically by your employer. The time to set up a system is now, before you retire. The issue is control. You need to track what's coming in, what's going out, what's growing, and what's shrinking. You would never ignore warning signs of an illness. Similarly, you'll want to be on top of your finances on a daily or weekly basis. Chapter 6 gives you easy ways to gain control of your finances.

When you retire, you may have to file a quarterly tax return to cover the taxes you owe on self-employment or investment income. No longer will a company payroll department deduct taxes automatically, making tax withholding simple. And if you're self-employed, you'll face a different tax table, along with the complexity of multiple earnings sources.

You'll confront the physical issue of managing your retirement accounts, both IRA and 401(k) or 403(b) plans. You may want to roll them into a single account at one financial services company, just to simplify the tracking process and asset allocation decisions. There are online tracking and asset rebalancing programs; but since most firms still send out paper statements, you'll need to set up a filing system or face being buried in a blizzard of paper.

Consolidation will make it easier to deal with your next major hurdle: required minimum distributions from your tax-deferred IRA and 401(k) rollover retirement accounts. You'll need to aggregate the value of all your tax-deferred retirement accounts and choose a formula to determine the dollar amount required to be taken out each year. Then you have to decide which accounts to take the money out of and which investments to liquidate. See Chapter 11 for an explanation of the rules governing required minimum distributions.

But that doesn't end your retirement busywork. Once you start a program of withdrawals, you'll definitely have to stick to some sort of budget. What happens if you overspend? You can take an extra check from that tempting pile of money, but what's the impact down the road? You have to be even more vigilant about money management when there's a finite amount of money and an infinite amount of spare time.

Clearly, you won't be able to throw away your desk and computer once you retire! In fact, those tools become even more valuable in minimizing the time and energy you need to devote to retirement financial issues. Because that's what retirement is supposed to be all about—less stress, not more.

WHAT IF I HAVE MONEY LEFT OVER WHEN I DIE?

Although you may think it unlikely—after reading about rising costs, inflation, and longevity—it's possible that you may be below average, after all. Instead of living to nearly 100, you may be one of those who balance the averages by going on ahead earlier than you expected.

Or your investments might catch an updraft and grow faster than you can spend them.

It's wise to have a plan for what's left over, if only to keep your hard-earned, hard-saved, and dream-filled dollars from going to the government. Instead, you'll want those benefits to go to your family, friends, or the charity of your choice. A simple estate plan based on a revocable living trust is the key ingredient. And even if you don't have a lot of assets, you'll want to have a health-care power of attorney for medical emergencies and a living will, which instructs on your wishes when life support is required.

After all, why go to all the trouble of planning and accumulating for your retirement without taking the final step of contemplating the end result? It's just a question of timing. And I've always believed that timing favors the most prepared. You'll find a simple estate planning checklist in Chapter 18.

It's likely that the estate tax law will change dramatically in the next couple of years, making planning difficult. But if you believe the government will become more aggressive in taxing the fruits of your labor one more time, after death, then you need to be thinking about having life insurance—outside your estate—to provide liquidity to pay those taxes. For that reason, and also in case your money runs out at the end but you still want to leave cash to your kids, you'll be interested in the life insurance section of Chapter 18.

GETTING THE ANSWERS

Now that we've talked about the questions you must confront in planning your retirement, what about finding the answers? That's a lot easier than you might think. While managing all these variables can overwhelm the human brain, it's relatively simple for a well-programmed computer.

Financial companies—ranging from banks to brokerage firms to mutual fund companies to insurers to individual planners—have turned their focus to helping people calculate how much they need to save, how the savings should be invested, and then planning how the money should be withdrawn to maximize your retirement lifestyle. You'll find the very best staring point described in the box at the end of this chapter: Getting Your "Ballpark Estimate."

But it's not all about technology. Computer results are only as good as the information you put in and the programs that manage the data. We all want our hands held by a knowledgeable person.

So whether you've saved a bundle and don't know what to do with it or haven't started saving at all, this is the time to face up to the future. It may take major changes in your current lifestyle and some adjustments in your expectations to make your dreams of retirement possible, but there's no reason to despair. The numbers aren't that Savage, after all.

GETTING YOUR "BALLPARK ESTIMATE"

You've started thinking about the questions in this chapter—how much you'll need, how long you'll live, how to invest, the impact of inflation. Now it's time to connect the dots, and understand the impact of the range of answers to each of these questions in your search for the "number."

Your number is a very personal one, and it depends on your financial circumstances and goals. Figuring it out will take time, but I know you're running out of patience. So here's a shortcut to a rough estimate of your number, and some insight into the impact of each of these factors on the outcome of your planning.

Go to www.choosetosave.org, a web site created by the national nonprofit Employee Benefit Research Institute.

When you get there, click on the green box "Ballpark Estimate" (see Figure 3.1).

Be prepared for some serious thinking as you work through this online calculator. It will ask you for your age, your longevity estimate, your desired retirement age, and your current income and savings amounts. Then there are the variables, including your inflation estimate and your estimated investment returns

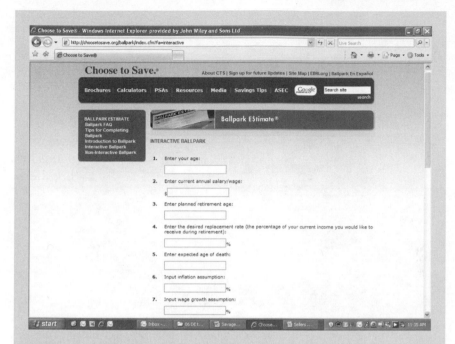

Figure 3.1 Ballpark Estimate
Source: www.choosetosave.org.

for before and after retirement. It even gives you a link to your estimated Social Security benefits, so that number can be included in the calculations.

With a click of your mouse you can see how much more you need to be saving each month to reach your goals. And as you change the variables—ranging from your life expectancy to inflation assumptions—you can get a rough idea or "ballpark estimate" of *your* Savage Number!

PART 2

MONTE CARLO YOUR MONEY

CHAPTER 4

THE SAVAGE ANSWER: MONTE CARLO MODELING

No, I'm not suggesting gambling. You want the answer to that key question: *How much money will you need in order to retire?*

The answer is simple. All you have to do is factor in your current assets, your future savings rate, how much those assets will grow in value based on your investment decisions, over your uncertain life expectancy, and how much they will be devalued by inflation. Then decide how much annual income you'll need to withdraw to maintain your lifestyle in retirement!

The complexity of this task, with all its uncertainties, is overwhelming—whether you're just starting to accumulate money or you're contemplating retirement. But there is a sophisticated computer you're modeling process that is designed to deal with all these variables. It is called *Monte Carlo modeling*.

MONTE CARLO MODELING: HOW IT WORKS

Despite the name, Monte Carlo modeling has nothing to do with gambling. It's simply the statistical science of modeling multiple alternatives to come up with a likely range of probable results. Monte Carlo was a code name for a technique employed during the

Manhattan Project to create the atomic bomb. Now it is being used to describe this simulation process, which has been made easier, faster, and more accessible by today's computers.

Stanford University professor and noted Monte Carlo modeling expert Dr. Sam Savage (no relation) explains the advantages of Monte Carlo modeling over the use of averages by telling the story of the man who drowned crossing a river that had an average depth of just three feet. Unfortunately, that average depth masked the fact that the water was ankle deep near the banks and nine feet deep in the center. On average, he would have crossed the river easily; in reality, he drowned!

Dr. Savage calls it the "flaw of averages," a fallacy he says is as fundamental as the old belief that the earth is flat. He notes that when faced with an uncertainty such as future sales, interest rates, or investment returns, many people succumb to the temptation of replacing the uncertain number with a single average value. Roughly translated, the flaw of averages states: *Plans based on average assumptions will be wrong on average.*

Monte Carlo modeling goes far beyond the law of averages. It's useful because in practice there is no one average number that is sufficient for making good investment decisions. The beauty of Monte Carlo is that it illustrates the range of probabilities so that you can observe the trade-off between risk and return. In fact, if you make forecasts and take action based only on the average results, you're making a big mistake.

BEWARE OF AVERAGES

If it were just a matter of simple math, you could create a plan that would look like the chart in Table 4.1. On the left is the income you might need, and across the top is the compound rate of return you might hope to gain from your investments. So if you need $20,000 a year in income and you expect to earn 6 percent annually, you will need $319,000 in an investment that continues to compound at that rate. (Zero coupon bond funds perform the job of compounding your money.)

Table 4.1   Assets Needed to Generate 40 Years of Income

	Rate of Return			
Income	2%	4%	6%	8%
$ 15,000	$ 419,000	$ 309,000	$ 239,000	$ 193,000
20,000	558,000	412,000	319,000	258,000
25,000	698,000	515,000	399,000	322,000
35,000	977,000	720,000	558,000	451,000
50,000	1,395,000	1,029,000	797,000	644,000
75,000	2,093,000	1,544,000	1,196,000	966,000
100,000	2,790,000	2,058,000	1,595,000	1,288,000

But it's not so simple. This table uses averages, but none of us lives in the average. Sometimes there are ups, and sometimes there are downs. So unless you're using a computer program especially designed to look at all those probabilities—everything from the variability of investment returns of various asset classes to the likelihood of different levels of inflation—a simple chart with average returns is very misleading.

If you want a picture of how dangerous the use of averages can be when it comes to financial planning for retirement withdrawals, consider the story of Joe, who retired in 1969. When he reached the age of 65 back in 1969, Joe went to a retirement planner with his $250,000 in savings. The planner advised a conservative allocation: 60 percent stocks, 30 percent bonds, and 10 percent cash or money market accounts, as shown in Figure 4.1.

Based on historical averages, the planner told Joe he might expect an average annual return on his investments of between 10 percent and 12 percent over the next 30 years. In hindsight—which we have, since Joe's portfolio was created in 1969—we see in Figure 4.2 that his portfolio did indeed have an average annual return of 11.7 percent over that 30-year period.

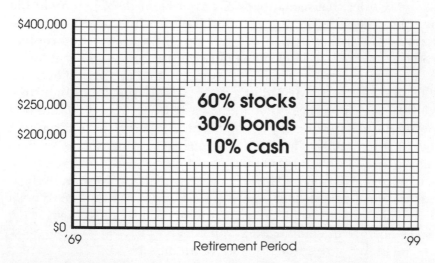

Figure 4.1   Joe's Retirement Portfolio in 1969
Source: T. Rowe Price Associates, Inc. Reprinted with permission.

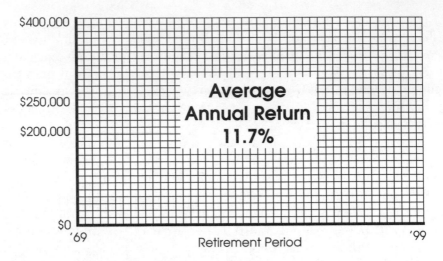

Figure 4.2   Portfolio's Average Return, 1969–1999
Source: T. Rowe Price Associates, Inc. Reprinted with permission.

Back in 1969, the retirement planner told Joe that based on his forecast of an average annual return of between 10 percent and 12 percent, he could take out 8.5 percent of his principal every year to live on. Under that scenario, depicted in Figure 4.3, Joe would not run out of money for 30 years, at which time he would be 95. The planner noted that if Joe were still alive at that age, he probably wouldn't notice that he had run out of money!

But that forecast was based on averages, and the period between 1969 and 1999 was a period of extremes. The Dow Jones Industrial Average, which was below 800 in the early 1970s, stayed around that low level until 1982 before taking off on an incredible bull run that took it over 10,000. The average annual return for stocks (including dividends) in that period was nearly 12 percent. However, if Joe had started withdrawing his 8.5 percent cash in those early bear market years, as shown in Figure 4.4, his account would have been so depleted that he would have run out of money in just 11 years (by 1981)—before the bull market even began.

The moral of this story: Beware of averages!

That warning is even more apparent after the stock market crash of 2008–2009. Those who were planning to retire, or had just

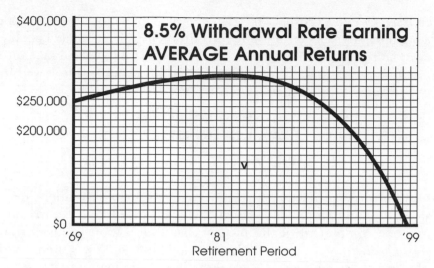

Figure 4.3   Planner's Withdrawal Advice
Source: T. Rowe Price Associates, Inc. Reprinted with permission.

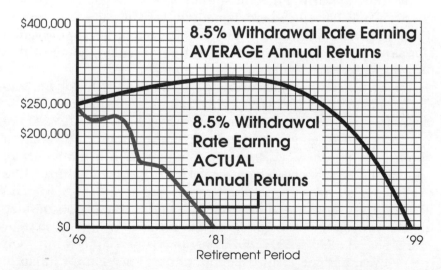

Figure 4.4   What Really Happened: Joe Ran Out of Money in 11 Years
Source: T. Rowe Price Associates, Inc. Reprinted with permission.

retired, face the prospect of trying to plan their withdrawals from a significantly smaller amount of retirement assets. It has become even more apparent that you need a planning tool that will take into account the possibility of steep market declines, perhaps followed by extensive periods of sideways activity or extreme volatility.

MONTE CARLO MODELING AND RETIREMENT PLANNING

Obviously, you can't use simple averages to make investment decisions for your retirement security. Average investment returns are just one component of the picture. You'll also want to know how those averages were created. For example, how long was the period of time used to compute the average return? You'll want to know the range of extremes from that average midpoint. Statisticians call it the *standard deviation*, but it's helpful just to think of it as the "range of highs and lows."

That's where Monte Carlo modeling comes in. The basis of Monte Carlo financial planning is to take all those variables related to investment returns, inflation, and income goals and evaluate the range of possible outcomes when these variables are matched in different ways. It's the kind of analysis that requires a sophisticated computer program and a great deal of information. Some of that information is easily available.

We know about the historical performance of stocks and categories of stocks such as large capitalization and small companies. Computers can also track returns on various types of bonds. There is historical data about the range of interest rates and inflation numbers. The Monte Carlo computer models run thousands of simulations to see how a strategy plays out over all the various combinations.

Figure 4.5 shows the results of Monte Carlo simulations modeling the probability of maintaining a retirement spending strategy over a period of 30 years, withdrawing only 4 percent of your assets the first year and increasing that amount by 3 percent for inflation each year.

Success Rates: 4 Percent Withdrawal Rate / 30-Year Retirement Horizon

Stock Allocation in Portfolio (rows) × Bond Allocation in Portfolio (columns)

Stock \ Bond	0%	5%	10%	15%	20%	25%	30%	35%	40%	45%	50%	55%	60%	65%	70%	75%	80%	85%	90%	95%	100%
100%	82%																				
95%	82%	83%																			
90%	83%	83%	84%																		
85%	83%	84%	84%	85%																	
80%	83%	84%	85%	85%	86%																
75%	83%	84%	85%	86%	86%	87%															
70%	83%	84%	85%	86%	86%	87%	88%														
65%	83%	84%	85%	86%	87%	87%	88%	88%													
60%	83%	84%	85%	86%	87%	88%	88%	89%	89%												
55%	83%	84%	85%	86%	88%	88%	88%	89%	90%	90%											
50%	83%	84%	85%	86%	88%	88%	89%	89%	90%	90%	91%										
45%	81%	83%	86%	87%	88%	88%	89%	90%	90%	91%	91%	92%									
40%	81%	83%	84%	86%	88%	89%	89%	90%	91%	91%	92%	92%	92%								
35%	79%	82%	84%	86%	87%	88%	89%	90%	91%	91%	92%	92%	93%	93%							
30%	77%	80%	83%	85%	87%	88%	89%	90%	90%	91%	92%	92%	93%	93%	93%						
25%	73%	77%	82%	84%	86%	88%	89%	90%	91%	91%	92%	92%	93%	93%	93%	94%					
20%	66%	73%	80%	83%	85%	87%	88%	90%	91%	91%	92%	92%	93%	93%	93%	94%	94%				
15%	53%	68%	76%	80%	82%	85%	87%	89%	90%	91%	91%	92%	92%	93%	93%	93%	93%	93%			
10%	26%	52%	68%	74%	79%	82%	84%	86%	88%	90%	90%	91%	92%	92%	92%	93%	93%	92%	93%		
5%	0%	4%	16%	34%	50%	62%	70%	76%	80%	83%	85%	87%	88%	90%	90%	91%	92%	92%	92%	91%	
0%	0%	0%	2%	13%	31%	47%	59%	67%	73%	78%	81%	83%	85%	87%	88%	89%	90%	90%	90%	91%	91%

Stock Allocation in Portfolio

Bond Allocation in Portfolio

Figure 4.5 Success Rates: 4 Percent Withdrawal Rate/30-Year Retirement Horizon

Source: T. Rowe Price Associates, Inc. T. Rowe Price, 100,000 Monte Carlo Simulations. The underlying long-term return assumptions are 10% for stock, 6.5% for intermediate-term bonds, and 4% for cash, which total 1.211% for stock, 0.726% for bonds, and 0.761% for cash. These results are not predictions but should be viewed as reasonable estimates. Reprinted with permission.

In the example you see the likely probability of success—not running out of money—depending on the mix of stocks, bonds, and cash in your retirement portfolio. Your assets can be invested in various combinations of stocks, bonds, and cash.

Looking at the bottom right corner of the chart, you'll see that if you invested 100 percent of your money in bonds, you would have only a 91 percent chance of not running out of money over your lifetime. Yes, high-quality bonds are safe and secure. But as you get to the date when you sell your last shares of your diversified bond fund, there is still a very small possibility that interest rates will be at a high level, causing lower bond prices. So those final withdrawals may not be able to give you complete certainty of not running out of money.

The modeling shows that there were a few periods when you would not have earned enough on your bond portfolio to sustain the payments. That's a slim chance, based on a broad range of modeling history. But in a period of massive inflation, prices of older, fixed rate bonds could fall sharply. That's the risk in "safe" bonds. On the other hand, there's an even larger chance that you, or you and your spouse, won't live the full 30 years.

Obviously, living longer adds greater risk to your goal of lifetime income. Given the choice (which we aren't), most of us would choose to live longer! But longevity adds another degree of uncertainty to your goal of lifetime income. If you expect to spend more years in retirement, you'll have to adjust both your mix of investments and your *withdrawal rate.*

Table 4.2 shows a broader range of withdrawal and investment probabilities, also based on Monte Carlo modeling. The table is broken into three segments representing withdrawal periods of 20, 25, and 30 years. Within each segment, you have a range of investment opportunities—a balance between stocks and bonds. (Figure 4.5 has a cash component, but Table 4.2 does not; so the success percentages in the two graphics vary slightly.)

As you can see from Table 4.2, if you are willing to withdraw only 4 percent per year (and increase that amount for inflation each year thereafter), you can pick almost any investment scenario and probably not run out of money over any withdrawal period. But can you live on those smaller withdrawals, or do you need more?

Table 4.2   How Much Can You Spend in Retirement?

The table shows the estimated probability of maintaining several spending or withdrawal rates throughout retirement, depending on the investor's asset allocation and time horizon. The analysis assumes pretax withdrawals from tax-deferred assets and can be applied for any size retirement portfolio.

Initial Withdrawal Amount	Stock/Bond Mix*			
	80/20	60/40	40/60	20/80
	20-YEAR RETIREMENT PERIOD Simulation Success Rate			
7%	56%	52%	44%	26%
6	74	75	75	71
5	89	92	95	97
4	97	99	99	99
	25-YEAR RETIREMENT PERIOD Simulation Success Rate			
7%	39%	30%	17%	4%
6	57	53	44	25
5	77	78	78	73
4	91	94	97	98
	30-YEAR RETIREMENT PERIOD Simulation Success Rate			
7%	28%	19%	7%	1%
6	45	38	24	7
5	65	63	57	40
4	84	87	89	89

*The following asset allocations include short-term bonds: 60/40 includes 60% stocks, 30% bonds, and 10% short-term bonds; 40/60 includes 40% stocks, 40% bonds, and 20% short-term bonds; and 20/80 is comprised of 20% stocks, 50% bonds, and 30% short-term bonds.
Source: T. Rowe Price Associates, Inc. Reprinted with permission.

Withdrawing a larger percentage has a major impact on the probability of sustaining income streams over your projected lifetime. That's one of the trade-offs you have to make, and that's where you may need guidance beyond the perspective the numbers give. Most financial services firms that offer Monte Carlo modeling also provide advisers to help you decide on a suitable investment and withdrawal strategy.

MONTE CARLO AND YOU

Monte Carlo modeling has become widely available through professional financial advisers, whether mutual fund companies, brokerage firms, or financial planners. But while the term "Monte Carlo modeling" has become generic for this process of weighing variables, you should know that not all "models" use the same inputs and weightings. Some use longer periods of market history, for example. Others assign minuscule odds to extreme market events. Yet those extreme events do happen, as we've recently seen. And they can dramatically impact your chances of success!

That doesn't mean that Monte Carlo modeling isn't useful. In fact, as you've seen it is far more useful than simple averages or guessing. It just means that, as in life, there are no guarantees. There are only probabilities. You have to go with the odds! That said, using this type of planning tool dramatically increases the odds that your investments and withdrawals will be balanced so that your money will last your lifetime.

What varies most in Monte Carlo modeling is *your* input—your personal information and goals, dreams and fears. After all, these programs can't offer a personal retirement scenario without taking into account your own goals, risk tolerance, and priorities. So whether you go through the planning process with a financial planner or a large mutual fund company or an online calculator, you're going to be asked some tough questions. For example, you might be asked to decide what's more important: having a check for $5,000 a month or not running out of money for as long as you live. You probably want to choose both, but you have to order your priorities.

Let me give you an idea of how this works. Suppose you're 65, married, ready to retire, and have $1 million in retirement assets. If your top priority is not to run out of money, you could buy an immediate annuity today for the rest of your life that would pay $6,160 a month. Assuming you buy from one of the safest, top-rated insurance companies, your income is secure. You can sleep well, you think.

But wait. What about your spouse, who is the same age? Don't you want that income to cover his or her lifetime as well? In that case, you'll get a smaller monthly check—$5,415 a month—but a promise to pay as long as the surviving spouse lives. Now can you both sleep well?

Not yet. That monthly check might cover your expenses right now; but remember that with an immediate annuity, you're locked into a fixed dollar amount. What if inflation returns with a roar? Even at just 3 percent inflation, your purchasing power will be cut in half in 25 years. Don't you expect to live at least that long? You need the ability to cope with change, ranging from inflation to investment returns. That's where Monte Carlo modeling becomes invaluable.

So while that fixed monthly payment—whether a pension check or an annuity check—gives one kind of security, it doesn't cover *all* your retirement worries. Now let's look at the other extreme.

We know that small-company stocks have a historic average return of nearly 12 percent for the past 80 years. Well, if you invested all your cash in speculative stocks, you might make a lot of money; but you certainly wouldn't trust anyone to invest your retirement savings in that risky manner. If you had to withdraw money during a market decline, your plan would be in deep trouble. Small-company stocks might be suitable for only a small portion of your retirement funds.

The answer to creating a secure retirement plan is to use a combination of investment vehicles: some for growth, some for income, some for diversification, and some for certainty. It is that *mix* of investment choices and a realistic assessment of how much you can spend that Monte Carlo modeling is designed to provide.

When you seek counseling from a financial services firm that uses Monte Carlo modeling, you'll receive a matrix of investment possibilities and a ranking of the probabilities that you'll reach your financial goals by using each of the possible investment combinations. Those goals might range from a certainty about lifetime income to leaving an estate for your children. The planning process takes into account your other income from pension(s) and Social Security and then determines a withdrawal rate to combine with the investment plan. The combinations give you an overall range of success probabilities. You choose.

Then you have to implement the plan by reallocating your investment assets. And you have to be disciplined about withdrawing money only at the prescribed monthly rate, or all your planning will have been in vain. Self-discipline trumps information when it comes to using your assets wisely in retirement.

So go back over the 10 key questions in Chapter 3—the great uncertainties that exist in planning your financial future. You should feel a lot better knowing that there are solutions available. But first you need to gain some perspective.

DO-IT-YOURSELF MONTE CARLO: TOOLSFORMONEY.COM

In the chapters ahead, I'll be giving you resources to find financial firms and professionals to help you sort through this process of Monte Carlo retirement modeling and come up with various scenarios based on your personal situation.

I must admit that I'd be a bit intimidated to try this process of modeling multiple variables on my own. But maybe you're willing to give it a try. I'd be remiss if I didn't introduce you to two web sites that offer free, downloadable software that will let you take Monte Carlo for a drive.

At www.toolsformoney.com, financial professionals download dozens of software functions, which they use to do modeling for their clients. But software architect Mike Fulford, CFA, also wants to make a simple version of his retirement software available free of charge for those who want to play around and see the results of changing the variables—ranging from inflation assumptions to investment returns to withdrawal rates. You can easily download the program, using the spreadsheet on your own computer, keeping your information private.

At www.financialfate.com, Monty Hothersall has created a powerful, free tool that uses Monte Carlo and incorporates powerful cash flow calculations to help in your planning, including major life events, such as college for your children, a wedding, or a second home—as well as having enough money for retirement. This is a program that you easily download to your own computer, free of charge, to use at your convenience. No one is tracking your information or trying to sell you a product.

These two software programs are designed to be an exercise in "what-ifs"—a chance to see what happens when you change your assumptions about so many uncertainties in life. You'll probably still want advice from a professional who understands how to turn these statistical probabilities into investment activities. There are no guarantees with Monte Carlo modeling, or in life, but it is a way to expand your planning horizon.

CHAPTER

5

SAVING UP, DRAWING DOWN

T here are two key stages of the retirement planning process—accumulation and distribution.

During the *accumulation phase*, you're concerned about whether you're saving enough money and choosing the appropriate investment to reach your goals. You may even need help prioritizing those goals. Retirement should be a top priority, but you may also be saving for college for your children, or for a down payment on a home. With different goals, different time horizons, and different types of investment accounts, the process can be complicated.

Then, during the *withdrawal phase*, you need to know not only how much money you can take out every month or year, but how the remainder should be invested. Suddenly, your risk tolerance may change, as you realize that in retirement you will no longer be contributing new money to your plan, but only hoping to stretch your assets to cover your retirement lifestyle—and lifetime. Once again, you need to set priorities, either for lifetime income or to have money left over for an estate.

The two phases are complementary parts of the same project: your retirement. And, as you'll see, there is no fixed moment in time when you make the switch from one to the other. You'll always have investments—assets accumulating—even as you start to withdraw your money for living expenses.

The twin virtues—saving and investing—are the cornerstone of your retirement planning and retirement living. The first step is the discipline to save. The second is the belief that—*over the long run*—you will come out ahead by letting your money work for you in a diversified investment portfolio. (More on that in Part 3.)

If you don't believe in the future of the American free enterprise system—as reflected in the growth of the stock market over the long run—then no amount of planning will make your retirement secure. Don't depend on the government to rescue you. The only way all those government promises can be kept is through a growing economy.

There have always been periods of economic slowdown and market decline. And through our history, those tough times have always been followed by better ones. Who could have predicted in the midst of the deep recession of 1981–1982, with double-digit unemployment, a 21 percent prime rate, and the Dow Jones Industrial Average trading at 800, that just 20 years later the technology boom would bring the Dow to 14,000? Today, who knows what technology—nanotech, or new energy sources—will fuel the next boom? History says something great will come along. America *will* survive and prosper—and you'll be glad you invested for the future!

ACCUMULATION PHASE

Decades ago, there was a single goal: retirement. You could pretty well anticipate your retirement date—age 65—and your retirement income—your promised pension, plus a monthly check from Social Security. But all that changed about 25 years ago when corporations started switching from defined benefit plans, which offered a fixed monthly check, to defined contribution plans, which required the employee to make contributions to a 401(k) plan.

Now, the amount of money you'll have in retirement is largely up to you—and the stock market! That's a frightening thought for many people who had never lived through a stock market crash. But in recent years this new generation of retirement plan investors has lived through *two* significant market declines: the dot-com bubble bursting in 2000, and the bear market brought on by the credit crisis that started in 2007. In each case, investors have been shocked to find their money—not only their profits, but their hard-earned contributions—has simply disappeared.

Or as one wise old trader explained to me many years ago when I asked what happened to all that money lost in falling stock prices: "My dear, it went to money heaven!"

If you lose 50 percent of your account value in a market decline, you have to then make 100 percent—just to break even. That is a daunting task for those who had hoped to retire early. Now they're wondering if they can retire at all.

But the stock market crash has definitely created a lifetime opportunity for younger investors. Their regular monthly contributions to the company retirement plan or individual retirement account are buying more shares for each dollar invested. When the market does rebound, and it will, they will have a chance at greater wealth, because they own more shares (more in Chapter 8).

Whether you've saved only a few dollars or are well invested in a retirement plan at work, you're in the accumulation phase if you are still contributing. Your company 401(k) retirement plan (or 403(b) savings plan for nonprofits) isn't the only place you could be saving. If you're self-employed or own your own small business, you can set up a Keogh plan, an IRA, a SEP-IRA, or an individual 401(k) plan. These plans differ in their contribution limits and in whether those contributions are made by employee or employer. You can find definitions and instructions for opening these accounts at any major mutual fund or brokerage web site because they also offer the mutual funds and stocks to make your retirement plan grow.

The accumulation phase won't stop until you stop making contributions to your IRA, Keogh, or 401(k), and that may be longer than you think—even past your official retirement date. If you're still working in retirement, you may continue making contributions to grow tax deferred in a company plan or in a Roth IRA—even as you are required to start taking distributions from your previous retirement plans after you reach age 70½. (Remember, there are no withdrawal requirements for a Roth.) The more money you continue to save, the more you'll have to grow and eventually to live on.

When you're in the accumulation stage, you basically have two issues to confront: how much to save, and where to invest.

Let me respond to the first question by saying that I have never, ever heard anyone complain about having saved too much for retirement! Money not spent in retirement can be passed on to the next generation, or left to a worthy cause. It's far better than the other alternative of having to scrimp on food, medicine, heat, or air-conditioning—circumstances that many of today's elderly face daily. Yes, presumably you may have regrets about all the money you saved if you die at an unexpectedly young age—but that's a long shot.

That brings us to the next issue: where to invest.

Suddenly investors are learning that there's no magic to the stock market, just long-term investment principles. The twin bear markets early in this century have both confused and angered those trying to save for retirement. They started with unrealistic expectations, and also misunderstand the nature and risks of the stock market. New investors had no idea about important issues like diversification and asset allocation—or the possibility that *all* sectors could decline together.

Now the industry focus will turn to investor education and tools to make sure those retirement assets will grow in both bull and bear markets. Those financial products are expensive and time-consuming to create. You'll find new forms of annuities that give upside growth, while protecting against losses. (See Chapter 12.) There is no product that can give a complete guarantee against loss, while promising protection against both bear markets and inflation. That's why some form of Monte Carlo modeling will be needed to assist investors in the accumulation phase—as they have more choices of investments and need to balance their hopes for growth against their fears of loss.

You'll find this advice through your company 401(k) plan, your bank, brokerage firm, mutual fund company, or financial planner. They'll help you track your investments, check the allocation among different asset classes, and model whether your current rate of savings and investment allocations will allow you to reach retirement age with enough assets.

That's the first half of the challenge. Withdrawal is the second.

WITHDRAWAL PHASE

The huge loss of assets facing those who had planned to enter the withdrawal phase is an immediate challenge. It will mean that those who can should work longer, and continue contributing to retirement plans. And for those who can't work longer, it will mean withdrawing less each year. So while the focus is on rebuilding assets, the financial services industry is ready to target the next great shift for this generation—the move from accumulation to withdrawal.

If building a pool of retirement assets caused anxiety, the withdrawal phase will be even more challenging. Taking an early approach will be critical to avoiding surprises. And modeling retirement withdrawals will give new insight into the importance of delaying retirement versus increasing investment risk. Even at this stage of life, time is far more important to your financial plan, and it gives more opportunity for success.

So withdrawal modeling is the next big use for Monte Carlo simulations. Now that you have a fixed sum in your retirement account, how should it be invested? How much can you take out every month? Where does Social Security fit in? And how much should you continue to earn by working? The trick is to make it come out even—your money *and* your life.

You could take your retirement assets and buy an immediate annuity—a check every month for life, like the old-fashioned pension plans. But do you remember the woes of people living on fixed incomes when inflation soared in the 1970s? They couldn't keep up with rising electricity bills and property taxes. Clearly, you need some exposure to stocks or real estate—assets that tend to keep pace with or increase in value during periods of inflation.

Or we could have *deflation*, a period of very slow economic growth in which prices actually fall, much like what Japan saw in the 1990s, and was feared most recently in America. If that happened, you'd be thrilled to have locked up 5 percent or 6 percent corporate bonds, while the Fed cut other rates to near zero to stimulate economic growth.

No one has a crystal ball to know whether inflation or deflation is in your future, so financial modeling is designed to create a balance that will get you through all extremes.

THE RIGHT BALANCE

When you look at the accumulation and distribution phases, you may recognize that they are one and the same, two distinct aspects of the same problem. You can't solve one without the other. That's why the sooner you start planning and modeling both your accumulation and distribution phases, the better off you will be.

Before going on to the specifics, I'd like to leave you with this word picture. It's an explanation I've used for many years to explain why I lost my active interest in mathematics somewhere during high school algebra.

The teacher drew a problem on the chalkboard that had to do with a bathtub. The hot water was running in at x. The cold water was running in at y. The tub drain was open, and the water was running out at z. The idea was to solve for all those values so you would know exactly when the tub was filled before it started to run over and so the bath water would be tepid, neither scalding nor frigid. My reaction was: What a waste of time! Why not just put your hand in the water to monitor the temperature and keep your eye on it so you can turn the water off before it runs over? Well, that works in bathtubs, but it didn't work very well with my math teacher. And it doesn't work very well in financial planning, either!

Think of it this way: The water running in is your accumulation phase. The hot and cold are the various choices in your investment mix. The water running out the drain is your withdrawal phase. And what's left at the end of your life is your estate. Do you want to chance your retirement going down the drain? I don't think so. So it's time to get started on your plan. The first step is getting organized.

SEVEN BEST WAYS TO SAVE FOR RETIREMENT

Here's the most important advice for the accumulation phase of your retirement planning: *Small contributions can add up to big money over the years.* That's especially true inside a retirement plan where you get a tax deduction for your contribution, and growth is not taxed until the money is withdrawn at retirement.

(A Roth plan offers an after-tax contribution, but the money is withdrawn tax-free.)

Automatic deductions are the best way to organize your retirement savings. Remember: If you don't see it, you won't spend it! If your company doesn't have a retirement plan, sign up for automatic contributions to an IRA with a mutual fund company, bank, or brokerage firm.

Once you've put money into your retirement plan, it's out of reach, since it is costly to withdraw early. There is a 10 percent federal penalty for early withdrawal before age 59½ from most retirement plans. And withdrawals are taxed as ordinary income, except for Roth IRAs and Roth 401(k) plans.

Here are highlights of how these plans work.

1. **Individual Retirement Account (IRA)**
   - Contribution limits: $5,000 in 2009 or $6,000 if over age 50. Contribution limits will be indexed to inflation in 2010, and beyond.
   - Earnings grow tax deferred; withdrawals are taxed as ordinary income.
   - Contributions are tax deductible at any income level if you are not covered by a company plan.
   - Contributions for those covered by a company plan are tax deductible below certain income levels: $55,000 maximum income for 2009 for the full deduction, $65,000 for a partial deduction) for single filers. Joint return income limits are $89,000, full deduction, and $109,000 partial deduction, even if one spouse is not covered by a company plan.
   - Distributions are required after age 70½.

2. **Roth IRA**
   - After-tax contribution, but tax-free growth and withdrawals.
   - Income limits: You may make a full contribution if your modified adjusted gross income (MAGI) is below

$105,000 for singles and $166,000 for joint filers in 2009. Less than full contributions can be made to a Roth IRA for those with MAGI below $120,000 on a single return and $176,000 on a joint return.

- Contributions must be made by date tax return is due for that year.
- No required distributions at age 70½.
- Special opportunity to convert a traditional IRA to a Roth in 2010, regardless of income levels. Taxes paid on the conversion can be spread over two years, 2010 and 2011. Taxes should be paid using money held *outside* the plan. Consider this if you believe tax rates will rise in the future.

3. 401(k) or 403(b) Retirement Plan

- Pretax salary deduction, with tax-deferred growth.
- Possible company match ("free" money!).
- Loans are available; but if you leave the company without repaying, the loan becomes a withdrawal, subject to taxes and penalties.
- Rollover to an IRA at retirement or when you leave company.
- Some 401(k) plans may allow *after-tax* Roth contributions.

4. Profit-Sharing Plan for the Self-Employed (Keogh)

- Discretionary annual contributions based on income.
- Maximum contribution is $49,000 in 2009.
- Account must be established by December 31 of tax year.

5. Tax-Deferred Annuities (see Chapter 12)

- After-tax contributions; tax-deferred growth.
- Drawbacks: Early-withdrawal penalties, surrender charges, high fees and costs.
- First withdrawals are taxed as ordinary income unless you annuitize with a monthly lifetime check.

6. Life Insurance

- Cash value borrowed is not taxed as income.
- Borrowings reduce ultimate insurance coverage.
- Variable policies build cash value, but no guarantees.

7. Your Home

- Builds cash value inside a growing asset, instead of using it as a piggy bank through home equity loans.
- Lifetime withdrawals are available through a reverse mortgage after age 62 (see Chapter 14).
- Drawback: Paying off mortgage eliminates tax deduction for interest.

Note: Many large and small companies have miscalculated the amount of fixed monthly pension checks owed to retired employees. At the National Center for Retirement Benefits, Inc., the "pension detectives" will investigate without charge, unless they uncover additional benefits. In that case, the fee is 20 percent of the additional money recovered. Go to www .ncrb.com or call 800-666-1000.

A final thought: Remember to name a beneficiary for your retirement account. See Chapter 18 for information about naming the correct beneficiary for estate tax purposes.

CHAPTER **6**

GETTING IT ALL TOGETHER

Ever since the economy and the stock market became front-page headlines in the midst of the deep recession, people have been talking about "financial literacy." That's a bit like locking the barn door after the horse is out! But amid all the problems, it's good that there's finally recognition that personal finance is an important part of everyone's education. And now there are new techniques and technologies that make it much simpler to gain control of your money—and your financial planning.

The first step in planning is getting organized. It will help you in your everyday money management, as well as planning for your future. Don't be afraid of technology. New devices and new online services give you an incredible edge in watching, managing, deciding, and organizing your finances.

You can avoid expensive over-limit charges on your credit card, by using your cell phone to get an instant view of your account. You can pay your bills on time, by scheduling them on your bank's web site, or through a computer program. And you can easily track your daily spending to see if you're exceeding the budget you've created. There are even web sites that let you compare your spending habits with others in similar circumstances—taking social networking to a new level.

Having your finances well-organized is a must, whether you're doing your own planning or seeking advice from others. You'll save time and energy if you can present your advisers with your complete financial picture all in one place. It doesn't make any sense to get advice only on your current 401(k) plan if you also have money in previous employers' plans or in an individual retirement account (IRA). Any advice on investing has to be in the context of your total financial picture—including the value of your home, business, and other savings. There are a few simple ways to put this picture together so you can present it to your advisers and track it yourself.

ONLINE, ON PAPER, ON YOUR COMPUTER

You can't reach your goals if you don't know where you stand now. Before we get to web sites and computer programs, try an easy exercise. Take out a sheet of paper and draw a line down the middle. On one side list what you *owe* and on the other side list what you *own*. On the "own" side, include the current value of your home, your retirement accounts, your savings, and anything that you could sell and turn into cash. On the "owe" side, list your debts, including the outstanding balance and the interest rate on your mortgage, car loan, credit cards, medical debt, student loans, and any other debts. That's the basic framework of your *balance sheet*—the big picture of where you stand financially today. Confronting that reality may be frightening, but it is the first step in gaining control of your money.

Now, take one more sheet of paper to create your *cash flow statement*—a picture of what's coming in, and what's going out every month. This is a more complicated task, because there are so many spending categories. Some like mortgage or rent are the same every month. Others, like phone, electricity, or gasoline, may arrive monthly, but in irregular amounts. And some payments, like homeowners or auto insurance, may come once or twice a year. If you're having trouble listing all those expenses you can purchase a simple budget book. Or, maybe now you can see why you're ready for a very simple computer program or a secure, helpful web site.

There are three ways to use your computer to track your personal finances: (1) Keep all your financial information on your own computer and then go out to the Internet to various web sites to update and download your banking and investment information. You can safely store all this information in a password-protected program on your computer, remembering to back up the data regularly. (2) View your financial information on your financial institution's web site, securely protected by your personal identification number (PIN). Then, if you are away from home and need to pay a bill, check your credit card balance, or sell a stock, you can access your account safely from any computer. (3) Use your iPhone, cell phone, PDA, or any computer to securely view your entire financial information from your various banks and credit card companies, as well as track your cash and check it against your personal budget. You can do this all in real time as you make spending decisions anywhere!

We've come a long way from budget books! Now I'll show you how easy it is to be on top of your spending, saving, investing, and every financial obligation, no matter where you are or when you want to take a look.

Free Online Money Management

In the past few years, technology has given you a new power over your money—if only you're willing to take advantage of it instead of being intimidated by it. Two leading web sites—Mint.com and QuickenOnline.com—download, categorize, and graph all your spending and finances automatically, every day—and compare them with your personal spending plan they helped you create. They'll even contact you with warnings about overdrafts or falling stock prices or bills coming due.

These web site services are *not* just for the techies and the younger generation! Even if you're approaching retirement, it's not too late to give these web sites a test drive. In fact, they could become a terrific retirement hobby, since now you have both the time and the motivation to pay close attention to your spending and investment accounts.

The proof of their usefulness is in their growth. Mint.com boasts that it is used by more than one million people, tracking $175 billion in spending transactions and more than $47 billion in assets in users' investment accounts. QuickenOnline has nearly as many users and offers similar features.

Currently these sites are not for transferring money or paying bills. Instead, they act as your personal bookkeeper, getting current information directly and securely from your banking, credit card, and investment companies.

You can create your own categories to organize your spending, or use their preset categories. You can even track the ways you spent the cash you withdrew from the ATM, so it won't be forgotten but instead will factor into your "spending trends."

The real value of these web sites goes beyond just getting your account balances. It comes from their tools, which are designed to make the numbers useful. They organize your information into a useful, graphic format—and help you analyze your spending. They'll even send you e-mail or text alerts to let you know when you have low balances or a regular bill payment coming due.

The Mint.com investment section allows you to compare your investments to major market indexes. You can see your asset allocation graphically, track your profits and losses compared to your cost basis, and even export all this information to a spreadsheet. As you'll see later in the discussion on portfolio tracking, Mint.com gives you all the current information, helpful graphics, and useful tools of desktop software. It puts the information literally at your fingertips and reminds you to take a look!

These online financial web sites are absolutely secure and private. It takes minutes to set up your account, and you're not committed to use it in the future. But you'll be hooked, I'm sure. Best of all, they're *free*! They are supported by advertising, so you don't pay for these services. Odds are they will actually *save* money for you, by showing you where you waste it and keeping you from making unwise impulse purchases. Mint.com even presents you with money-saving opportunities, such as CDs with higher interest rates or credit cards with better terms than the one you're using.

Some web sites include a social networking format that can be intimidating to those who grew up keeping personal finances very private. But web sites like Geezio.com and Mvelopes.com incorporate the ability to interact, anonymously, with other users to compare spending patterns or get advice from peers who are trying to reach similar goals.

You picked up this book because you wanted to do something different, learn more about your money, and get control over your finances. This is the place to start changing your money life. Take five minutes to tour Mint.com and give it a try (see Figure 6.1)!

Figure 6.1   Mint.com Spending Trends
Source: Mint.com.

THE BASICS: PAYING BILLS ONLINE

While all the technology just described is exciting, it can be a bit over-whelming if you're just getting started. So let's go back to the basics. The first step is online bill payment. If you haven't started paying all your bills online, you're missing out on the most basic way to save time, save money, and gain visibility and control over your finances. Most banks, savings and loans, and credit unions offer free online bill payment to their good customers, saving you the cost of stamps and printed checks.

If you go to your bank's web site, you will see a button to click to get more information and to sign up for online banking services. Don't be afraid that you'll get lost in cyberspace. Every bank has a toll-free help line where trained professionals can view your accounts and help you with any problems. In fact, help is faster with online banking because the customer service representatives can see everything in your accounts, and so can you—at the same time.

You are 100 percent guaranteed against fraud when you use online bill payment. You'll use your own password and PIN to gain access to the world's most secure money transfer network—one that the banking system uses to transfer trillions of dollars every day. If you've been tricked into revealing your PIN, contact your bank immediately. The bank will change your access code, and you will be completely protected against fraudulent withdrawals.

Your online bill payments are much more secure than paper checks. Just think about how many people handle a paper check, whereas your online transfer is just a series of securely transmitted digits. And your payment is guaranteed to arrive on time if you allow enough lead time. No more late fees for missing deadlines.

You can write an online check to *anyone.* Phone companies and utilities can receive electronic transfers to be credited to your account, but many individuals and small businesses are not set up to receive money that way. So if you want to write a check to your sister in another city, you can issue instructions online, and a paper check will be printed at the bank and mailed to her at no extra cost to you.

We've long anticipated the paperless society; and when it comes to checks, we're well down that road. In fact, the Federal Reserve has closed down several check-processing centers because of the decline in paper check writing. The next new thing will be online bill *presentation.* In fact, it's already starting.

Many large corporations already make it easy for you to visit their company web sites to view and pay your bill. But the next generation in online bill presentation allows almost all of your bills to be sent to *your* bank's web site. They are posted there so you can review the charges and dispute them, if necessary, before paying the bill directly from your bank web site. You can specify the date and the amount to be paid. Some banks will even send you an e-mail reminder that bills have arrived at your web site. Of course, it's all done with complete security.

No more waiting for the bill to arrive in your mailbox or having mail forwarded to you when you're on vacation. Online bill presentation allows you to view and pay bills securely from any computer, even when you're away on vacation. This is where the banking industry is going, and it's moving quickly. So get started today—and think of all the trees we'll be saving when we eliminate paper bills as well as paper checks!

How does this new technology of money management help you in retirement planning? Actually, it's a central part of planning how much money you'll need to spend in retirement and of tracking that spending once you are retired. If you start now, you'll have a complete financial record of your cash flow, and you'll be able to pay down debt more easily. You will also be able to accurately assess your future needs.

ORGANIZING YOUR ONLINE FINANCIAL LIFE

You can pay bills at your bank web site from any location or initiate payments from a software program you install on your home computer. You can instantly track your spending and current status at web sites like Mint.com or QuickenOnline.com. But you might also want to *keep* those records in a more permanent fashion, stored on your own computer and backed up on a disk that you can send to your accountant at tax time.

That's where a program like Quicken desktop is useful, not only to pay your bills online but also to track your spending and organize your data on your personal computer. One of the helpful pages from Quicken Deluxe is shown in Figure 6.2.

There are two ways to use Quicken: (1) You can pay bills at your bank's web site and then download your check payment information into Quicken. Or (2) you can start the bill-paying process at your home computer and use Quicken to send payment instructions securely to your bank. Either way, you'll now have all your bill payment information organized, stored, and backed up on your home computer. It's a good idea to back up the program on a separate disk every time you use it. It's simple—just a click of your mouse to do it—and you'll be prompted to back up every time you exit the program.

Quicken automatically creates a check register, subtracts your balance, and reconciles your account as checks clear. (You can even print out the check register to remind you of the old days of writing

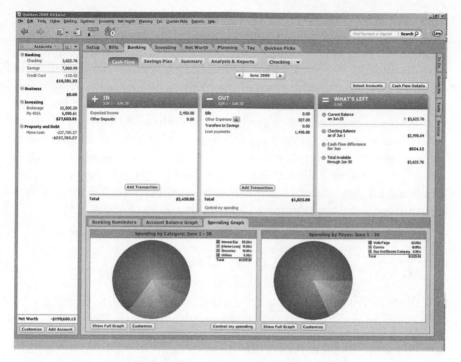

Figure 6.2   Quicken Deluxe 2009 Cash Flow
Source: Copyright © 2009 Intuit Inc. All rights reserved. Used by permission.
Quicken is a registered trademark of Intuit Inc.

paper checks and then rewriting everything in a check register!)
But what's most helpful about the electronic check register is that
you can assign a category to each of your checks and view your spending by category with a click of your mouse. Or you can click to track
your checks by payee. As you download your checking information,
you'll also see your ATM and debit card activities, showing where
the card was used or the location of the ATM withdrawal. Then you
can assign each debit to a category. Now you have no excuse for not
knowing where all the money went.

Quicken uses all this information to help you create your own
budget and your own spending categories. It guides you to pay down
your debt, and helps you create and track a very important category:
saving! Then other sections of the Quicken desktop program guide
you through the basics of financial planning.

There are several versions of desktop Quicken, and they are updated every year. To get started, you might try Quicken Deluxe, which you can buy in stores or download from www.quicken.com for about $60. There are also expanded programs with additional features for those who own small businesses. All allow you to set budgets and to make projections about paying down debt and building savings for college or other goals. You wouldn't track your cash flow today using an abacus or a slide rule. Similarly, the old-fashioned paper checks and register system can't begin to compete with a debit card, online bill payment, and the Quicken program. (Note MicrosoftMoney offers similar features, but the parent company has announced it will no longer support this software after 2012.)

A CREDIT CHECKUP

If you're planning and saving for retirement, you already know the importance of paying down debt. Unfortunately, that's a lesson many Americans are learning the hard way. Americans have nearly $1 trillion in unsecured credit—and default and bankruptcy rates have been soaring.

Card issuers face new restrictions on raising rates and fees, but that won't solve the problem of growing debt for the estimated half of all cardholders who make only minimum monthly payments. If you currently owe $1,000 on a credit card, with an annual percentage rate of 18 percent, and are making a minimum monthly payment of 2 percent of the balance, even if no further charges are ever added to the account, you won't have that $1,000 paid off for 12 years!

Here's a tip for paying down your credit card debt. If you double the current monthly minimum payment, keep paying that same amount monthly, and never charge another penny, your balance will be paid in full in fewer years.

Credit and bankruptcy is a huge subject, and many books exist to help you deal with those issues. Among the best is Gerri Detweiler's *Ultimate Credit Handbook*. But I must add a word of warning here about companies that promise to help you negotiate a lower payoff for your credit card debt. Yes, it might be possible to negotiate—but only if you have some cash on hand to offer as a settlement. Most of these companies suggest you stop making card payments and divert the money to an escrow account. Then they'll take their fees out of that account. And *then* they'll help negotiate on your behalf. By that time, your credit is ruined!

The one resource I recommend for help in this area is Consumer Credit Counseling Services, the national, nonprofit organization with member agencies in every state. Call 800-388-2227, and you'll automatically be connected to the nearest local agency. You can either get counseling (in person or over the phone) or work through their debt repayment program, which will help you out of debt, instead of getting you into deeper trouble. If you don't need this information, pass it on to adult children, co-workers, and friends. The toll-free number is always on the home page at www.TerrySavage.com.

PORTFOLIO TRACKING

Can you bear to look at your investments after the market crash? Well, you should do that on a regular basis—even if it is painful to see your hard-earned dollars disappear in a declining market. In fact, taking more interest in your investments will help you understand the benefits of continuing a regular program of retirement savings. (See Chapter 8.)

You probably receive either paper or online statements of your holdings from your company retirement plan, brokerage firm, and mutual fund companies. That creates the job of opening the envelope, perusing the statement, and filing it in some drawer where you'll accumulate quite a pile. While I'm not advising that you discard your monthly statements, there is a better way to track your investments.

Almost every major web portal, including MSN, AOL, MarketWatch, Motley Fool, and Google, offers a free service for investment tracking. They know you'll come back on a regular basis to view your portfolio and update your progress. And in the process, you'll view their ads. Not all tracking services are alike in the ease of inputting your investments or updating security values and prices. So where should you start?

Some services exist merely as a convenient place to view and update your holdings, but others provide more than just tracking the bottom line in each of your investment accounts. They add value, by giving you comparison tools so you know how your fund's performance compares to its benchmark, or how much of the bottom line increase in your account comes from growth versus your additional contributions. And on the downside, they'll let you know how much of a decline is a result of the market, and how much is taken out for fees!

In other words, there are some portfolio tracking opportunities that help you with your investment planning, and even integrate that information into your overall savings and retirement planning. Here are a few:

QUICKEN

Quicken is more than a free online tool, or a software package that can manage your finances. Within Quicken desktop there is a tool that can securely gather and track information about all your investments—from almost every brokerage firm, bank, mutual fund company, or other investment provider. If you want to do the online bill payment described earlier and the portfolio management explained here, you should probably purchase Quicken Premier, a step above Quicken Deluxe.

It can instantly collect updated information about your investment and retirement accounts from over 6,100 financial institutions, including 401(k) providers. All you have to do is contact each institution and set up online access, getting a user name and a PIN.

It's easy to add a new investment account into your Quicken software and set up the download procedure. As you enter the name of the financial institution, you will see the web address and toll-free number. If you don't have an ID number and a PIN, you can get them immediately and start downloading in minutes.

Then, you can safely store your PINs for all your accounts in the secure PIN Vault that's part of this software. When you go online to perform a one-step update, you can click on the PIN Vault, and the program will go directly to each financial institution to access the latest information. No more logging on to several sites and gathering information one account at a time.

The Investing Center in Quicken software gives you access to tools in the Performance and Analysis Views, which let you see how your portfolio is doing compared to major market benchmark indexes. In Performance View, you can compare your investments to major market benchmark indexes, average annual return, and your investing activity. In Analysis View, you can run through asset allocation and review Morningstar fund ratings.

You can get the average annual return for each of your accounts or over the entire portfolio for the past one, three, or five years. You can sort your accounts between taxable and retirement accounts, or you can view the portfolio as a whole and evaluate whether your asset allocation is on target and see how to rebalance your portfolio. Using data from Morningstar and provided by Quicken, you can compare the funds you own to others in the same category. You can see whether your investment performance is driven by actual portfolio gains or just by additional contributions you've made to your accounts.

Once you've downloaded your portfolio information into Quicken, you can view your entire financial net worth, including the equity in your house, your credit card debt, and the balances in your checking and savings accounts. All of your financial information is securely stored in one place where you can get a complete view of your total financial picture and use some basic tools to make projections for the future.

MORNINGSTAR

Morningstar.com is the outstanding web site for investment information on mutual funds and stocks. And it has a terrific online portfolio tracking section, complete with proprietary tools that analyze your portfolio and provide advice. A good portion of the information on the site is free, but there is a premium membership that costs $174 a year (or $18.95 a month). It's worth it if you want more personalized advice and analysis for your investments.

The Portfolio section of Morningstar.com, shown in Figure 6.3, is an excellent place to organize and track your entire investment portfolio. You can access it from any computer. And you can use your iPhone, BlackBerry, or cell phone to access your portfolio at any time.

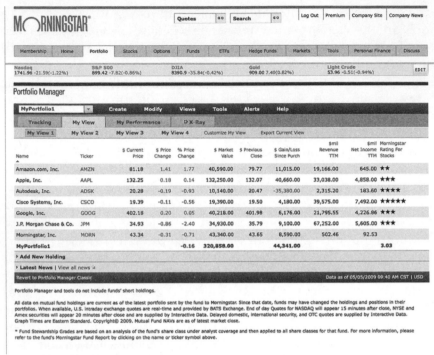

Figure 6.3   Sample Portfolio
Source: © 2009 Morningstar, Inc. All Rights Reserved. The information contained herein:
(1) is proprietary to Morningstar and/or its content providers; (2) may not be copied
or distributed; (3) does not constitute investment advice offered by Morningstar; and
(4) is not warranted to be accurate, complete or timely. Neither Morningstar nor its
content providers are responsible for any damages or losses arising from any use of
this information. Past performance is no guarantee of future results. Use of information
from Morningstar does not necessarily constitute agreement by Morningstar, Inc. of any
investment philosophy or strategy presented in this publication.

You'll be able to see not only the current prices of your stocks and
mutual funds, but also use some of the tools that let you track performance, compare to benchmarks, and check the Morningstar ratings
on mutual funds and individual stocks. Premium members can also
access the latest analyst reports and alerts directly from their PDA.

To get started, all you have to do is click on the "Portfolio" tab on
the home page at www.morningstar.com. Then you can set up one or
more portfolios. This can be done by "importing" your account data
as a direct download from most financial services providers and web

sites, including MicrosoftMoney, and from online portfolio trackers at AOL, MSN, Quicken, and Yahoo!, as well as brokerage firms such as Fidelity, ScottTrade, T. Rowe Price, and Bank of America. (There is a complete listing of firms online.)

Or you can simply take your latest monthly statements, and directly input your securities or funds, the number of shares, and your cost basis if you have it. There's even a "copy and paste" service to make this easier. (If you don't know the cost, but do have your purchase date, there is a special tool "Get Price" that will retrieve the closing price on the date of purchase.) Remember, cost basis is not as important inside a retirement account, since all withdrawals will come out as ordinary income.

You can set up more than one portfolio, and even create a "watch list" portfolio to follow stocks or funds that you're considering buying. Once you've set up your portfolio, the next step is to use the free tools that help you go beyond just tracking your investment performance, to help you understand the characteristics of your portfolio and warn you against overconcentrating in just one category of stocks.

Once you've created your portfolios, the fun begins. You can sign up for a daily e-mail service, letting you know how your portfolio is performing, along with links to news articles of interest. They'll also send e-mail alerts with at least 40 different triggers. For example, if your security moves up or down 10 percent in one day, has a change in its Morningstar Rating, or has a change in fund manager, you'll be notified. Because Morningstar tracks more than 22,000 different funds and 24,000 stocks, the data is readily available for this analysis.

The most useful feature of the Morningstar portfolio tracker is Portfolio X-Ray. To the get the full benefits of this service, you must be a premium member. (But there is a limited Instant X-Ray feature available to free users of this web site.) Once you've created a portfolio, click on the X-Ray tab, and you'll be given a wealth of information. (See Figure 6.4.) This feature looks *inside* your mutual funds to see the investments that each holds. Then all of that information is presented in a series of graphics that let you know how well you're diversified and how your portfolio stacks up against major indexes in terms of sector weightings. You can see the overall tilt of your portfolio—whether to large cap companies or smaller companies, whether toward companies considered growth-style or value-style

Figure 6.4   Sample Portfolio X-Ray

Source: © 2009 Morningstar, Inc. All Rights Reserved. The information contained herein: (1) is proprietary to Morningstar and/or its content providers; (2) may not be copied or distributed; (3) does not constitute investment advice offered by Morningstar; and (4) is not warranted to be accurate, complete or timely. Neither Morningstar nor its content providers are responsible for any damages or losses arising from any use of this information. Past performance is no guarantee of future results. Use of information from Morningstar does not necessarily constitute agreement by Morningstar, Inc. of any investment philosophy or strategy presented in this publication.

investments. And you can see how your sectors (consumer goods, health care, financial services, technology, etc.) stack up against the weighting of the Standard & Poor's (S&P) 500 stock index. You even get a report on the fees and expenses you're paying, compared to the average mutual fund.

Having your entire portfolio organized and analyzed will come in very handy in the next chapter, when we move from merely tracking to getting advice on your investments, and strategies to meet your retirement goals.

MOVING BEYOND TRACKING— TO ADVICE

Once you have your financial information organized, it's time to move to the next level—getting good advice. Now, we're going back to the concept of Monte Carlo modeling.

RESOURCES FOR GETTING IT TOGETHER

- QuickenOnline.com (free)
- Mint.com
- Geezio.com
- Morningstar.com
- Quicken.com (to download software)

CHAPTER 7

A ROAD MAP TO MONTE CARLO

At the start of this section, you had an introduction to Monte Carlo modeling—the computer simulations that can generate a range of likely outcomes from a large number of variables. Now it's time to put that great process to work for you, combining technology with financial planning.

Mutual fund management companies, independent online financial advice firms, financial services companies, and financial planners all offer some form of Monte Carlo modeling services. The advice may differ slightly from one service to the other, but here's what they all have in common.

- *Reaching goals.* You may have one significant goal—retirement. Or you may have a series of goals—college for your children, a vacation home, travel plans, or a child's wedding, for example. The best services allow you to model for reaching multiple goals and to see the impact your decisions have on each one.
- *Varying strategies.* The main benefit of Monte Carlo modeling is that it allows you to see instantly what happens when you change the variables. For example, you could decide to take more risk in your investment portfolio, to increase your contributions, or to delay your retirement. Each decision has a different impact on reaching your retirement goal. When you use online simulations, you can see the impact of changing one or more of these variables with just a click of your mouse, so you can make better decisions.

- *Investment allocation.* If the model knows your goals, it can forecast how a change in the investments within your portfolio is likely to affect your ability to reach those goals. Whether you're limited to the funds offered inside your company retirement plan or can choose from a large universe, the best advice models can direct you to an investment allocation that will give you a good chance to succeed.
- *Withdrawal scenarios.* Here's where Monte Carlo simulations get interesting and add the most value. Your model will help you create an investment portfolio *and* a withdrawal scenario that will last your lifetime.

I'm sure you have one big question about this process: Will all the models provide the same advice if I provide the same input about my age, goals, and retirement savings? The answer is no. Each model might use slightly different data about market history, perhaps because of different time ranges. And each model might run a different number of simulations to create the range of probable outcomes. (The more simulations you run—several thousand at a minimum—the more reliable the projections will be.) And each model might weight the variables in a slightly different formula. The resulting investment and withdrawal advice could be moderately different, depending on the model used. And since this is a relatively new process, we won't be able to determine which service is best for many years to come. By that time, you will be well into your retirement.

After the recent stock market crash, many criticized Monte Carlo models for assigning relatively low probabilities to extreme market moves. Statisticians argue about bell-shaped curves, and fat tails (the chances of extremes at either end of the curve). We've just lived through one of those "least likely and most extreme" market events. But that's missing the point. We could always eliminate risk of market declines, simply by staying in cash! However, we'd then take on a greater risk by not having investment growth to create enough money to carry us through retirement. You can only do that—stay in safe cash equivalents—if you have "more than enough" money to last through a long period of retirement.

For most retirees, Monte Carlo modeling provides guidance to the trade-offs between risk and reward, so you can have a reasonable degree of confidence in your plan. These tools give you probabilities, not guarantees.

There is one thing you can be sure of: No matter which modeling program you choose from those mentioned in this chapter, you'll be far ahead of those who are using guesswork to figure out how much money they need to retire and how they can best withdraw their money to finance their lifestyle.

THE BEST ROUTES

No matter how you do it—whether you work independently with online tools, use online calculators with help from a financial firm, or get all your results and advice from an accredited financial planner—Monte Carlo modeling will be the basis for the best financial planning. So here are a few places to get this advice, recognizing that the competition for your retirement dollars is fierce and ever-changing.

Many corporate 401(k) plan providers offer Monte Carlo modeling and advice services to their employees from independent, third-party providers. Companies that offer their plan participants online modeling through any of the services discussed in this chapter solve the problem of data entry; the plan provider does it for you and automatically updates the data for new contributions, dividend payments, and changes to investments within the plan.

Although employer plans can offer third-party assistance for the accumulation phase, they are generally less useful for modeling withdrawals. That's because good withdrawal advice requires more investment options, such as immediate annuities for a portion of your money.

In fact, you probably don't want to leave your money in your company 401(k) plan after retirement because you will have a limited choice of investments, many of which are suitable for the accumulation phase rather than the more conservative withdrawal phase. Another reason to roll your company retirement plan into an IRA is because many company plans require an immediate distribution of funds at the death of the participant. That deprives your heirs of the ability to spread out distributions and to delay taxes on withdrawals. (See Chapter 18 on estate planning.) So it is better to roll your company retirement plan into an individual retirement account (IRA) at retirement, and seek advice that is appropriate for generating both an investment and a withdrawal strategy.

If your employer doesn't provide advice for your retirement investments and planning, you still have several providers from which to choose to get individual access to investment allocation advice. Here are a few you should consider.

Financial Engines

If you're in the accumulation phase, Financial Engines has one of the best modeling services, giving specific investment advice modeled for your own situation. This web site was created by Dr. William Sharpe, the Nobel Prize–winning economist who was honored for his contributions to modern portfolio theory. It was built to offer the same sophisticated tools used by money managers to employee retirement plan participants, who otherwise had little guidance in making fund choices.

Financial Engines' guidance is offered directly to plan participants by more than 750 corporate plan sponsors, including 112 of the Fortune 500 companies. Through these 401(k) plans, more than 7.4 million plan participants have access to Financial Engines' Monte Carlo modeling services for personalized investment advice. They also offer managed accounts to company plan participants.

Individuals can access the same tools online at www.financial engines.com for $39.95 a quarter or $149.95 a year. That includes modeling for all your tax-deferred accounts, employee stock options, and multiple goals, such as college savings, home down payment, as well as your retirement forecast. A premium service at $300 a year will also model your non-tax-deferred accounts. You can get a free, one-year trial subscription to Financial Engines by clicking on the box at www.TerrySavage.com.

When you sign up, you'll be asked to complete an online questionnaire. You'll need to input specifics, such as your age, current rate of contributions, and the investments you have in your retirement plans. (If your company plan offers Financial Engines, the investment data will be entered automatically.) This process will take a little thinking

Figure 7.1   FinancialEngines.com Forecast
Source: www.financialengines.com. The simulation pictured is hypothetical and provided for illustrative purposes only. This illustration should not be relied upon as investment advice.

because you'll also be asked about your goals, including retirement and other objectives.

The computer screens for Financial Engines allow you to move sliders to see the impact of changing variables on your retirement outlook. Your outlook is visualized as a weather forecast that ranges from dark and cloudy to bright and sunny, depending on your financial forecast. (See Figure 7.1.) More specific investment advice regarding switching individual funds is given with the forecast.

Whenever you return to the web site to check your forecast—sunny or partly cloudy—you'll be given advice about rearranging your portfolio. You might want to revisit every quarter or every six months to see how their engine suggests you rebalance your portfolio. If you are using no-load mutual funds, you can easily follow their advice to stay on track to reach your goals.

Since the majority of Financial Engines' subscribers are corporate employees, this program has concentrated on giving advice for the accumulation phase of retirement planning. It does not offer modeling for retirement withdrawals.

Morningstar Asset Allocator

Earlier in this section, I recommended Morningstar.com as an excellent place to track your portfolio and to get information on individual mutual funds and stocks. But once you've started tracking your portfolio on Morningstar.com, you can access some very simple tools to guide your retirement investment planning. This is a do-it-yourself version of basic Monte Carlo modeling, which is available to "premium" Morningstar members.

Simply click on the "Portfolio" tab, and then choose "Tools" from the menu. From there, click on "Asset Allocator." That lets you analyze your portfolio(s) in terms of your financial goals. You can move a slider to see the impact of changing your asset allocation. You can model for allocations that will allow you to reach a specific lump sum—your "number"—or for a specific stream of income at retirement. (Inflation adjustments are automatically programmed in, so you can use today's required income number for your goal.)

Then you move on to the second stage of planning, the Portfolio Allocator tool. It advises you on the appropriate allocation of your money among the funds and stocks you own (or the limited list of choices in your 401(k) plan). Or you can ask the tool to choose new funds or stocks based on the Morningstar analysts' picks of best-performing funds. (The Portfolio Allocator tool does not require premium membership.)

If you're feeling alone in your investment woes, Morningstar. com offers an easy way to share views with others. Simply click on the "Discuss" tab on the top line, and you'll find many investment topics and an individual view. Then if you click on "Sharing," you can actually post your own portfolio, minus dollar amounts, and get the thoughts of members. Or you can follow the most successful investors' portfolio choices.

If you're willing to make your own investment decisions based on independent research, Morningstar.com should be your home base for portfolio tracking and research. Or bring it to the attention of your company retirement plan executives. Morningstar offers similar advice to more than 17 million retirement plan participants as an adviser to 140,000 company plans, either helping them select a menu of funds or creating portfolios of mutual funds designed to be appropriate for various retirement goals.

T. Rowe Price

T. Rowe Price Advisory Services (www.troweprice.com) was one of the earliest entrants into the Monte Carlo modeling arena for withdrawal planning. Although the firm is best known for its top-performing and wide-ranging group of mutual funds, it has long provided individualized investment advice. The latest version of its Monte Carlo modeling tool is capable of running 100,000 iterations, or hypothetical market scenarios, to illustrate the probability of different retirement income strategies (e.g., asset allocation and withdrawal amount combinations) designed to keep you from running out of assets in retirement.

The tool can also be used to determine the amount to save each month in order to achieve an income goal in retirement. For investors getting close to retirement, it can demonstrate the potential benefits of waiting a year or two more before retiring. You can do basic modeling of your retirement planning strategy using its online retirement calculator for free at www.troweprice.com/ric.

If you'd feel more comfortable discussing your plans with an adviser, T. Rowe Price also provides Advisory Planning Services to individual investors with at least $100,000 in investments. They advise clients on how much they need to save each year, how they should be invested, and how much they can afford to spend annually in retirement. Clients pay a one-time fee of $250 for both an initial recommended retirement planning strategy and all ongoing annual checkups. (If you have at least $500,000 invested with T. Rowe Price, the $250 fee is waived.)

T. Rowe Price advisers don't focus a specific number or dollar amount you should have saved in order to have a comfortable retirement, but on the percentage of your current salary you will be able to withdraw from your investments when you retire. With their Monte Carlo–based Advisory Service, an extensive online questionnaire elicits information about your investment risk tolerance, priorities, goals, and time horizon. Then the computer generates a range of individual investment and withdrawal scenarios, sorted by varying probabilities of success.

An individual adviser is assigned to each client to provide a personalized strategy, which includes an asset allocation strategy and a dollar amount to contribute or withdraw each year. The adviser will also help you with that critical decision: when it may be financially optimal for you to retire, given your personal goals and the money you have accumulated to provide for retirement income. Your individual adviser is available to help implement the strategy if your assets are held at T. Rowe Price.

T. Rowe Price views the accumulation phase and the withdrawal phase as integrated parts of the advice process. And, it's an ongoing process, so there is no cost for an annual checkup.

Fidelity

Fidelity Investments has perhaps the most ambitious retirement planning service. It's far grander in scope than just Monte Carlo investment and retirement income planning. In an effort to capture the assets of America's baby boomers, Fidelity has decided it will provide an all-encompassing service for this generation.

The Fidelity Retirement Income Advantage program provides the framework for learning, planning, investing, and withdrawing all your retirement assets, from Social Security and pension checks to IRA rollover assets and other savings, whether invested with Fidelity or elsewhere. The starting point is a Monte Carlo planning tool that guides individuals to deal with risks ranging from inflation and rising health-care costs to investment risk and concerns about outliving assets. Then, using your individual input on expenses and sources of income, it will generate both investment and withdrawal scenarios. There are also a number of what-if scenarios that you can run to understand the impact of potential changes to your retirement plan.

The investment strategies model both taxable and tax-deferred accounts. The resulting recommendations present both Fidelity and third-party investment products, ranging from money markets to equity and bond funds to annuities. And with $50,000 or more to invest outside a company plan, Fidelity will actually manage your mutual fund portfolio for a small annual fee.

The Retirement Income Planner guides you through the risks I mentioned earlier in the book—outliving assets, inflation, investment risk, and the rising cost of health care—and creates a sustainable model of regular withdrawals. You can do all the work online by following the steps of the computerized program, which offers explanations along the way to help you make intelligent choices as you input data. A Fidelity planning consultant is also available to guide you through the process, either by phone or in person at one of Fidelity's many branches nationwide.

Recognizing that baby boomers want consistent attention and advice, Fidelity takes retirement modeling one step further. Once the plan is created, it can be tracked online, and you can choose to receive an alert if and when your account moves away from your selected target asset allocation.

Fidelity consultants will help you determine required minimum withdrawals from IRAs and will suggest which accounts should be drawn down first, even from non-Fidelity accounts such as bank IRAs. With Fidelity's online bill payment service, you can have pension and Social Security checks deposited directly to your account. You can pay your bills from that account or send yourself a planned monthly distribution from your retirement funds.

This service is offered free to Fidelity customers, and noncustomers can create a free "membership" account to gain access as well. (See Figure 7.2.)

Vanguard

The Vanguard Group, which manages some of the largest funds and specializes in index funds, has provided a type of Monte Carlo modeling to its clients for many years. Its web site—www.vanguard.com—has an online retirement accumulation calculator powered by Financial Engines.

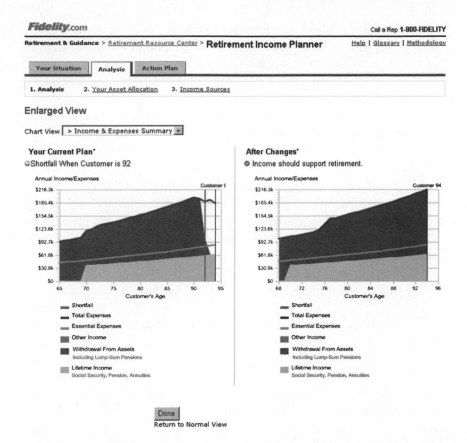

Figure 7.2   Retirement Income Advantage Income and Expenses Summary
Source: Fidelity Investments. Copyright © 2004–2009 FMR LLC. All rights reserved. Used with permission.

Vanguard also offers a more personalized service to clients. It uses a variation of Monte Carlo modeling called "time pathing" to generate a range of probable scenarios. That strategy orders returns from every 20- or 30-year period for every asset class under consideration; then it calculates the likely probability of running out of money for various investment and withdrawal scenarios. You choose the scenario with the probability that lets you sleep.

The fee for this service at Vanguard ranges from free to $1,000, depending on the aggregate account balance in Vanguard products. The fee covers a one-time consultation with a certified financial planner who will walk you through the choices and help you develop a plan, using both Vanguard and non-Vanguard investments. They also have a complete and ongoing money management service at a higher cost.

Financial Planners

The personalized services that professional financial planners provide will continue to be a critical resource for baby boomers in spite of the tools, advice, and information to be gained online. For many people who are unfamiliar with both finance and technology, there's no substitute for a professional who can deal with both of those issues while giving you the personal reassurance to create a plan and stick with it.

But you want to make sure you're getting advice from someone you can trust. That search starts with a professional organization that trains, tests, and certifies individual planners. Just as you wouldn't go to a physician who was not an M.D. or a surgeon who was not board certified, you should look for the initials CFP—certified financial planner—when considering a financial planner. It's not a perfect guarantee, but it does keep you away from product salespeople who only call themselves financial planners. You can learn more about CFPs from their web site, www.cfpboard.org. You will find a search engine there that allows you to check a planner's credentials and disciplinary history or to get a list of CFPs in your area.

Not all planners are compensated in the same way. Many charge an hourly fee for creating and updating a plan—plus, they receive commissions on products they sell, such as life insurance or mutual funds. Fee-only financial planners do not accept commissions or compensation of any kind on the products they sell. Fee-only planners are credentialed through the National Association of Personal Financial Advisors (NAPFA), which awards the RFA—registered financial adviser—designation. NAPFA members can be reached at www.feeonly.org.

There's a big difference between a product salesperson and a true financial planner. Banks, brokerage firms, and mutual fund management companies have created all kinds of names and titles for their salespeople. It's up to you to ask questions about their registrations, training, experience, references, and compensation; and your questions should elicit an honest response. Trust your instincts. If you have any doubts, walk away. You may not know much about financial planning, but you haven't reached this point in life without learning an awful lot about people.

ARRIVING IN MONTE CARLO

So now you've seen the future of financial planning. Guesswork, estimation, and paper-and-pencil calculations are a thing of the past. There's mystery inside those computer black-box programs, but they're being designed by mathematicians and statisticians. Monte Carlo modeling is simply the process of rolling the dice a huge number of times to see the likelihood of different outcomes. A computer can roll those dice millions of times in just a moment or two and give you results.

Keep in mind that your personal circumstances can change over time. What might be a good plan at age 60 or 65 could be impacted later by a variety of circumstances, including unexpected medical expenses, a death in the family, or even an unexpected increase in your assets from an inheritance. Planning is a process, not an event. You'll want to return to your planning adviser, perhaps annually, to update your data and to consider changes to your plan.

The companies I've mentioned in this chapter are just a recommended few of the many financial services firms that offer Monte Carlo modeling. Always choose a reputable and responsible provider. As I noted, there will be slight differences in the scenarios and recommendations provided by the various firms mentioned here. What's really important is that you're doing something statistically significant about planning for your investments and withdrawals during retirement. For sure, your odds of coming out ahead are much greater.

CHOOSING A FINANCIAL ADVISER

The recent financial crisis and stock market crash have led to calls for more regulation of financial services firms, and even a new entity to serve as a consumer watchdog. Currently, stockbrokers, registered investment advisers (RIAs), and certified financial planners (CFPs) have different credentials and are held to different standards of fiduciary responsibility. And they are compensated differently. Just because someone calls himself an "expert" doesn't mean he has the same level of experience or proficiency. Until common standards are established, and monitored, you have to do your homework. Here are some resources that will help:

- **www.finra.org**   This is the web site of the Financial Industry Regulatory Authority. It explains the arbitration process, by which every investor has agreed to resolve disputes. There's a direct link to the Office of the Whistleblower. Click on BrokerCheck to find a salesperson's background.
- **www.sec.gov**   The Securities and Exchange Commission web site has a section called Enforcement, where you can see the names of suspended firms, read about suspected scams, or report an abuse.
- **www.morningstar.com**   Click on "Stewardship Grade" to evaluate a mutual fund in terms of its shareholder responsibility.

- **www.cfpboard.org** The web site of certified financial planners allows you to search for credentialed planners and to check on their registration and disciplinary history.
- **www.feeonly.org** This is the web site of credentialed financial planners who do not charge commissions on products they sell but work on a fee-only basis.

PART

3

INVESTING
FOR
RETIREMENT

CHAPTER 8

STOCKS, BONDS, AND CHICKEN MONEY

D on't give up on the stock market! If you do, you are effectively giving up on America. The stock market represents the growth and opportunity of our free enterprise system. The valuation of stock reflects our optimism—or pessimism—about the future. As you'll see in this chapter, over the long run a diversified portfolio of American stocks has been a great investment. And history also tells us that just when things look worst for the country and the stock market, the best buying opportunities are created.

It has been painful to see hard-earned dollars go down the drain in stock market losses. It's one thing to lose profits, but far more devastating to lose the money you invested, when you realize the hard work needed to earn those dollars in the first place. On the other hand, no one ever questioned their growing "wealth" when the stock market was rising.

Being a successful stock market investor requires great self-discipline and a confidence in the future that only comes with historical perspective. It's an old Savage Truth: "The lessons that cost the most, teach the most." The past few years have taught an expensive lesson. But don't learn the *wrong* lesson from this experience. Don't give up on America and the stock market.

For most Americans, the stock market is the greatest opportunity to grow your own hard work into wealth, by letting your money go to work for you. If you're just starting out, you've been given a great point of entry. If you're close to retirement, it's tempting to belatedly become very conservative. As I've written for years, the concept of having enough "chicken money" (as described in this chapter) should take place *before* a crisis—so you don't panic and sell your long-term investments at the wrong time.

Speaking of timing, a word to the wise: No one has perfect timing when it comes to stock market investing. There's a great and long-running debate about whether you can come out ahead by picking the turns in the stock market. Trading successfully is difficult because you have to be right three times—when you get in, when you get out, and when you get in again! Markets turn quickly at tops and bottoms, and typically when least expected. So your timing has to be nearly perfect to capture the gains.

There's another reason it's difficult to trade successfully. It's because of those two most devastating emotions: fear and greed. These emotions only emerge when it comes to money decisions. And they destroy all rational thought. Greed seduces you into believing you are smarter than the market. No one wants to listen to sensible advice at the top. In the fall of 2008, Jim Cramer was excoriated when he suggested people have five years of living expenses set aside so they could ride out a bad market. Not bad advice, in hindsight!

No one can tell you where the bottom of a bear market will ultimately be made—although many will try to "call the bottom." Again, you'll only know for sure in hindsight. But if you stick to your plan of regularly investing on a monthly basis, for sure *you* will be buying near the bottom—unless you think the market and America are going straight down forever. And that's a bad bet, based on history.

Bottom line: You don't have to become an investment expert in order to make smart retirement decisions. You simply have to make a sensible plan—in terms of asset allocation, risk assessment, and investment diversification. And then you have to stick with that plan, over the long run, and not fall victim to those emotions that always lead people to buy at the top and sell at the bottom.

You also have to know enough to ask the right questions and to judge which investments are appropriate for your situation and your own risk tolerance. There are shelves of books about investing (including three of my own) and a vast array of web sites to give you detailed explanations. But this section is meant to give you realistic expectations—and some easy strategies—for retirement investing.

The balance among different types of investments, such as stocks, bonds, and what I call safe, chicken money, will change as you move toward retirement and then into your withdrawal phase. Most people will become more conservative as they age, but you'll always need some investments in stocks because of their potential for growth.

Even within the category of stock market investments, you'll want to have exposure to different sectors of the market. You might use mutual funds to diversify into international stocks or natural resources stocks, for example. As you move into retirement, your investment choices aren't limited to the funds offered by your company retirement plan if you roll your retirement assets into an individual retirement account (IRA).

Investing is always about creating a balance between risk and reward. To do that, you need perspective. And you may very well choose to have professional advice. But how can you recognize good advice if you know very little about the subject yourself? That's why it's so important for you to understand the basics of investing and to have realistic expectations.

REALISTIC STOCK MARKET EXPECTATIONS

Stocks—or mutual funds that own stocks—will probably be the core of your retirement portfolio. Given the devastation of the bear market, that may be an unappealing fact. But it is also your greatest opportunity to grow your wealth. Most companies no longer offer pension plans that will generate a monthly retirement check. And since many existing corporate and government pension plans are seriously underfunded, more responsibility for retirement savings and investments will be placed on individuals through individual retirement accounts and 401(k) or 403(b) plans at work. All of those retirement plans are built primarily around the stock market.

Think of the need for stock market investments as a trade-off. Either you cut your lifestyle dramatically now to save enough for your retirement or you save enough to invest in the stock market, and let your money work for you, growing over the long run, to reach your goals. The answer for most people will be a combination: save more and keep investing!

Because you have read the earlier chapters on Monte Carlo modeling, you now have an idea of the needed amount of savings to reach your retirement goals. Now, let's face the issue of what to do with those savings. Depending on your age, and stage, in life, you'll want to become an investor.

There are good reasons for making stocks the core of a retirement investment plan. Stocks make it easy to diversify your investments across sectors of the economy. Stocks are a liquid investment, meaning you can get in and out easily. And stocks are easily valued at the closing price every day, so you don't have to worry about getting an estimated value if you could sell. Finally, stocks have a long-term record of keeping up with, and even surpassing, the effects of inflation—a fact that's important to remember in the wake of recent losses.

Stock Market Returns—Then and Now

What kind of returns can you *really* expect from your stock market investments? Just a few years ago, there was a widespread belief that 15 percent or greater annual returns were relatively easy to achieve. After all, that's what investors had come to expect based on their experience in the late 1990s.

For the bull market period between 1982 and 1999, the average total return of the Standard & Poor's (S&P) 500 was an unprecedented 18.7 percent. It's no wonder that watching the stock market became the national pastime, and rising stock prices sparked dreams of wealth and easy retirement. It was as if everybody had a winning lottery ticket.

Then, two successive bear markets brought investors back to reality. The dot-com bust of 2000 seemed obvious in hindsight. Did anyone really believe that earnings didn't matter—and that it "being first in the space with eyeballs" was a good investment metric? After that crash, the market managed to make new highs by spring of 2007. Helped by a flood of liquidity facilitated by the Federal Reserve, money flowed into the stock market. The Dow Jones Industrial Average topped 14,000 in midsummer 2007.

That liquidity also helped create an economic boom in the housing markets, as financial institutions leveraged the housing market—and the political pressure—to create mortgages for people who had little in the way of savings or income that would have justified the loans. Again, in hindsight, it is clear that the housing bubble could not expand forever, as I wrote at the time. But because the mortgage loans were securitized, passed on to global investors, and held off bank balance sheets, it was not so easy to measure the size of the bubble or the devastating impact of the subsequent collapse.

The bear market in 2000–2001 wiped out $7.2 trillion in total market value of stocks It's estimated that the bear market that started in fall of 2007 wiped out $30 trillion of global stock market assets, and perhaps an equal amount in real estate assets, both residential and commercial. By March 2009, the Dow Jones Industrial Average had fallen below 6,500—matching losses posted by almost every global market index.

Such an extreme boom-and-bust cycle is bound to cut into investors' confidence. People are wondering what stock market returns to expect for the future. The answer lies somewhere between the extremes of euphoria and despair, and it hinges on your time horizon.

Historic Returns—The Big Picture

First, let's look at the lessons of history. From 1925 through 2009, the S&P 500 stock index had an average annual total return of 9.6 percent. ("Total return" includes dividends and price gains.) The chart of long-term market returns in Figure 8.1 shows that $1 invested in a diverse portfolio of large company stocks in 1926, with dividends reinvested, gives you that average annual return. There were big ups and downs in the market along the way, and you've lived through some of the most dramatic ones.

That top line on the chart represents the value of $1 invested over the years, but it also represents the U.S. economy. And, taking the long-term perspective, you must be struck by the overall uptrend represented by that line.

Are you willing to bet against that huge uptrend, against the U.S. economy and its future? Think of all those people who swore they'd never buy another share of stock after going through the Depression of the 1930s. What a ride they missed! Similarly, those who were

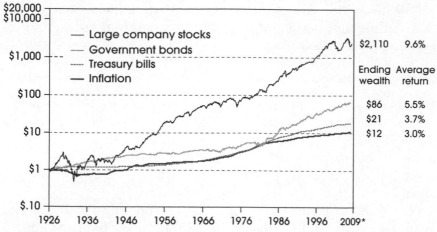

Hypothetical value of $1 invested at year-end 1925. Assumes reinvestment of income and no transaction costs or taxes.
*Data through June 2009.

This is for illustrative purposes only and not indicative of any investment.
An investment cannot be made directly in an index.
Past performance is no guarantee of future results.

Figure 8.1   Stocks, Bonds, Bills, and Inflation, January 1926–June 2009
Source: Copyright © 2009 Ibbotson Associates, Inc. Reprinted with permission.

burned in the stock market crash of 1973–1974 would have missed out on the entire 1990s bull market if they had stayed on the sidelines. What future gains will you miss if you're scared out of the stock market by your most recent experience?

It's important to note that the long line represents a *diversified* portfolio of large company stocks, with *dividends reinvested.* The S&P 500 stock index didn't exist back then, but today it would represent that diversified portfolio. If you invest in an S&P 500 index-tracking mutual fund (and almost every major fund company offers one), you could reinvest your dividends very easily.

And don't discount the importance of dividends. During the period of this chart, going back to 1926, dividends have represented 43 percent of the total return of the S&P 500 index. Dividends might not seem important in recent history, as corporate managers used their excess cash to buy back stock so they could push share prices higher and make their stock options more valuable. Now as companies cut costs in an effort to return to profitability, there will be more incentive to return cash to shareholders—especially if demand remains low and there is little reason to invest the cash in building productive capacity.

Long Term—Do You Have 20 Years?

We can't predict the future for the stock market, but the past should be a good guide if you believe in the future of America. (If you're a pessimist about America's future, then you certainly aren't thinking about retirement!) And based on the past, there's a strong argument for investing a significant portion of your retirement funds in stocks—*if you have at least a 20-year time horizon.*

Figure 8.2 explains why. It takes that top line in Figure 8.1 and breaks it up into time periods. The bar on the far left shows that if you hold stocks for only one year, you have about a 50-50 chance of making or losing money. The bar on the far right is the ultimate argument for stock market investing. *It shows that there has never been a 20-year period—going back to 1926—where you would have lost money on a*

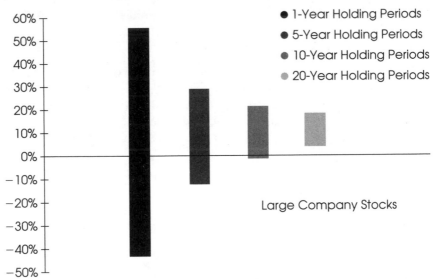

Each bar shows the range of compound annual returns for the period 1926–2008.

This is for illustrative purposes only and not indicative of any investment.
Past performance is no guarantee of future results.

Figure 8.2 Reduction of Risk over Time, 1926–2008
Source: Copyright © 2009 Ibbotson Associates, Inc. Reprinted with permission.

*diversified portfolio of large company stocks with dividends reinvested—even
adjusted for inflation.*

You can pick any 20-year period, even a time during the Depression
and even the time in the 1970s when the market stayed below 800
for almost a decade. No matter what period you choose, you would
not have lost money at the end of 20 years, even adjusted for inflation. That's held true throughout stock market history, going back to
1926. Do you really think it will be different this time?

This is not to say stocks are the only sound investment for a retirement portfolio. Stocks can be devastating over shorter time periods,
as you've seen. You'll need some balance. Alternative investments,
such as real estate and commodities, may outperform the stock market from time to time. In fact, they may shine far more than stocks
in a period of high inflation. And, of course, some sectors of the
market may at times outperform the major indexes.

That acknowledged, if you do plan to live at least another 20 years,
these two charts are a powerful argument that you need to have a
substantial portion of your retirement fund invested in that diversified portfolio of stocks, while continually monitoring the appropriate proportion of stock market investments as you approach the age
at which you'll need to start withdrawing money.

What is your appropriate proportion to be invested in equities?
That's an individual question, one that's answered personally by the
Monte Carlo retirement modeling described in Part 2 of this book.
It's important to know that your model will be different from that
of your neighbor, your sister-in-law, or your coworker. And the stock
market itself will have its own behavior, regardless of your personal
needs. So you need realistic expectations about the market in order
to make—and live with—your own investment decisions.

Persuasive Perspective

One thing to be learned from the long-term charts is that every generation had its own fears for the future, its own worries that this time
around things were different. That's why you'll appreciate Figure 8.3,
a Morningstar chart showing that even though the recent bear
market was both costly and frightening, it was not unique! There
have been eight bear markets that sustained losses of more than 20
percent, and the most recent was the worst since the stock market

Month-End Results as of March 2009 (since 1925)

Peak	Trough	Decline	Recovery
August 1929	June 1932	83.41%	January 1945
October 2007	February 2009	50.95%	To be determined
August 2000	September 2002	44.73%	October 2006
December 1972	September 1974	42.63%	June 1976
August 1987	November 1987	29.53%	May 1989
November 1968	June 1970	29.25%	March 1971
December 1961	June 1962	22.28%	April 1963
May 1946	November 1946	21.76%	October 1949

Figure 8.3   Peak-to-Trough Declines of Over 20 Percent on the S&P 500
Source: © 2009 Morningstar, Inc. All Rights Reserved. The information contained herein: (1) is proprietary to Morningstar and/or its content providers; (2) may not be copied or distributed; (3) does not constitute investment advice offered by Morningstar; and (4) is not warranted to be accurate, complete or timely. Neither Morningstar nor its content providers are responsible for any damages or losses arising from any use of this information. Past performance is no guarantee of future results. Use of information from Morningstar does not necessarily constitute agreement by Morningstar, Inc. of any investment philosophy or strategy presented in this publication.

crash of 1929. That statistic is sad comfort. But the chart is posted here because of its final column—the time from trough to recovery. You will notice that while patience was required, there eventually *was* a recovery from every bear market—and in each case the stock market rose to make substantial new highs!

So, as you become a long-term investor, there are likely to be many times when you might ask: *Is it different this time?* It's another way of asking whether you should stop investing in the stock market at a given point because things have changed. They never have before. I believe that as long as our free enterprise system remains intact, the long uptrend will remain intact. It's possible that it will be different in the future, but do you want to bet your retirement on it?

Opportunity of a Lifetime?

And that brings up the opportunity for younger investors. While they may not have as much money as their parents, they do have more time. And as noted earlier, time is the most valuable asset. A recent study by T. Rowe Price shows that those who start investing during a severe bear market gain a substantial advantage by investing regularly over those decades until retirement. That's because they have two powerful forces in their favor: the cyclicality of markets, and the ability to accumulate more shares earlier in their investing career. If you have the discipline to maintain a program of regular investing, even as the market remains discouraging, you will reap greater rewards over the long run. Here's the historical proof.

Compare the results of four investors who each contributed $500 per month (15 percent of a $40,000 annual salary) invested into a retirement account invested in the S&P 500 index, regularly over a 30-year period. Two of those investors started out just before two of the worst bear markets in history—1929 and 1970. The others started in 1950 and 1979—just before two great bull markets (see Figure 8.4).

The surprising result: The ending account balances of the two investors who started in bear markets were more than double those

This chart illustrates the account fluctuations of four different investors contributing during four different 30-year periods. Each investor contributes $500 per month (or 15 percent of a $40,000 annual salary) into a retirement account invested in the S&P 500 index over a 30-year period. A hypothetical $10 share price was used at the beginning of each period and was indexed to follow the monthly fluctuations of the S&P 500. All dividends were reinvested in additional shares.

The investors who began contributing in 1929 and 1970 started at the beginning of decades with ferocious bear markets. Yet their ending account balances were more than double those of the two investors who began contributing at the start of decades with strong bull markets, in 1950 and 1979.

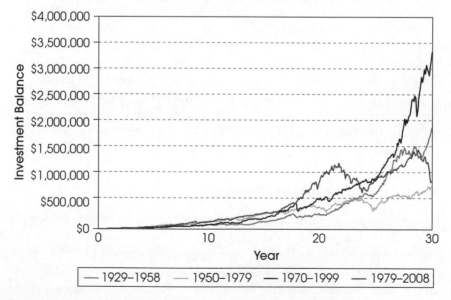

Figure 8.4   Advantages of Bear Market Investing
Source: T. Rowe Price Associates, Inc. Reprinted with permission.

of the two investors who began contributing at the start of decades with strong bull markets!

Then, as now, it was discouraging to keep investing monthly in a market that showed poor returns. The S&P 500 had a negative (–0.9 percent) return from 1929 to 1938, and only a 5.9 percent return in the stagflation of the 1970s, as these investors were starting out. Yet the bear market investors stuck to their plan—and that provided a huge benefit:

At the end of 30 years, the portfolios of those who started out in the bear markets were worth more than double the value of the two investors who started out in bull markets! All those years of buying shares at low prices put them in a better position to gain from *future* bull markets, after the initial bear market.

Are you thinking that's ancient history? Well, let's project the retirement portfolio results for today's investor, taking a starting date of 1999 and continued regular investments through 2008. Suppose today's investor *never makes any more investments*, but simply maintains her account for the remaining 20 years from 2009 until retirement. We'll project that she earns only the same, relatively low 8.5 percent annualized return that was realized between 1929 and 1958, a very sub-par period in stock market history. Even so, at the end of 30 years her account will have gained a 1,208 percent return on her contributions!

Take another look at Figure 8.4, which shows the results for the four investors. As T. Rowe Price demonstrates: "A poor start doesn't necessarily equate to a smaller nest egg. History, indeed, demonstrates just the opposite—assuming they maintain their investment program."

(The T. Rowe Price study used a hypothetical $10 share price at the beginning of each period, and it was indexed to follow the actual monthly fluctuations of the S&P 500. All dividends were reinvested in additional shares.)

What to Expect—The Next 20 Years

People facing retirement have tough decisions to make. History is interesting, but we live in the present, and we plan to retire in the future. Even if you believe in the long-term uptrend of the stock market, every period has its own characteristics that create the overall average. So what can long-term investors reasonably expect from their large company stock funds over the coming 20 years?

Twenty years is a critical time frame not only because, as Figure 8.2 showed, there has never been a 20-year losing period for large company American stocks (with dividends reinvested), going back to 1926. But it's also significant, because if you retire at age 65, you're likely to live another 20 years—and you'll need some growth in your investments to counter inflation. But how much growth can you reasonably expect—and what's the potential risk?

As you've just read, the stock market has gone through many periods of extremes—both on the upside and on the downside. In fact, whenever a market goes to extremes in one direction, you can certainly expect opposite and equal extremes in the other direction as the market reverts to its long-term trend line. That's exactly what has happened in the recent stock market crash.

The issue becomes one of figuring out where that trend line or "mean" return lies. And you also want to know how far it has gone in the extreme, and what future market returns might be likely, in an effort to return to the mean. If you'd like to get some historic pricing perspective for individual stocks—or major market averages—go to www.bigcharts.com, where you can see prices historically and graphically to give you that perspective.

Forecasting future stock market results is not a subject for crystal balls or astrologers, although some do try to predict the market using those tools. But there is a certain cyclicality, and—some say—predictability to market action by using charting techniques. This is certainly not an exact science, or there would be many more stock market gurus with real track records to back up their claims.

We can, however, look at the results of the past to get perspective. A 2005 study by B. Grady Durham, president of Monticello Associates, gave a useful analysis of the nearly 20-year bull market that ran from 1982 to 2000. Durham pointed out that the 18.7 percent average annual return of that bull market was almost double the Ibbotson long-term rate of return that goes back more than 80 years.

Where did those extraordinary returns come from? There were three components to that soaring bull market that peaked with the Dow Jones Industrial Average at 12,000: dividend yield, valuation change, and earnings growth.

Yield refers to the dividend payout, which contributed 3.2 percent per year to the average annual bull market return of 18.7 percent.

Earnings growth is the traditional driver of stock investment returns, and it contributed 6.6 percent to that 18.7 percent average annual return, only slightly above the long-term trend line.

Valuation change is simply the change in price/earnings (P/E) multiples—the ratio of stock price to company earnings each year. Amazingly, this component contributed 8.9 percent of the average annual market return during the 1982–2000 bull market—a reflection of the demand for stocks, and the willingness of investors to pay for future, predicted earnings. Both predictions and enthusiasm contribute to an expansion of P/E multiples—and thus to the bull market.

When the bull market began in 1982, stock prices were close to an all-time valuation low, with P/E ratios at 7 times earnings. By the time the bull market ended, valuations had been pushed to nearly 30 times earnings (see Figure 8.5). The long-term average P/E ratio of the S&P 500 stock index is 14.19 percent, according to Ibbotson.

What does that mean for investors in the future? At midyear 2009, the S&P 500 had a P/E valuation of 31.4 times current earnings and 12.4 times forecasted 2010 earnings—still high by historical standards. It also had a historically low dividend yield of 2.3 percent, compared to the long-term average dividend yield of 3.8 percent.

There's one more thing investors might have to contend with in the years ahead: changes in *volatility*. When the market is booming,

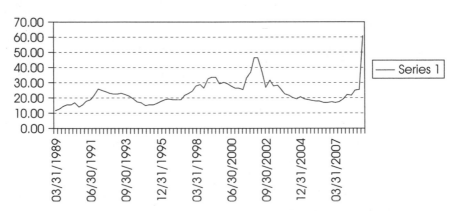

Figure 8.5   Stock Market Valuation, P/E Ratio of S&P 500, March 31, 1989, to March 31, 2007 (Quarterly)
Source: Standard & Poor's, S&P Index Services. Reprinted with permission.

investors feel more comfortable with high volatility. After all, most of the volatility in a bull market is on the upside. But in a period of lower expected returns, high volatility can be downright scary since it is leading to actual losses.

Volatility is such an important component of market expectations that there is actually a tradable index that tracks the level of market volatility: the Chicago Board Options Exchange VIX. It's sometimes referred to as the "fear index." But it can also be seen as an index of opportunity, since it reflects investors' implied anticipation of future market extremes.

Then there are years of both low volatility and low returns. In those years, like the 1970s, investors may actually be bored by the meanderings of a flat market. When the market enters a period of lower expected returns or lower volatility, it requires more discipline to stick to your investment plan.

Maybe now it's payback time for all those bull market years. In the next decade or so, stock market returns might be at or below the 9.6 percent long-term historical average. That doesn't mean you should completely give up investing in the stock market—even if you're close to retirement. It just means you'll have to adjust your expectations to more modest returns for a while. Knowing the context of market history will help you control your emotions even though you can't control the stock market.

UNDERSTANDING BONDS

When you're creating an investment portfolio, bonds are often seen as the alternative to stocks. Bonds are debt; stocks are equities. Bonds are viewed as safer, more secure investments because bondholders have a first call on a company's assets in case of bankruptcy.

But on a daily basis, bond prices move up and down, just as stock prices do. You can lose money on bonds even if a company doesn't default on its obligation to repay its debt and interest. Since bond prices fluctuate, if you sell when bond prices are down, you could take a loss. And even if you don't sell, your bonds or bond funds could show a paper loss of value, which you will see when you receive the monthly statement for your retirement account.

How You Can Lose Money in Bonds

There are several reasons bond prices could decline, and they apply to all bonds, including corporate bonds, government bonds, and tax-free municipal bonds issued by cities and states. A multi-trillion-dollar bond market trades every day between dealers, even though prices are not posted as prominently as prices on a stock exchange. And, as with stocks, when there is an excess of desire to sell, prices will be pushed lower.

The most obvious reason for price declines in bonds is that the borrower has financial problems. Many bondholders don't want to risk owning bonds through a bankruptcy because there may not be enough assets to pay off principal and interest that is owed to the lenders. As sellers rush to unload those bonds, the price will drop.

Suddenly people are not as worried about the return *on* their principal as they are about the return *of* their principal. No one will pay you $1,000 for your bond if the company's assets are worth only $600 per bond. Eventually, as sellers push bond prices down, speculators may be willing to take the risk of buying, hoping to make a profit by selling when good news helps push prices higher.

Of course, you can prevent the problem of losing money on bonds of risky companies by sticking with highly rated companies that are unlikely to have financial problems. But you could still lose money, even on the bonds of top-rated companies. The reason is called *interest rate risk*, and it applies to bonds issued by even the best, top-rated companies and governments.

Suppose you purchase a 30-year bond from a good company that promises to pay you 6 percent interest every year. A few years later, inflation returns and brings higher interest rates. Other top-rated companies then sell new bonds that carry an 8 percent interest rate. Your old 6 percent bonds are still paying the promised interest, but investors would rather pay $1,000 to get one of the new, higher-interest bonds issued from an equally strong corporation. If you need to sell your bond, perhaps to pay for an unexpected expense, you'll find that its market price has dropped to $800. That price allows the buyer to get an investment return similar to current interest rates.

You don't have to sell your bonds and take a loss, unless you need the cash. If you hold your bonds to maturity, you'll get your principal—the face value of the bond—back. But in the meantime, you might have been stuck with returns that don't even match inflation. It's a scenario that happened to many bond investors in the late 1970s.

The rule is simple: *When interest rates rise, bond prices fall.* The reverse is true as well. When interest rates fall, bond prices rise. When rates dropped to 4 percent, older bonds of similar quality and maturity with interest rate coupons of 6 percent traded at a premium to their $1,000 face value.

In the fall of 2008, there was a rush by frightened global investors to the safety of U.S. government Treasury securities. The demand for these bonds pushed prices up, and the yields went down. Then as fears of inflation returned, some investors decided they didn't want to lock their money up for the long term at current low rates. So they sold Treasury bonds, pushing yields higher.

Most investors are so focused on the relative safety of bonds' promise to ultimately return their principal that they forget about these market risks to the *current prices* of bonds. But just like the stock market, bond prices can rise and fall—giving rise to profits or losses.

How *much* will your bond price rise or fall as interest rates change? That depends on the length of time until the bond matures. The longer the maturity of the bond, the larger the swing in price will be when interest rates change. It happens to all bonds. And this principle explains how you can lose money in perfectly safe bonds. The greatest mistake is to fool yourself into thinking you can't lose money in bonds or bond funds.

The Advantage of Bond Funds

If you're thinking of investing in bonds, there's another concern to keep in mind. When it comes to buying and selling bonds of individual companies or of states and municipalities, individual investors face many pitfalls. Small orders may not get the best prices when you are buying and may find illiquid markets when it is time to sell. The huge bond market is not as price transparent as the stock market. That allows dealers to purchase bonds for inventory, then mark up the prices, and sell them to you. You will never know how much money the dealer made on the transaction beyond the

commission that shows on your confirmation. There is a web site, www
.investinginbonds.com, that allows investors to track bond prices on a
real-time basis. The site gives current prices and information on corporate, government, and municipal bonds. You can search by name to
see recent trade prices of bonds you may want to buy or sell.

For most investors, a better strategy is to buy a bond fund, such
as those offered by major mutual fund companies. These are *open-
end* bond funds, meaning that the money you invest at any time is
used to purchase new bonds for the fund. You can buy funds that
specialize in corporate bonds or government bonds or even bonds of
international companies or governments. For a small annual fee, a
professional manager will choose the bonds and get the best prices.

The typical bond fund sticks to bonds of a specific maturity: long-
term (10 to 20 years), intermediate-term (3 to 10 years), and short-
term (less than 3 years). Funds that buy debt of even shorter-term
maturities, less than one year, are typically called *money market funds*.
Funds may also specialize in one type of bond—foreign, municipal,
or even a low-rated category called *junk*, or high-yield, bonds.

The portfolio manager of your bond fund has the responsibility
of buying and selling the best bonds in the category. But you'll still
have interest rate risk, especially if you are invested in a long-term
bond fund. Remember: The shorter the maturity of the bond or
bonds in a fund, the less price volatility your portfolio will have.
When rates rise, bond funds with shorter-term investments will
always have some bonds maturing, which provides cash to reinvest
at higher yields. Longer-term bond funds will be stuck with low-
yielding investments, unless the portfolio manager decides to sell.

Some bond funds are closed-end funds, listed and traded on
exchanges. These are just a fixed package of bonds with no portfolio
manager. Municipal bond investment trusts are a kind of closed-end
bond fund. Although it's easier to buy and sell these funds, they do
carry the same interest rate risk as individual bonds—falling in price
as interest rates rise. And prices of these funds may also rise or fall
based on investor demand.

Total Return, Total Risk

By now you realize that it's best to buy bonds when interest rates
are at their peak for the cycle. Obviously, that's as difficult as buying

stocks at their lows. No one knows for sure when those moments have arrived, except in hindsight! If all this is a bit complicated, or even downright scary, here's the point. Investing to get a fixed interest rate can be enticing because the risks aren't obvious. For many years, people touted the safety of bonds for widows, orphans, and retirees. But back then, interest rates didn't move up or down very much.

In the past three decades we've seen dramatic swings in the interest rates, or yields, on even the safest government bonds. And those huge swings in yields mean commensurate swings in bond prices. Remember, when interest rates rise, bond prices fall.

In the late 1970s a tremendous fear of inflation gripped the bond market. No one wanted to lock money away in 30-year Treasury bonds. To attract buyers, the Treasury had to pay rates that soared to over 12.5 percent in March, 1980. Don't you wish you had locked up some of those bonds in your portfolio? You'd still be collecting high interest rates, and you get your principal back in 2010 when the bonds mature.

In more recent years, the situation has reversed. The credit crunch that started in the summer of 2007, and grew into a worldwide panic in the fall of 2008, caused a rush to the perceived greater safety of U.S. government IOUs—Treasury bills, notes, and bonds. Yields on the 30-year Treasury bond fell below 3 percent in early January, 2009. (See Figure 8.6.) The world was preoccupied with *de*flation, not inflation. So in the huge global bond market, the rush to safety pushed Treasury bond prices up, and yields went down dramatically.

It's as difficult to predict the bond market as it is to predict the stock market. Will all the borrowing and money printing done to rescue the economy result in another period of inflation? In that case, you'd want to stay away from bonds, knowing that inflation brings higher interest rates in its wake. On the other hand, if the U.S. economy were to stay in a deflationary state, much as Japan has been in since the 1990s, then rates will stay low, and you'd be delighted to get a 4 percent yield on Treasury bonds.

There's one more factor affecting values of U.S. government bonds: the willingness of foreign central banks to keep lending to the United States at current interest rate levels. The United States has become a huge borrower, and very dependent on foreigners to lend us money. That worked well when Americans were shopping and importing "stuff" from China, Japan, and other global markets. They

Figure 8.6 Treasury Bond Interest Rates
Source: From CME Group based on data from Global Insight.

collected dollars when we paid them, and their central banks were happy to put the money to work buying U.S. government debt.

But as the U.S. government borrows more, and creates more money to rescue sectors of the economy, there is growing global concern that perhaps the value of the U.S. dollar will not be worth as much in the future: inflation! And among our creditors, there's growing concern about being "stuck" with U.S. dollar bonds at low interest rates. The bond market may require higher interest rates to attract money to fund our deficits.

Because bond prices can move up and down, you need to understand the concept of *total return* to understand the risk you might be taking when you invest in any type of bond. This risk applies to individual bonds; to bond funds; to bond-like investments such as Ginnie Maes; and to government, municipal, and corporate bonds.

Interest rates could go up, and bond prices could fall. In fact, falling prices could completely offset the interest you earn on the bonds and result in an actual *loss* of capital. Your total return could easily become negative if you own bonds in a rising-interest-rate environment.

Stocks versus Bonds—An Alternative?

You might think that stocks and bonds are the perfect way to balance out the risk in an investment portfolio, but they are not each other's alter ego. Rising interest rates can be bad for stocks because they reflect a higher cost of doing business for a company. And rising interest rates eventually make bonds a more attractive investment than stocks. If you have cash and can get an 8 percent or 10 percent return on a bond, why take the risk of owning stocks?

But history shows that in some periods rising rates are not bad for the stock market, especially when rates do not increase enough to impact business profits or to provide an enticing alternative investment. In fact, if moderate inflation pushes interest rates higher, stocks may actually benefit because this type of environment allows companies to raise prices, thereby increasing their profits and growth. But rising interest rates are *always* bad for bonds because even if rates rise just a little, bond prices will fall. That's why investing is not that simple. If it were, everyone would be a winner.

KEEP YOUR NEST EGGS SAFE WITH CHICKEN MONEY

"Chicken money" is money you can't afford to lose. It's nothing to be ashamed of. Everyone should have some chicken money set aside for emergencies or just for peace of mind. The percentage of your assets that falls into this safe money category depends on your individual situation.

Having chicken money is partly a function of age: If you're older and not working, you can't replace investment losses. But it's also a function of time horizon: If you need the money within a year or two, you can't afford to take risks with it. And it's partly a function of your personal risk tolerance: You'll need some money put away safely so that you can take appropriate risks in the stock market.

These safe investments are limited to short-term insured bank certificates of deposit (CDs), money market deposit accounts in banks and thrifts, money market mutual funds that buy only short-term government IOUs, Treasury bills from the U.S. government, and even Series I U.S. savings bonds. If you are in a top tax bracket, you might also buy a fund of very short-term (less than 18 months), top-rated, tax-free municipal bonds for safety and liquidity.

These chicken money investments all have a few things in common:

- They are safe and insured.
- They pay very low interest rates relative to other investments at any time. (If you have to pay taxes on the interest you earn, you may barely break even with inflation.)
- They are very *liquid* investments, meaning that you can get your cash quickly and with minimal penalties for early withdrawal.
- There will be no fluctuation in the value of your principal.

The yields on these chicken money investments are always lower than on other, riskier investments. If someone offers you an investment with a higher yield or interest rate and says there is no risk, you can be sure there is a catch or a lie in that statement. When interest rates are low, the people who can least afford to take more risk are tempted by other products, or outright scams, because they want to earn higher rates.

You don't get rich with chicken money investments, but you won't get poor, either. You can sleep well with chicken money investments, knowing that you always have access to your full investment.

Chicken Money Investments

The easiest way to invest your money safely is in short-term, federally insured deposits at your bank. If you need access to your money, keep your CDs in maturities of less than three years or use the bank's money market deposit account. You'll want to make sure you're earning the best rates for that maturity. Sometimes banks pay lower rates because there's not a lot of competition for deposits. To check rates in your area (or outside your area if you're willing to wire a substantial deposit), go to www.bankrate.com.

There is a limit to Federal Deposit Insurance Corporation (FDIC) insurance on accounts. Generally speaking, the limit is $250,000 per account, although the limits can be increased through the use of joint or trust accounts. (A link on the home page of my web site, www .TerrySavage.com, will take you directly to the section of the FDIC.gov web site with complete deposit coverage rules.) If you have more than the insured limit and want to spread the money to several banks, you might be interested in www.cdars.com, a service that distributes your deposits to remain under the insured limits.

United States Treasury bills are the ultimate chicken money investment. These are short-term IOUs directly from the government, with maturities of one year or less. There is an auction of T-bills every Monday (except holidays) and the rates are set by global bidders based on economic conditions and inflation expectations. The easiest way to find the current yields on Treasury bills, notes, and bonds is to go to www.finra.org (the Financial Industry Regulatory Authority) and click on the "Market Data" tab. There you'll find closing prices for major market averages, and Treasury yields.

To learn more about buying U.S. government Treasury bills, go to www.treasurydirect.gov. You can open an account and buy Treasury bills with as little as a $100 investment. The interest you earn is taxable on federal income tax returns but is free from state income taxes.

To buy U.S. savings bonds directly from the government, go to www.savingsbonds.gov. Since May 1, 2005, Series EE savings bonds pay a fixed lifetime rate. For that reason I no longer recommend the purchase of new Series EE bonds, although you definitely should keep older Series E bonds, which still have a rate that fluctuates to keep up with the general level of interest rates on five-year Treasury notes. Series I savings bonds are a better investment, because the interest is calculated on a slightly different basis. There is a fixed base rate plus a semiannual adjustment based on inflation as determined by the consumer price index (CPI), and no federal income taxes are paid on savings bond interest until you cash in the bonds. Depending on their income, parents may cash savings bonds to pay for college tuition without being subject to any income taxes on the interest. Because of penalties for early withdrawal, you should plan to hold your savings bonds for at least five years.

As a result of the credit crisis, most money market mutual funds, which were not previously guaranteed by any agency, now carry federal backing. I have always recommended choosing a money market mutual fund that invests in only U.S. government and government agency securities. You can find them through all major fund companies and brokerage firms. Yields change daily, but because of the guarantee the share price will always be one dollar per share, so you will not lose principal.

Chicken Money and Risk

Keeping most of your money in chicken money investments is definitely not a long-term investment strategy. You can't escape risk in life, no matter how hard you try. Even with these safest investments, you run the risk of losing out to taxes and inflation over the long run.

So use these investments as a safe harbor when you have an immediate need for money or when you are concerned about the risks of other market investments. Or set aside an appropriate portion of your assets to allay your fears of risk while your other investments work harder in appropriate, but riskier, investments.

Never be chicken out of ignorance. Understand risks by asking questions, and take appropriate risks to make your money grow. And always listen to that small voice inside you that warns you about risks others don't see—or don't bother to explain.

A Minute on Mutual Funds

You can buy individual stocks, bonds, or chicken money investments; or you can hire a professional money manager to do it for you in a mutual fund. By this point, you've heard a lot about mutual funds and how they work, so I won't try to explain the advantages of professional money management and diversification. But I do want to make three important points about mutual funds.

1. Fund choices matter. Using a mutual fund doesn't absolve you of the responsibility for making investment choices and for monitoring those choices. If you're choosing among the mutual funds offered by your company retirement plan, the possibilities are limited.

As noted earlier, some retirement plans even offer individualized advice services to help you choose appropriate funds. If not, stop at my web site, www.TerrySavage.com, and sign up for the free trial offered by FinancialEngines.com, to get a start on choosing the most appropriate funds for your goals.

If you're opening an individual retirement account, or simply searching for a place to start investing, you'll be faced with an entire universe of mutual funds—more than 22,000 of them. Finding the right ones can be a daunting task, which is why you might turn to a financial adviser. Or you can do your own research to find recommended funds.

The place to start your search for mutual funds is Morningstar .com. There you can research a fund's investment objectives, track record, and fees and other costs. They'll even offer advice on constructing a portfolio of recommended funds. And, as you'll see in the next chapter, you might choose "target-date" funds that are appropriately invested for your hoped-for retirement date.

2. Understand mutual fund costs. Many mutual funds are sold on a no-load, no-commission basis. You contact the fund company directly, through its web site or toll-free phone lines, to request information and an application as well as to have a fund company representative answer your questions. You may also purchase your funds through a financial adviser or stockbroker. In this case, you may pay an up-front (or back-end) fee or commission for the adviser's advice and service. It's always worth paying for good financial advice, but you don't want to overpay. Before you buy a mutual fund, ask about the commissions to the broker and also ask about the ongoing annual fund management fees. Especially in a period of modest investment returns, every penny counts.

3. Mutual funds have risks. There's another important lesson that, sadly, too many people have learned the hard way: A mutual fund doesn't limit your risk, but it does diversify your risks. Still, if a fund is invested in stocks, and the entire market falls, your fund shares will lose value. The portfolio manager will try to beat her benchmark index of market performance. And the fund manager will be considered successful and even rewarded for outperforming the benchmark, such as the S&P 500 index. If the fund shares lose less value in a bear market, or outperform in a bull market, the fund manager may get a bonus. You get the stock performance, which may be small consolation if you're losing money!

That's why it's so important to create a portfolio of mutual funds—covering different sectors of the investment markets. You may start with an index fund that tracks the performance of the S&P 500 stock index—a basic exposure to the major companies in the U.S. stock market. But you might want to also add a fund that buys only smaller companies, or one that invests in foreign companies. There are mutual funds that are designed to add income to your portfolio, and others that are meant to be one-step investing, managing the task of portfolio allocation for you. More on those in Chapter 10.

These are the basics, but you still need a bit more knowledge. If you're going to manage your own investment portfolio—or understand the advice that others give you—you'll want to know about different investment tools that can diversify your exposure to risk. We'll discuss those tools in the next chapter.

RESOURCES FOR STOCKS, BONDS, AND CHICKEN MONEY

For Investment Education about Stocks and Mutual Funds

Every financial services firm has a web site filled with useful information, tools, and calculators. Following are some independent sites.

- **www.morningstar.com**   Click on the "Personal Finance" tab, and then on "investing classroom" for a variety of online tutorials and workshops on every investment topic.
- **www.bigcharts.com**   Free charts of historical stock prices, and major market indexes.

For Real-Time Bond Prices

- **www.investinginbonds.com**
- **www.finra.org** Then click on "Investors" and then on the tab for "Market Data."

For Chicken Money Investments

- **www.treasurydirect.gov** Then click on "Individual" and from there you'll find a menu explaining everything from buying Treasury bills to purchasing savings bonds. There's even a bond calculator so you can find out the current value of your old savings bonds.
- **www.bankrate.com** To search out highest CD yields (as well as lowest credit card rates and mortgage rates in your area).
- **www.cdars.com** To diversify your bank CDs, keeping below the insured limits.

CHAPTER

9

BEYOND
THE BASICS

The core of your long-term stock market investments should be a mutual fund that holds a diversified portfolio of large company stocks, such as an S&P 500 index fund. But as you learn more about investing, you'll want exposure to other areas of the market—perhaps small company stocks or international stocks—to further diversify your holdings. You might want to add gold or real estate to your holdings, or place a special emphasis on energy or biotech, or on shares from one foreign country or another specific sector of the market. And maybe you don't want all of your investments denominated in dollars.

While you might seek diversification through some of these opportunities, your investments may not always be made through the choice of individual stocks or traditional mutual funds. Instead, you might choose a different vehicle, such as an exchange-traded fund (ETF) as described next.

You could use options instead of stocks to own shares for a limited period of time. Options have multiple uses, even allowing you to gain income and protect your investments in a market decline— or to profit from your belief that the market will fall.

If you're willing to accept more risk, you could even decide to trade futures on commodities and financial trends, such as interest rates or currencies. Futures give you more leverage—the chance to make more money on the upside, or to lose more on the downside. There are even options on futures!

If you're thinking that investing has just grown more complicated, take a deep breath. You don't have to go beyond the basics of stocks and traditional mutual funds to be successful. But if you want to add emphasis on one market sector, you need to understand the costs, risks, and opportunities that these products provide. All may have a place in your investment strategy.

EXCHANGE-TRADED FUNDS

You're probably familiar with traditional, open-end mutual funds that allow you to invest more money at any time, with fund share prices determined at the close of the day by valuing the individual securities owned by the fund. Exchange-traded funds (ETFs) don't work that way.

ETFs are fixed baskets of securities that are generally designed to track an index or hold stocks from a specific, narrow market sector. Like individual stocks, ETFs are traded on major exchanges. You can buy and sell shares in these funds throughout the day, with prices being set by bid and offer, as they are with all listed securities. Depending on demand, the shares in the ETF might be worth more than the securities in the basket, or they might trade at a discount to the underlying value of the securities in the basket.

ETF shares can be bought on margin and even sold short. If the basket of securities represents a major segment of the market, you have a convenient way to own that segment or, if you're hoping to profit from falling prices, to sell it short. Because most ETFs are passively managed, fixed portfolios of stocks, expenses within the funds are very low. You will, however, have to pay a commission to buy and sell the shares through your broker.

Exchange-traded funds allow a focused, yet diversified, exposure to various market segments in a cost-efficient format. They allow you to invest in targeted sectors of the market or in broad market indexes with one purchase. For example, you could purchase the equivalent of the Standard & Poor's (S&P) 500 index in the form of an ETF call the SPDR, popularly known as "Spiders." It is traded on the New York Stock Exchange under the symbol SPY.

QQQQ ("Cubes") is the symbol for an ETF that represents the NASDAQ 100 index of stocks, which is dominated by the tech sector.

Another ETF with the symbol DIA, called "Diamonds," replicates the Dow Jones Industrial Average. There are also ETFs for major market sectors, from health care to real estate to financial services to natural resources. There are many fixed-income (bond) ETFs, including corporate bonds and Treasuries, as well as ETFs that replicate foreign stock and bond indexes. There are also ETFs that either hold physical commodities or track commodity indexes using futures and swaps.

There are even leveraged ETFs and inverse ETFs, which are daily trading vehicles that can be very volatile and expensive. The leveraged ETFs are designed to give you more return—or losses—for your small investment. And the inverse ETFs are designed to let you profit from a move to the downside in an index or group of stocks. But, by design, the returns are amplified far more than you might expect.

Because these portfolios of stocks are prepackaged, or created, they typically have a sponsor or provider. For example, Barclays Global Investors created iShares ETFs (which are now owned by BlackRock). Vanguard sponsors a series of ETFs, most of which are considered a separate share class of a Vanguard mutual fund. State Street Global Advisors sponsors the "Spiders" group of ETFs, which track not only the well-known S&P 500 index, but many sectors of the market. And Merrill Lynch sponsors HOLDRs (Holding Company Depositary Receipts), a series of stock sector ETFs. No matter which company created, or sponsors, your ETF, you must buy and sell your shares on the exchange where they are listed.

For tax purposes, ETFs are treated just like other securities. You pay capital gains taxes on the sale of your ETF shares based on your profit or loss and on the length of your holding period, just as you would with any other security. Because these portfolios are fixed, there are rarely capital gains distributions to shareholders unless the manager has to sell a security inside the portfolio, as in the case of a merger.

The low expense of ETFs makes them attractive to long-term investors. But if you're planning to invest a fixed amount every month, you'd probably want to avoid those trading commissions and send your monthly check to a low-cost traditional index fund at a no-load mutual fund company, if there is one that represents the same portfolio.

You can find more information on ETFs, including advice on creating a portfolio of ETFs, in a special section tab at Morningstar.com.

REAL ESTATE INVESTMENT TRUSTS

Investments in real estate, beyond the family home, should be an important part of a diversified investment portfolio. One of the easiest ways to invest in a diversified portfolio of real estate is through a real estate investment trust (REIT). These trusts save the time and expense of buying individual properties. There are more than 140 publicly traded REITs, with nearly $186 billion in market capitalization—the price of the shares multiplied by the number of shares the companies have outstanding.

REITs are simply a form of holding company for real estate properties and services. Typically, equity REITs concentrate ownership in one type of property: apartments, offices, shopping malls, hotels, or even storage units. Other REITs offer mortgages to existing properties. The shares of these publicly traded companies are listed on major exchanges, and dozens of mutual funds invest primarily in the shares of REITs.

The attraction for investors is twofold. First, REITs offer a chance to own diversified pieces of choice properties that could appreciate in value, especially if inflation returns. Second, these companies are required by law to pay out 90 percent of the rents they collect in the form of dividends to shareholders. So REIT shares offer a tempting regular dividend payment that is higher than most other equity investments.

A portion of that dividend may be ordinary income, capital gains, or even return of invested principal. That creates some beneficial tax opportunities as well as a stream of income. (Under the 2003 tax law changes, the ordinary income portion of a REIT dividend does not qualify for the maximum 15 percent tax rate.) This flow of dividends is based on the flow of funds from operations (FFO), which is the traditional measure of REIT earnings.

REITs add balance to a portfolio. In times of inflation, REIT shares may become more valuable, reflecting the increase in value of underlying properties. And in a slowing or deflationary economy, the dividends—secured by rents—make REIT shares attractive.

Of course, there are risks in REITs. If the economy slows dramatically, vacancies may increase, and tenants may be evicted or go bankrupt. Consumer spending may decline, causing problems for REITs that specialize in shopping malls. Business travel may decline, causing problems for hotel REITs. But although income may decline, the REITs still own the properties. That's the attraction of REITs and the mutual funds that specialize in them.

At the National Association of REITs (NAREIT) web site, www .reit.com, you can get a list of all publicly traded REITs and a quick link to their web sites. You can search by category. There's also a list of mutual funds that specialize in REITs. You can also research REIT funds at Morningstar.com.

GOLD AND NATURAL RESOURCES

We think in dollars and plan for our future in dollars. But what will the dollar be worth when it comes time to retire? It's a question that Americans never had to worry about because the dollar has been the world's reserve currency since 1971. Oil is priced in dollars, and so is most of the world's trade. But during the economic crisis, so many new dollars were created to bail out the financial system that the world began to question the future value of the dollar.

The creation of too much paper money is the very definition of inflation—the loss of purchasing power. The United States had a taste of inflation in the 1970s—when it expanded the money supply to pay for the Vietnam War and at the same time pay for the Great Society. Lenders demanded higher interest rates to offset the expected loss of buying power, pushing Treasury bond yields to more than 12 percent in 1980. Prices of gold and other natural resources soared as they became a more attractive alternative than paper money.

There's a natural fear that we could have another huge round of inflation in the United States. As I write in the summer of 2009, the inflation fears are offset by fears of deflation—a contraction in the economy caused by debt write-offs and stock market losses. But a look back shows that no government in history could resist the power to print paper currency to solve its financial problems. Most recent examples include not only Germany after World War I, but Zimbabwe, which in 2009 issued a 50 billion Zimbabwean dollar banknote that could purchase only a loaf of bread!

Gold and natural resources have always been seen as a hedge against inflation. Unlike paper money, gold cannot be created out of thin air—much as medieval alchemists and even Rumpelstiltskin tried. For centuries, gold has been a safe haven in times of trouble and a hedge against inflation. But natural resources stocks and the mutual funds that specialize in them are also in demand during periods of global economic growth. That's why you might want a portion of your investment portfolio invested in gold or other natural resources.

There are many ways to purchase gold. You can buy bullion bars in small denominations, but they are heavy and expensive to store. You can buy gold coins: either *numismatic* coins, which are valued for their rarity, or *bullion* coins, which are currently minted around the world and valued only for their gold content. Among the most popular gold bullion coins are the one-ounce American Eagle and American Buffalo coins, as well as the Canadian Maple Leaf, Australian Kangaroo, and Austrian Philharmonic. Some of these coins are also available in smaller sizes, such as a half ounce of gold. A note of caution: Buy only from reputable dealers, take delivery of your coins instead of leaving them with the dealer, and store them in a bank vault.

There are some stocks that directly represent the price of gold. For example there is an ETF traded on the New York Stock Exchange with the symbol GLD. It holds gold bullion and is designed to track the price of gold on an intraday basis. In a slightly different format, Central GoldTrust (GTU) also holds gold bullion.

It is perhaps easiest to buy shares of gold mining companies. The advantage of owning gold mining shares when gold prices are rising is twofold: First, shares of gold mining companies typically pay dividends; and second, gold mining shares leverage increases in the price of gold. If a mine is already operating profitably, a higher gold price does not force the company to add new workers or incur other expenses in order to increase profits. As gold prices rise, all the profit drops to the bottom line, making the shares even more attractive.

You can search Morningstar's web site for mutual funds that will give you a diversified portfolio of gold shares, as well as funds that specialize in natural resources, such as oil, gas, timber, and farmland. Or you can check out the gold and natural resources funds at www.usfunds.com.

Beware of penny stock speculations. They abound when gold prices rise. You can diversify your portfolio into precious metals and natural resources without becoming a speculator or a target for scam artists.

THE U.S. DOLLAR

Suddenly, we're all far more aware of the value of the dollar versus other currencies, such as the yen or Canadian dollar or euro or British pound sterling. It's not just a matter of what things cost in a foreign currency when we are shopping—or of what things cost to foreigners when they are shopping here. We've learned that when the dollar loses value, foreigners take the dollars we've sent to their countries and come back to buy bargains—from real estate to luxuries—made cheaper to them because as the dollar falls in value, their currencies buy more.

Americans have always felt the world revolved around the dollar. But in recent years the countries that have collected the dollars we spent as we shopped globally are now starting to get worried about holding so many dollars. With nearly a trillion U.S. dollars in its reserves, China is one of our largest creditors. They've publicly commented that maybe the world needs a different reserve currency, or basket of currencies on which to price global transactions. They feel there are just too many dollars floating around out there, and the United States owes too much money, to maintain confidence in the dollar.

However, when the global financial markets were on the verge of collapse, there was a giant rush to the presumed safety of the U.S. dollar. Perhaps the lesson is that the world doesn't trust the dollar, but it trusts other currencies even less!

Although most of us will always make financial transactions in dollars, there is a good reason to watch the value of the U.S. dollar against foreign currencies. The value of the dollar impacts not only the cost of imported goods, but the price we pay to "import" capital. That price is interest rates. If our global creditors demand higher interest rates as an offset to feared inflation, it will impact the entire U.S. economy, from mortgage loans to credit card rates.

As long as the world is willing to hold those dollars and reinvest them in U.S. Treasury bills or other government securities, at low rates based on confidence in the future value of the dollar, there's no problem. But if you have a global business, you need to hedge against the possibility of a falling dollar. Similarly, if you have an investment portfolio, you'll want to protect against that same risk.

To hedge your need for foreign currencies or simply to speculate on the value of the dollar (and indirectly on global interest rates), you can use futures contracts traded on the Chicago Mercantile Exchange. (See the section on futures later in this chapter.)

There's another easy way to speculate on the future value of the dollar. At www.everbank.com, you can buy certificates of deposit (CDs) that are denominated in a wide variety of foreign currencies and that are insured by the Federal Deposit Insurance Corporation (FDIC). Your dollars are converted to the currency when you purchase the CD. The interest rate is set based on competitive rates in that currency. When the CD matures, you will have earned the promised rate of interest plus or minus changes in the value of the currency if you choose to convert back to dollars.

OPTIONS

Options on stocks provide a handy way to invest with a small amount of money or to protect the investments you've already made. For example, a call option gives you the right to buy a specific number of shares in a company at a specific price for a specific period of time. The option gains in value if the price of the underlying stock rises before the time runs out (expiration).

If you believe a stock will rise, you can buy a *call* option instead of paying for the full 100 shares or paying the 50 percent margin required to buy 100 shares of stock. If you believe the stock will fall, you can buy a *put* option. With a far smaller investment, you get all the benefits of owning the stock (call) or selling short (put), but only for a limited amount of time. If you guess right about the direction of the stock but your timing is off, you can lose all the money you spent on the option.

You can buy options on a single stock, or on a major market index, or on most ETFs, which are typically indexes related to a specific sector of the economy. So options allow you to diversify your portfolio, for a relatively small amount of money. The trade-off is that you only own the option for a limited amount of time. When it comes to investing in options, truly timing is everything!

There's another use for options. As an investor, you can use options to protect your portfolio. You can sell (write) options on a stock you already own, and you can pocket the amount (the premium) you are paid. But by selling the option, you are granting the buyer of the option the right to purchase your stock at a specific price during a specific period of time. So you have to be ready to give up your stock to the owner of the option during the period of time the option is outstanding.

For example, if you own a stock that is trading at 50, someone might pay you $5 for a six-month option (price is determined by the market). If the stock rises, the option holder will then call the stock away from you, paying you $50 a share. But since you collected the option premium, it is as if you sold the stock at 55. You'll have to decide in advance if that's enough profit for you.

If you change your mind and don't want to sell the stock at 55, then you can buy the option back. Again, the price of the option will be determined by the market, which weighs the time left until the expiration of the option against the likelihood that the stock will move higher. If the stock has moved up, and there is time left on the option when you buy it back, then you will suffer a loss on your option trade—but you will still have the stock.

Selling options on stocks you own can increase your income in retirement. You can learn more about this strategy of adding income to your portfolio in Chapter 11. And there's help learning about options at the end of this chapter.

FUTURES

Futures markets exist to allow producers and users of products to hedge against risk. Many of the products traded in these markets are tangible commodities, such as oil, natural gas, corn, wheat, cattle, coffee, and pork bellies (bacon). But there is also risk in the future value of intangibles, such as interest rates, currencies, stock prices, and the relationships among these vital parts of the financial system. So there are futures contracts to hedge against financial risk as well as commodity risk.

Futures markets exist to transfer that risk, at a price decided on by global market participants. While your mental picture of futures trading might be one of wild shouting and hand waving on a physical trading floor, most futures trading today takes place electronically. But wherever a transaction is made, there are two sides—a buyer and a seller. Only when they come together is a contract made. Thus, it could be said that futures trading is a zero-sum situation: For every side of the contract that wins, there is an opposite side that posts a loss.

Among the futures market participants are users of that commodity, who need to hedge prices for the future. A U.S. manufacturer that is selling products in Europe needs to know what the dollar value of euros will be when it is paid for its product in a few months. Speculators, who participate merely to make a profit if they are correct in forecasting the direction of prices, also provide liquidity.

Since futures are traded with a very small cash margin, there is a lot of leverage to the money invested. Leverage works both ways: You can easily double your money, but you can also lose all of your initial investment, or even more. The major futures exchanges have web sites with educational features to explain how futures work. Check out the Chicago Mercantile Exchange's site at www.cmegroup.com.

Although you may never be a speculator, you might want to use futures to hedge against the stocks and mutual funds in your retirement portfolio. If you believe that the market will decline but don't want to sell your stock funds, you could easily sell a futures contract that roughly represents the stocks in your portfolio or buy a put option on a stock futures contract.

If you're interested in commodity futures, you will have to do your homework and deal with a reputable brokerage firm. The first place to start is at the web site of the National Futures Association, www.nfa.futures.org. There you can research individual brokers, firms, and money managers that specialize in futures.

Or you may choose to add commodities exposure to your portfolio through an index fund that does not speculate but simply tracks an index of physical commodities. Several funds provide this service: The PIMCO Commodity Real Return Strategy Fund (PCRAX) uses a portfolio of derivatives to simulate the performance of an index. The Oppenheimer Real Asset Fund (QRAAX) uses the Goldman Sachs commodity index as its benchmark. And the Rogers International Raw Materials Fund, LP, created by global investment guru Jim Rogers, uses a proprietary index to track more than 35 commodities used in global trade. Go to www.rogersrawmaterials. com for more information.

HEDGE FUNDS

By now you've realized the dangers of hedge funds—dangers I warned of in the first edition of this book! So I'll let most of this section stand unchanged—but add one more word of warning. Once a hedge fund has had a couple of losing years, the smart money—and the maybe-smart *managers*—leaves! After all, the terms of these hedge fund agreements typically state that *all losses must be recouped before managers can take their cut!* That means there is no incentive for the managers to stick around to recoup *your* money. Instead they've probably moved on to manage new hedge funds, hoping you have a short memory.

Hedge funds are *not* mutual funds. They are private investment partnerships that operate with relatively little government regulation. With the exception of antifraud standards, they are exempt from Securities and Exchange Commission (SEC) regulation under federal securities laws. And they are not required to disclose information about their holdings and performance to either individual investors or regulators.

These partnerships are called hedge funds because they use specialized investments to protect against a downturn in the market or even to profit in a downturn. For example, hedge funds may *sell stocks short*—a technique that involves selling shares you don't own, with the aim of repurchasing them at a lower price and booking a profit. Or hedge funds may use derivatives such as put and call options, as well as futures, to profit from declines in stock prices. And they may use *leverage*—buying stocks or futures on margin, thus increasing the amount of profit or loss relative to the capital invested.

Even after the market crash, in 2009 there was nearly $3 trillion invested in hedge funds, even as the number of hedge funds declined because of closures and consolidations. It's relatively easy to start a hedge fund, because hedge funds are not subject to the stringent SEC disclosure requirements that must be met when offering shares in a traditional mutual fund to the investing public. And, unlike traditional mutual funds, where the objective is to get the best performance for the lowest management fees, hedge funds charge investors huge performance fees. The typical arrangement calls for the fund manager to receive as much as 20 percent or more of the fund's profits, but not necessarily to share in the losses.

Some additional warnings apply: Hedge funds are not only opaque but illiquid. You may not be able to withdraw your money until the end of a quarter or even a year. In the interim, you may not be able to get a valuation for your shares. And while there have been some spectacular successes, there have also been astounding and costly hedge fund failures.

Because of the inherent risks in hedge funds, investor participation is usually limited to high-net-worth individuals—those with at least $1 million net worth, exclusive of personal residence. Many pension funds and other institutions invest a portion of their assets in a variety of hedge funds. They can afford to turn over a relatively small portion of their holdings to aggressive, discretionary managers.

To diversify their risk, sophisticated investors may invest in several different hedge funds that use different strategies. Funds might specialize in securities related to merger arbitrage, emerging markets, or the technology sector. They might use market timing techniques, or they might try to remain market neutral, profiting no matter what the direction of the overall market is. There are even funds of funds that allow some degree of diversification.

You can learn more about performance of the larger hedge funds at www.marhedge.com and at www.hedgefund.net. But many of the funds that lose money do not report to these services, or they liquidate the partnerships and obliterate their records. Before becoming enchanted with visions of huge gains, take a cold, hard look at the costs and the risks of investing in a hedge fund.

In fact, that last bit of advice holds true for all the investments mentioned in this chapter. Many of them might be considered more sophisticated, but that does not mean that they are more risky. Indeed, some of these alternatives might be used to actually lower the risk inherent in your investment portfolio. Don't skip over these possibilities, but do research the products—and the people—before you invest your money.

RESOURCES FOR INVESTING

Your broker or financial adviser may suggest some of the strategies or investment alternatives presented in this chapter. Each has a place in a sophisticated portfolio. But never invest blindly. Always do your own research, and don't be afraid to ask questions. Here is a list of resources for alternative investments:

Real Estate Investment Trusts

- www.reit.com

Gold, the Dollar, and Natural Resources

- www.morningstar.com
- www.dinesletter.com
- www.everbank.com
- www.usfunds.com

Options on Stocks

- www.cboe.com
- www.iseoptions.com
- www.thinkorswim.com

Futures

- www.cmegroup.com
- www.nfa.futures.org

Exchange-Traded Funds

- www.morningstar.com
- www.nyse.com
- www.ishares.com
- www.etfconnect.com

Hedge Funds

- www.marhedge.com
- www.hedgefund.net

CHAPTER

10

ONE-STEP RETIREMENT INVESTING

Whether you are just starting your career or are rapidly approaching retirement, you may be looking for the easy way out. Aren't we all? I have two suggestions that can simplify your investment program, recognizing that they don't necessarily take the place of professional investment advice. Then there's a third strategy designed for those who think that it's too late to start investing for retirement and that they don't have enough money to get started.

These one-step strategies will work for you—*if* you don't give up on the stock market. That's a big "if" when you've seen the market collapse. It's tempting to lose your trust in the future. But that's what planning is all about—a belief that you can make some basic decisions today that will make tomorrow better. As I've said throughout this book, the stock market reflects the future of our American free enterprise system, which has created a better standard of living for more people than any system on earth. Don't bet against America—or the stock market that represents our economy.

The first strategy simplifies stock market investments. You just buy the "whole market." That's easy these days, since the advent of mutual funds that were designed for this purpose. The second strategy solves the problem of diversifying your retirement investments and reallocating your assets as you approach your retirement date. There are funds that will do the job for you. The third strategy lets you start a diversified investment program with as little as $100 or buy a few shares of individual stocks for just $4.

BUYING THE WHOLE MARKET

Instead of hedging your bets through options or investment alternatives, you might want to just buy the whole market. It's really very simple to do. To make the task easier, let's define the whole market as the Standard & Poor's (S&P) 500 stock index (although there are many broader indexes, such as the Vanguard Total Stock Market Index, or indexes that replicate sectors of the market, such as the Russell 2000, which represents smaller companies). Here are three different ways to invest in the S&P 500 index, each with different costs, liquidity, and leverage.

Index Mutual Funds

Almost every 401(k) retirement plan has an S&P 500 index fund as one of its choices. And if you're investing on your own, major mutual fund companies such as Vanguard and Fidelity offer index funds on a no-load, no-commission basis. Contact them through their web sites or toll-free numbers.

When buying or selling shares in a no-load index fund, your order will be executed at the day's closing price. So if the market falls late in the day, you can't take advantage of earlier prices. For long-term investors, one day's price fluctuation shouldn't make much difference anyway.

Vanguard prides itself on very low annual costs. Its S&P 500 index fund subtracts just 18 basis points (0.18 percent; 1 basis point is $\frac{1}{100}$ of 1 percent) to cover operating costs. Since index funds don't trade stocks, there are very low transaction costs inside the fund. Major changes occur only when new stocks are added to the index or others are deleted. Otherwise, the fund managers simply purchase more shares of every company in the index as new dollars arrive from investors. Buying an index fund is the easiest way to own the market, but there are other ways, too.

Exchange-Traded Funds: Spiders

The one drawback to an index fund is that your order is executed at the end of the day. But what if you want to own the stock market right now? Many traders or market timers want to get in and out quickly. They don't want to wait until the end of the day. As noted in Chapter 9, exchange-traded funds (ETFs) have become a popular way to trade the whole market or smaller sectors of the market. Specifically, the Standard & Poor's Depositary Receipts—SPDRs, or Spiders—are a package of the S&P 500 stocks. This ETF is traded on the New York Stock Exchange under the ticker symbol SPY. You can buy just 100 shares or even a smaller amount.

These units are designed as a security with a market value of approximately one-tenth of the value of the underlying index. Thus, if the S&P 500 is trading around 900, the SPY would trade at 90. So 100 shares would cost $9,000. If you're buying on margin, you have to put up only 50 percent of the face value.

There are some drawbacks to Spiders. As with any other stock, you pay a commission every time you buy or sell. That cost can be minimized by going through a discount broker. The advantage of Spiders is that you can buy and sell throughout the day, acting on your instinct about where the market is going.

Futures: E-mini S&P 500

There's another, more leveraged way to buy the whole stock market. It's done by trading the E-mini S&P 500 futures contract. (Full disclosure: These contracts are traded on the Chicago Mercantile Exchange, a publicly traded company where I am a director.)

The advantage of using the futures is that you can control a much larger position in the market for a relatively small amount of money. The current value of one E-mini S&P 500 contract is about $45,000. The margin requirement is $5,600, or about 12.5 percent of the total value of the contract. (To purchase $45,000 worth of Spiders, you would have to put up $22,500.) Of course, leverage works both ways. If the market declines, you can be called to put up more margin money.

The E-mini S&P 500 contract is traded electronically, and the market is open virtually around the clock. It has average daily trading volume of $112 billion in market value, compared to the Spiders, which trade about one-quarter of that market value, or $27 billion per day. Individual investors place their orders through a futures broker or through one of the many stock brokerage firms, such as Charles Schwab and Merrill Lynch, that offer trading in futures contracts. Commission costs vary.

Buying the whole market using one of these techniques gives you exposure to equities and diversification within the equity category. It isn't a substitute for an asset-allocation plan that crosses between stocks, bonds, and money market alternatives. For that, the next section gives you one simple strategy for growing your retirement investments.

RETIREMENT INVESTING MADE EASY: TARGETED RETIREMENT FUNDS

The idea of "target-date" retirement funds is to make it easy for the novice investor to choose a mixture of mutual funds that are suitable for building a retirement portfolio. Recognizing that younger investors, farther from retirement, have a longer-term perspective, target-dated funds for those retiring in 2040 have a larger component of stocks than more conservative funds designed for those retiring in 2010 or 2015. The idea is that the portfolio managers of the funds would automatically adjust the balance of risky holdings to become conservative as retirement drew near.

The concept was approved by Congress in 2006, when it passed legislation authorizing employers to automatically enroll employees in 401(k) plans—and to put that investment into a target-date fund, unless the employee chose other alternatives. This so-called safe-harbor rule fostered the expansion of target-date funds inside company retirement plans, and made them more appealing to those making their own choices for individual retirement accounts.

Target-date funds are designed to do the work of asset allocation for you. They are, in effect, a sort of one-stop, no-decision retirement investment opportunity being offered by the best-known and most respected names in mutual fund management: Vanguard, Fidelity, T. Rowe Price, American Century, and others. You can use the targeted retirement funds for your individual retirement account (IRA), for your rollover IRA, or for after-tax investments that you have set aside for retirement. Some are even found as investment choices in 401(k) plans. These funds allow maximum diversification along with an automatically changing mix of assets that's appropriate to your own targeted retirement date.

How Targeted Retirement Funds Work

The fund company creates a series of targeted retirement funds in five-year increments ranging from 2005 to 2050. All you have to do is pick your expected retirement date and invest in the fund. Inside each fund is a mix of mutual funds run by that company. It's a fund-of-funds concept, meaning that the target series funds invest not in individual stocks but in a variety of well-known stock, bond, and international mutual funds. Other targeted retirement funds use a mix of individual stocks and bonds. The fund changes its mix of investments to become more conservative as you approach your targeted retirement date. Each fund family also offers a final fund choice as you actually move into retirement—a very conservative portfolio to support withdrawals for your retirement income.

There is no set allocation for stocks versus bonds versus money market investments for a target-date fund. The mix of investments varies from one fund family to another, reflecting disagreement on how much equity exposure is desirable at each age. The average holding of stocks in 2010 target-date funds from various fund families was 45 percent in 2008, reflecting experts' belief that even those close to retirement needed a significant exposure to expected stock market growth during their retirement years. But that average masks a range of 21 percent to 70 percent equity in similarly dated target funds.

When the market crashed in 2008, many people nearing retirement realized that they would not be able to recoup those losses, since at retirement they typically stop investing and start withdrawing. Target-date funds were widely criticized because people didn't understand the risk of their exposure to stocks. But in reality, what they didn't understand was the possibility of the impact of a stock market crash just before they retired. There have been major market declines several times in the past century. And the only way to hedge against this risk is to also have a significant portion of your assets in low-yielding "chicken money" investments, in addition to your stock portfolio.

Once you understand that target-date funds are designed to make investing easier, but are not designed to manage your entire nest egg, you can use them with the correct perspective. But you should also investigate the mix of investments *within* your chosen target-date plan. If the fund chosen by your company 401(k) plan seems aggressive, it just means you need to build up additional savings in money market accounts outside your plan, or in a "stable-value" fund, if it is offered inside your company plan.

One other thing to keep in mind: When you reach your target retirement date, you might not want to sell your target-date fund. Most will continue to be managed *during* your retirement—which may last as long as 30 years. As you move through retirement, the ongoing management of your funds will become even more conservative. Other target-date funds simply turn into income funds after the target date is reached.

It isn't difficult to check the investment mix within target-date funds. Just go to the fund company web site. For instance, the Vanguard fund targeted for those who will retire in 2045 has 90 percent stocks and 10 percent bonds. But for those in the 2010 fund, the mix is roughly 52 percent stocks and 48 percent bonds. The T. Rowe Price Retirement 2040 fund is invested similarly to the Vanguard longer-dated fund—with 89 percent in stocks. But the T. Rowe Price Retirement 2010 fund has a mix of 58 percent stocks and 36 percent bonds.

Whichever fund family you choose, you will be far ahead of the guesswork that most people employ to build their retirement investments. And once you reach the threshold of retirement, you can employ the Monte Carlo modeling programs offered by these companies to reallocate your investments and to calculate withdrawals that your portfolio will support for your lifetime.

Comparing the Companies

Vanguard. Vanguard's program is called the Target Retirement Funds. Target dates on these funds range from 2005 to 2050. Vanguard, which is known for its low-cost money management services, uses its own index funds in each series. So, for example, the Vanguard

Total Stock Market Index is combined with investments in the Vanguard European Stock Index Fund and the Vanguard Pacific Stock Index Fund for the stock portion of series investment. The well-known Vanguard Total Bond Market Index Fund combines with the Vanguard Inflation-Protected Securities (bond) Fund and the Vanguard Prime Money Market Fund to form the bond portion of each fund. The annual management cost for this series is by far the lowest of any company, ranging from 0.18 to 0.19 percent. The minimum investment for an IRA is $3,000.

Fidelity. Fidelity's Freedom Funds, as its targeted retirement series is called, use investments in up to 25 of its well-known funds such as Fidelity Blue Chip Growth Fund and Fidelity Equity-Income Fund, newly created dedicated portfolios like the Series 100 Index Fund, Series All-Sector Equity, and Series Large Cap Value, as well as international funds such as the Fidelity Europe and Fidelity Diversified International funds. The bond portion is based on a newly created dedicated Series Investment Grade Bond Fund. The Freedom Funds also utilize the Strategic Real Return Fund, which invests in inflation-hedging securities such as Treasury Inflation-Protected Securities (TIPS), real estate investment trusts, floating rate notes, and commodities.

It is the Freedom Fund manager's job to implement and to manage portfolios to a predetermined "rolldown," which is sometimes referred to as a "glidepath," which alters the exposure to stocks and bonds over time. The annual management cost ranges from 0.49 percent to 0.80 percent annually and is made up of the underlying fund management fees. Minimum investment for an IRA is $2,500. Or you can open a Fidelity SimpleStart IRA (Roth or traditional) for a minimum contribution of $200 per month.

T. Rowe Price. T. Rowe Price Retirement Funds also use well-known equity funds, ranging from the Growth Stock Fund and the Value Fund to the International Fund, as well as their mid-cap and small-cap stock funds. They also use up to five of their own highly respected bond funds. The T. Rowe Price Retirement Funds are noticeably more aggressive in using equity funds, even during the years closest to retirement. They say their modeling studies indicate that people facing a 30-year retirement period initially need at least about a 55 percent exposure to equities in order to sustain withdrawals. The mix is actively managed through retirement, and the allocation keeps changing until the equity portion is down to 20 percent after 30 years in retirement. The annual management fee runs from 0.60 percent to 0.81 percent, based on the mix of funds in the series. The minimum investment for an IRA is $1,000.

American Century Investments. American Century offers LiveStrong Portfolios, part of a $6 million contribution agreement with cyclist and cancer survivor Lance Armstrong for the use of his trademarked name. (Investors are not charged extra for this contribution to the Lance Armstrong Foundation, which is made out of the profits of the management company.) The portfolios do not invest in tobacco products. They are otherwise similar to most target-date funds, with five-year intervals ranging from 2015 to 2050, plus an income portfolio for retirees. The funds are rebalanced each year, and the mix grows more conservative as you near your designated retirement age. Annual management fees are less than 1 percent, depending on the fund choice. Minimum investment is $2,500, but American Century will waive the fund minimum if you make an initial investment of at least $500 and continue to make automatic investments of at least $100 a month until reaching the fund minimum.

If your company retirement plan is managed by one of the fund companies mentioned here, ask to have the targeted retirement funds included among your 401(k) choices. If you've lost money in an IRA rollover account and don't know what to do about it, switch to one of these plans and let time—and the fund management company—do the work for you.

STARTING SMALL—NO EXCUSES!

Even if you don't have a lot of money to invest, or a lot of time until retirement, there's no excuse for not starting an IRA with a few dollars a month. Most mutual fund companies have minimum investment requirements of around $1,000. Many brokerage firms require significant minimum investments or charge huge commissions on small transactions. Here are two ways around that problem.

U.S. Global Funds—ABC Plan

There is one mutual fund company that has consistently befriended the small investor by offering access to its mutual funds with a starting investment of as little as $100. U.S. Global Investors (www .usfunds.com) offers a wide variety of no-load mutual funds that can be purchased using their ABC Plan, which stands for "automatically building capital." If you invest $100 in any of its funds and agree to an automatic monthly withdrawal of at least $30 from your checking or savings account into your mutual fund account, you can get started on this plan. The fund most suitable for growing an IRA is the All-American Equity Fund, which invests in a diversified portfolio of large company stocks. But U.S. Global Investors also has international funds, natural resource funds, and even fixed-income and money market funds that can be purchased using the ABC Plan.

ShareBuilder

If you want to buy individual stocks or exchange-traded funds but have only a small amount to invest, go to www.sharebuilder.com, which is now a division of ING Direct. At this online brokerage firm, you can start a regular weekly or monthly investment program for just $4 a transaction, and no minimum balance or investment amount is required. There are several programs, ranging from the $4 single fee to a monthly fee of $12, which gives you six free automatic investments each month. There is also an "advantage" plan, which gives up to 20 transactions monthly.

The shares you buy are held in your name or in an IRA. Transactions are executed twice a day, which means you cannot specify price unless you pay an extra fee. But you can execute a trade in real time for only $9.95 for up to 1,000 shares. For individual investors with small amounts to invest regularly, this web site is a cost-effective way to accumulate a portfolio.

Remember, time is money. Even a small amount of money, invested regularly over a long period of time, can make a big difference in your retirement lifestyle. Pass this information on to your children or grandchildren, or get them started on an investment program. Now there are no excuses!

MAKE THE CALL

Vanguard Target Retirement Funds
800-VANGUARD
www.vanguard.com

Fidelity Freedom Funds
800-FIDELITY
www.fidelity.com

T. Rowe Price Retirement Funds
800-638-5660
www.troweprice.com

American Century—My Retirement Portfolios
800-345-2021
www.americancentury.com

U.S. Global Funds
888-USFUNDS
www.usfunds.com

ShareBuilder
866-SHRBLDR
www.sharebuilder.com

PART

4

STREAMS OF RETIREMENT INCOME

CHAPTER

11

WHERE WILL
THE MONEY
COME FROM?

What matters most in retirement is income. Making your money *grow* takes a backseat to making your money *last*. And, unless you are very wealthy and are concentrating on leaving an estate to your children, the concept of making your money last includes drawing down all your assets at a rate that makes them last as long as you do. You don't want to drain your pool of assets too soon, so you'll spend some time replenishing the pool during your early years of retirement. In other words, you may have to keep working.

If you're approaching retirement, you have tough choices. If you're a younger reader, this section will help your resolve to save more and invest wisely. Basically the choices are limited for generating income in retirement. You can either work longer or spend less.

Given the recent losses in the stock market, the idea of working longer has become more accepted. In fact, you might want to go back to the web site mentioned in Chapter 3, www.livingto100.com, and rethink how long you're likely to live, and therefore how long you need to keep working—either before you officially declare your retirement or even during the early years of your retirement.

You may be planning to retire from your job, but statistics say you won't retire from earning some sort of income. And you're more likely now to delay that retirement. A midyear 2009 poll by AARP showed that 27 percent of those ages 55–64 had postponed plans to retire, and many feared that their jobs would be cut before they had a chance to retire.

In mid-2009, there were nearly 6 million seniors, over age 65, in the workforce. That's a dramatic increase from mid-2003, though even then, more than 4.5 million seniors 65 and older were working. And the 2003 figures were up 18 percent from 3.85 million in 1999, according to the Bureau of Labor Statistics (BLS). Clearly, more and more seniors are choosing, or needing, to remain in the workforce.

Since 1977, the number of seniors in the workforce has more than doubled. And the number of older women working into their senior years has jumped by even more—147 percent. Life clearly does not get easier as you age: Since 1977 the number of senior workers over age 75 and still working is up 172 percent! And baby boomers are just *starting* to retire!

Seniors currently make up 16 percent of the workforce, and the BLS predicts that by 2020, 24 percent of all workers will be 55 or older. In a recent Gallup poll, 60 percent of baby boomers said they expect to work once they reach retirement. In April 2009, the Gallup survey revealed that only 42 percent of Americans expect to rely on retirement savings as a major source of income—the lowest level in survey history.

Fewer and fewer Americans feel that the idea of "retiring early and enjoying life" is anything more than a dream. It seems the concept of retro-retirement—a long work career followed by income-producing part-time work, and then a relatively short period of idleness—is destined to be the future of the baby boomer generation.

The next step is to define just how to balance, and afford, these two opposing concepts of gainful employment and unpaid leisure.

THE BALANCING ACT: INCOME VERSUS PRINCIPAL

It's not just how much money you *have*, but how much money you can *spend* to maintain your lifestyle that counts in retirement. Whether you're staying in the family home, moving to a senior community, or dividing your time between winter and summer residences, it's *income* that turns dreams into reality. It's income that allows you to pay for the lifestyle you've chosen.

There are two ways to approach the concept of income. Very wealthy people can actually live off their income, without touching principal. They'll have a lot remaining to leave to their children or to charity. If that describes your situation, skip to Part 6, Estate Planning.

But most boomer retirees will have to do a careful balancing act between working, earning income on their investments, and drawing down principal at a rate that keeps them from running out of money before they run out of time. So let's examine your possible sources of retirement income.

GAINFUL EMPLOYMENT IN RETIREMENT

It's important to have multiple sources of income in retirement, and the odds are that they won't all come from your investments. In fact, the most critical source of income is likely to come from your continued, if part-time, employment. Finding that employment may take some creativity, but it won't be as difficult as some are predicting. When aging boomers are the majority, age discrimination will be less rampant. In fact, older workers are likely to be more in demand as the pool of younger workers shrinks. There is even a web site—www.seniorjobbank.com—dedicated to job seekers over 50.

Congress, which has so far been unwilling to deal with critical retirement issues, seems to have faced up to the likelihood that people will continue to work by repealing penalties in the Social Security Act that weighed heavily on seniors who work. Passage of the Senior Citizens' Freedom to Work Act of 2000 repealed penalties on those of full retirement age who earn income while collecting Social Security, even though your benefits may be taxable depending on your total income.

And there have been other changes. The federal Older Workers Benefit Protection Act (U.S. Code 29, § 623 and following) makes it illegal to use an employee's age as a basis for discrimination in benefits and retirement. This act protects people who are at least 40 years old. It tells companies that they cannot reduce health or life insurance benefits for older employees, nor can they stop their pensions from accruing if they work past their normal retirement age. The act also discourages businesses from targeting older workers when cutting staff.

Perhaps of equal importance to preretirees, the Older Workers Benefit Protection Act prohibits employers from forcing employees to take early retirement. The law states that an early retirement plan is legal only if it gives the employee a choice between two options: (1) keeping things as they are or (2) choosing to retire under a plan that makes the employee better off than previously. This choice must be legitimate, and the employee must be free to reject the offer.

In this era of corporate downsizing and rising unemployment, it is important to note these protections for older workers. But when job losses are taking place across the board, there is really no protection—as too many workers are finding out. Your current job may not be your dream position, but losing it would be a nightmare. So it's important to stress your experience and willingness to continue working, as well as your leadership abilities, to hang on as long as possible. The economy is cyclical—and eventually there will be growth and an economic recovery. This is the saving grace for younger workers—but it is added pressure for boomers who were hoping these would be their best earning—and saving—years.

Even if you have a job, you should start thinking about the challenge of creating a work scenario that suits your needs and your time commitment. A full-time job may be neither necessary nor appealing, depending on your assets and your health. Your retirement job may not be as an employee of your current company; or if it is, you may be an independent consultant, working flexible hours. Or you may start your own business, using the talents and skills you developed in the workforce. You could purchase a franchise, start a business from scratch, or teach others who want to start their own business. Sales opportunities will grow again in the financial services industry, where other boomers are less likely to be impressed by younger, inexperienced salespeople who are the age of the boomers' own children.

Now is the time to get creative—*before* you reach retirement age. Starting your own small business on the side while still working at your current job gives you the chance to do a test run on your concept. You still have the fresh contacts in your work life to get the support services you need for your business and to prospect for customers on your own time.

Again, it's attitude that counts. If you look at earning an income during retirement as an opportunity to earn rewards from your experience, interests, talents, and skills, you could have a much more rewarding second career. You know so much more than you did when you started out; you're worth so much more now. And people gravitate to those who have a positive mental attitude. It is the key ingredient in a successful retro-retirement. Even so, attitude is no substitute for income.

WITHDRAWALS FROM RETIREMENT ACCOUNTS

There are three basic sources of retirement income: money from (1) your *after-tax* savings, (2) your *tax-deferred* retirement plan savings, and (3) Social Security—if it still exists in its present form when you are ready to retire.

Those are the pools of money available for income drawdown that will be analyzed in your Monte Carlo modeling of retirement scenarios. Your advisers will look at the entire picture and suggest which accounts to draw down first. Even if you still have enough income so that you don't want to take money out of your retirement accounts (and what a great problem that would be), you're still required to make certain minimum withdrawals, except from Roth IRAs.

Where and When to Withdraw

Historically, the best advice—aside from the issue of required minimum withdrawals—was to spend your after-tax savings first, leaving your tax-deferred accounts more time to grow. After your death, your beneficiaries may be able to continue that tax-deferred growth for a while, making your retirement accounts even more valuable.

But it may be time to rethink the entire issue of taxes, as it becomes clearer that the government will be tapping the remaining pockets of wealth in this country to pay for its economic plans. And suddenly, *you* have become a deep pocket of wealth if you have retirement savings. Perhaps you should consider paying taxes *now*, if you have the cash, instead of later—when rates are likely to be higher.

There is a brief opportunity in 2010 to make that decision. Under current tax law, there will be a one-time chance to convert current IRA accounts to tax-free Roth IRAs, no matter what your income level—*if* you're willing to come up with the cash to pay the taxes over a two-year period, 2010 and 2011.

The money in your Roth IRA would then continue to grow—but tax-free, instead of just tax-deferred until you take withdrawals. (That withdrawal time will be at your discretion, since there are no mandated withdrawals from Roth IRAs.) You should have the cash to pay the taxes held in an account outside your retirement account—or else withdrawals to pay the tax will themselves be taxable and lose that chance for future tax-free growth.

Taking this big step of conversion relies on your belief that it is a smart move to give up your cash to pay taxes *now* to get tax-free withdrawals later. The government has been known to renege on such promises in the past. (Many municipal bond buyers were unaware that the government could add their interest to earnings in a way that would create taxes on their Social Security benefits.)

Estate tax laws are likely to change as well, impacting your retirement income planning (see Chapter 18). Under current tax law, your after-tax assets get a step-up in basis when you die. That means that if you have big gains in the value of your stocks, your heirs will inherit them with a new, higher cost basis as of the date of your death. That is scheduled to change in 2010, when instead of estate taxes, under current law, a new capital gains tax will be levied against the original cost basis on estates with assets above a certain level, with certain exemptions. The years after that are filled with uncertainty about everything except the fact that estate taxes are not likely to disappear, but are likely to grow. That's why personalized advice is so important. Depending on your situation, a different priority may be appropriate. But there will come a time, sooner or later, when you'll want to—or be required to—start taking distributions from your retirement plans.

Just don't start withdrawals from your tax-deferred retirement plan until after you reach age 59½, or you'll face a 10 percent federal tax penalty (unless you agree to take equal payments over your full lifetime). And you *must* start withdrawals in the year after you reach age 70½.

Three things to keep in mind:

1. The money you withdraw from your traditional retirement accounts will all come out taxed as ordinary income.
2. You can take as much money out of your tax-deferred retirement funds as you want without penalty once you reach age 59½.
3. You must set money aside to pay the taxes on these withdrawals—and you might even be required to make quarterly estimated tax payments.

Required Minimum Distributions and Required Beginning Date

As noted earlier, for seniors, life gets more complicated, not less, when it comes to finances. The rules for distribution of retirement accounts are among the most complicated. Thank goodness the financial services industry recognizes this and is competing to offer services to help you with distribution decisions.

Here are two key terms:

1. *Required beginning date (RBD)*. The deadline for the account owner's first RBD is April 1 of the year following the year the account owner reaches age 70½. Generally, it is wise to take the first distribution in the actual year you reach age 70½ to avoid a double distribution the following year, which could increase your tax bracket.
2. *Required minimum distribution (RMD)*. The amount of the RMD is based on the value of all of the tax-deferred retirement accounts owned by the person, although the distributions can be made from one or more accounts. The amount is calculated based on the Internal Revenue Service's (IRS's) Uniform Lifetime Distribution Table (except in the case of an owner whose spouse is sole beneficiary and is more than 10 years younger than the owner).

Getting It Right

It's important that you calculate your annual distribution correctly. The rules have been simplified in recent years, but mistakes can be costly. If you underwithdraw, you're subject to a penalty of 50 percent of the amount that should have been withdrawn. Your IRA custodian can help you calculate the exact amount of the required minimum distribution each year, using the factor from the IRS table. Just be sure to include *all* your retirement accounts in your calculation.

After you decide how much you *must* withdraw—remembering that you can always withdraw *more*—you then must decide which accounts to draw down first. This is not a matter of guesswork. You should have taken this issue into account as you went through the Monte Carlo modeling process described in Part 2 of this book. Still, you may want to revisit the subject every year as you consider rebalancing your accounts. Then you can withdraw more from the sector that has become overweighted because of gains—or because of losses in other sectors.

There's another issue to consider. Each year, your required withdrawal will be determined by the IRS table based on your age and retirement savings. What if you have investment losses? You may have smaller required withdrawals, or you may recognize that you're dipping into the bottom of the pot. That happened to many people after the last bear market. And that's why you need an overall plan, using Monte Carlo modeling, that covers both investments and withdrawals—a plan that should be updated every year.

As you consider consolidating all your IRAs, Keogh plans, and rollover accounts, this issue of modeling investments and calculating distributions should be a major consideration in your choice of retirement plan custodians. Life is complicated enough without agonizing over the proper withdrawal amount each year. Make it simple by using a financial institution that specializes in these services.

While we're on the subject of IRA withdrawals, please make sure you've named the appropriate beneficiary for any IRA assets that remain after your death. Your choice could make a huge difference in the future growth of that tax-deferred account. Details are in Chapter 18, Estate Planning.

Generating Income from Your Portfolio

Most of your retirement income will come from retirement plan distributions and from ongoing earnings. But you will also want to reevaluate your investment portfolio to see if it can generate more income. Perhaps the one strategy for generating income that has received the most attention is through the use of tax-deferred annuities. It is a subject that is so complex, and evolving so quickly with new products and guarantees, that it will be the focus of the next chapter.

First, though, a look at restructuring your current investment portfolio to provide a more reliable stream of retirement income. In Chapter 9, I explained income-producing investments, including bonds, real estate investment trusts, and the mutual funds that specialize in these asset classes. You can generate more income by giving these products greater weight in your portfolio. There are other strategies you can use to build income that will arrive on a regular basis.

Laddering: A Bond Strategy for Retirement

In stocks, you can buy a fixed dollar amount of mutual fund shares every month or quarter. You'll never pick tops or bottoms that way, but you will spread out your purchases and get the average price.

There's a similar strategy for bonds. It's called laddering, and it simply means that you stagger your maturities so that an old bond is always maturing and the cash can be reinvested at the current higher or lower yield. You'll never get the top rate for all your bond portfolio with this strategy, but you won't make the mistake of locking up all your money at low rates.

Laddering solves another problem. When you're retired, you want to count on both the income and the principal from your bonds. Yes, you'll hope to live off the interest income, but at some point you may need to sell some of your bonds because you need cash. It would be nice if that didn't happen in a period of rising interest rates, when bond prices are falling.

You can ladder a portfolio by buying short-term securities such as U.S. Treasury bills and staggering your purchases every few weeks. Or you can invest all at once and buy bonds of staggered maturities. Shorter-term bonds have smaller price swings because they're not locked in for such a long period. The principal will be returned to you as the bonds mature, and you can quickly reinvest at higher rates. And if rates are falling, you'll be less upset because part of your portfolio is still earning rates higher than those that are currently available.

It's relatively easy to buy staggered maturities of U.S. government bonds or shorter-term Treasury bills (T-bills). You can do it online at the U.S. Treasury web site, www.treasurydirect.gov. You can open a TreasuryDirect account at the site (minimum investment is $100) and create instructions to automatically roll over your T-bills or bonds when they mature, getting the prevailing rates at the time. In effect, you become your own disciplined bond fund manager. And the interest checks can be deposited directly into your checking or money market account at your bank.

Covered Call Writing to Add Investment Income

Owning stocks for growth is an important strategy in your retirement portfolio. You can increase your retirement income by concentrating on shares of companies that pay dividends. You can also increase your investment income by writing covered call options to collect more income on stocks you already own.

Most people think options are confusing, and perhaps risky; but quite the opposite is true if you use conservative strategies that actually minimize your investment risk. As noted in Chapter 9, call and put options give the buyer a chance to control shares of stock for a specific period of time without a large outlay of cash. For a small premium, the call buyer gets the right to purchase (and the put buyer gets the right to sell) a stock at a specific strike price for a limited period of time. If the stock doesn't move beyond the strike price, the option expires worthless, and the option buyer loses the cost of the option.

The person who grants that call option to the buyer is likely to be an individual with a portfolio of stocks who is searching for more income from the portfolio. If an investor writes, or grants, a call option, she collects the premium as income.

When you write a call option, there are only a few things that can happen. If the stock goes down or stays at about the same level, the option will expire worthless. You—the call writer—keep the stock *and* the premium income. The extra money you received for writing the call will cushion any stock losses. If the stock goes up, the person who bought the call will probably exercise the option and demand delivery of the stock at the promised strike price. You won't complain, though, because you are selling the shares at a price you thought acceptable when you wrote the call. And now you have more money to invest in more stocks, which allows you to write more calls and to earn more premiums.

You can start a program of call writing by purchasing individual stocks in round lots of at least 100 shares. You'll probably want to diversify your call-writing program over many stocks. The easiest way to do so is to buy 100 shares of an exchange-traded fund (see Chapter 9), a fund that represents an index such as the Standard & Poor's (S&P) 500—S&P Depositary Receipts (SPDRs), known as Spiders (ticker symbol SPY)—or the Dow Jones Industrial Average—the Diamonds (ticker symbol DIA). Then you can write a call against 100 shares of your fund. The premium you take in boosts your investment income. The costs of ETF transactions can cut deeply into your income. But if you execute the trades at a deep-discount brokerage that specializes in this type of activity, you can pay less than $1 in commissions for each 100 shares of the ETF and the same small commission for each option contract written.

In fairly steady markets, studies show that this strategy could easily add as much as 5 percent or more to an index fund investor's total return. In strong markets, the return could be even greater, although the written option limits the investor's gain on the upside. In a declining market, the call writer who gathers premium income will lose less than the buy-and-hold investor will—and may even earn a small profit. But in a real bear market, you may still have big losses on the underlying stock.

For information on this strategy, visit the Learning Center at the Chicago Board Options Exchange's web site—www.cboe.com. Also,

I highly recommend a book that's designed specifically to teach individual investors how to write covered calls: *The Rookie's Guide to Options*, by Mark Wolfinger (W&A Publishing, 2008).

Thus far, we've concentrated on creating your own income in retirement. Some of the most popular investments for doing that are insurance contracts—annuities. They create both opportunities for income and costs for guarantees, but the best of them is not without risk. More in the next chapter.

Then, the biggest retirement question of all: Will Social Security provide any meaningful income to you in retirement? Generations of Americans have relied on the promise of Social Security benefits as a foundation for their retirement income. After all, we've paid into the system over our entire working lives. But will those promises extend to the baby boomer generation over the next 40 years?

The topic of retirement income is fraught with uncertainty— whether we'll still have jobs, or can create another income through work, whether our portfolios can be restructured to provide both income and withdrawal of principal, and whether our promised government pensions will be there for us. It's no wonder people don't want to think about, much less plan for, a long retirement. But those who *do* plan will be in far better shape than those who rely on government coming to their aid.

INCOME RESOURCES

- **www.irahelp.com**   Ed Slott, IRA expert and author of *Parlay Your IRA into a Family Fortune* (Viking, 2008), answers individual questions on IRA issues at his web site.
- **www.treasurydirect.gov**   Create a portfolio of U.S. Treasury bills, notes, and bonds.
- **www.cboe.com/learning center**   Learn about covered call writing.
- **www.seniorjobbank.org**   For job seekers over 50.

- **www.seniors4hire.org**   Free membership for job seekers over 50.
- **www.aarp.org/money/careers/findingajob**   Shows you how to locate a Senior Community Service Employment Program (SCSEP) in your area.
- **www.snagajob.com**   This web site for part-time and hourly jobs has a special section for seniors.

ANNUITIES FOR INCOME AND TAX-DEFERRED GROWTH

One of the most important aspects of retirement income planning is the need for certainty. That's part of the appeal of the Monte Carlo process, a computerized evaluation of the likelihood that you will reach your goal of not running out of money before you run out of time (see Chapter 4). But you also need the certainty of having enough regular income to cover your retirement lifestyle. That's where annuities can play a role.

When you're planning your retirement, the topic of annuities is bound to come up. Annuities do have a place in most retirement plans. Immediate annuities can provide a regular, fixed stream of monthly income. And while you're still working, tax-deferred annuities can be a place to build tax-deferred growth when other options such as 401(k) or 403(b) plans or individual retirement accounts (IRAs) have been maxed out.

As a result of the market crash, many people are more anxious about protecting their investment gains. Even before the big market decline, insurance companies had started to create a wide variety of annuity products designed to combine the benefits of tax-deferred growth with certain guarantees against loss so that future streams of retirement income can be promised. Widely called "Guaranteed Minimum Income Benefits," these products, or riders to existing products, are becoming increasingly popular.

But a few words of warning when it comes to purchasing *any* annuity product. First, these are insurance company contracts and are backed only by the strength of the insurer, the willingness of other insurers to contribute to state-managed guarantee funds to back up these contracts, and the willingness of the federal government to support a failing insurance company.

Also, these products are complex and difficult to compare. They are laden with fees and penalties for early withdrawal, and adding contributions can extend the "surrender charge" period. You need expert advice to make sure you're purchasing the product most suitable for you. Unfortunately, because annuities can be structured to offer returns higher than those on bank CDs, many unsuspecting seniors have fallen into the trap of annuity salesmen who may not have their best interests at heart.

IMMEDIATE ANNUITIES

An *immediate annuity* promises a check every month either for life (or for two lives) or for a fixed number of years. The amount of the monthly annuity check is based on your age and life expectancy, current interest rates, and the rate the insurance company expects to earn on the money.

When you die, the checks stop and the insurance company keeps the balance in the account. You can arrange for the checks to continue beyond your lifetime to cover the life of your spouse or heir or to last for at least a certain period of time. You'll get less money in your monthly check if you make the insurance company promise to pay not only over your life but also over a second life, or for a definite period of time to your heirs, even if you die early.

Most Monte Carlo modeling scenarios will recommend that at least a portion of your retirement fund be devoted to this secure stream of income, especially if you don't have a regular monthly pension check or if your Social Security check does not provide enough protection for basic living expenses.

The downside of an immediate annuity is that once you *annuitize*—once you start taking monthly checks—you can never access your principal again or change the amount of the check. If inflation comes along and your monthly check doesn't cover future expenses, you're stuck with that same monthly check. Of course, you want to make sure you buy your annuity from a sound, highly rated insurance company because only state guarantee funds back these promises, not federal deposit insurance.

Once you have decided how much cash to invest in an immediate annuity, it pays to compare the monthly annuity amounts offered by different companies because they may use different assumptions. To use an easy online calculator to find out the amount you could receive monthly in an immediate annuity for your life, for joint lives, or for a guaranteed certain period, go to www.immediateannuities.com.

There is such a thing as an immediate *variable* annuity, where the money is invested in a mutual fund-like subaccount and your monthly check varies, depending on how your investments perform. These annuities do provide a minimum or floor payment amount, but this is usually lower than the investment amounts generated from the same amount deposited in a fixed immediate annuity. But that uncertainty belies the real reason most people opt for an immediate annuity: the peace of mind that comes from knowing that a regular monthly check will arrive in your mailbox or be deposited into your checking account.

And there is an *immediate annuity with inflation protection.* The Vanguard Lifetime Income Program (800-662-7447) solves the problem of inflation by adjusting payments over time to reflect changes in the consumer price index for urban consumers (CPI-U). You are guaranteed a minimum payment that will never decline in absolute terms or in relative terms to inflation. Every year on January 1, payments are adjusted upward. If the index were to decline, your monthly check could not be made smaller than your intial monthly payment amount, although it might drop below the previous year's payment level.

The cost of this protection is embedded in the monthly payment, which is initially smaller than you would otherwise get in an immediate annuity. For example, at current rates as of this writing, a 65-year-old male depositing $100,000 in a standard immediate annuity could expect a lifetime check of about $670 per month. The inflation protection program would reduce the monthly check to an initial $496 per month, although the amount would increase with inflation. If there were 20 years with an average CPI increase of 3 percent annually, the monthly check would grow to $896. It would grow to $1,087 if inflation averages 4 percent over a 20-year period. There's a big difference in your check when you pay for inflation protection. That should make you aware of the potential impact of inflation on a fixed monthly check.

TAX-DEFERRED ANNUITIES

Tax-deferred annuities should be used for additional retirement savings after traditional methods have been used. Your company retirement plan contributions reduce your taxes each year, and you might even get a matching contribution. But tax-deferred annuities are typically funded with after-tax money, because they provide tax-deferred growth.

With a tax-deferred annuity, you give the insurance company a check now and the insurer invests it, with all the growth compounding tax deferred. Eventually, you can take the money out, either in one withdrawal or in any amount you choose at any time. Or you can take a monthly check for life.

If you take money in one or more withdrawals, you'll pay ordinary income taxes *on the gains.* The first withdrawals are always considered ordinary income, and ultimately you can withdraw your original investment tax free. If you take a check a month for life, a portion is taxed as ordinary income and a portion is not taxed because it is considered a return of principal.

There are two more considerations with tax-deferred annuities that might make you think twice before buying. The first is *surrender charges.* Although these charges can be as high as 20 percent, they generally start at 8 percent and decline over the years, and they may last as long as the first eight years you own the annuity. The second concern is the federal rule that says withdrawals of earnings from tax-deferred annuities before age 59½ face a 10 percent *federal tax penalty.* (There are certain penalty exceptions for annuity withdrawas under age 50½, if the payments are taken in equal payments over your life expectancy, under Rule 72T and 72Q.)

So tax-deferred annuities are usually best for people over age 60 who don't need their principal for a number of years. Some annuities do allow withdrawals of up to 10 percent of the account value each year without surrender charges. There are other hardship consider-ations such as waivers if the money is needed for a nursing home or terminal illness. These make the annuity more liquid, but you'll have to read the fine print! Basically, if you're considering a tax-deferred annuity, you'll want to be sure you have no immediate need for the money you're investing—unless you're using a Guaranteed Minimum Income Rider to start the flow of retirement income.

There are two kinds of tax-deferred annuities: *fixed-rate* and *variable*.

Fixed-Rate Tax-Deferred Annuities

These products work like bank certificates of deposit (CDs) but with-out the federal deposit insurance. You get the insurance company's promise of either a fixed rate for a certain number of years or an initial high rate that may be adjusted in the coming years. It's easy to compare these annuities because all the fees are figured right into the yield you have been promised.

Remember to check those surrender charges, and look for an annuity in which the surrender charge doesn't last longer than the fixed-rate guarantee. For example, you may be promised a 5 percent annual yield on principal invested for five years, with surrender charges that end after five years. That way you won't be trapped in an annuity that doesn't keep up with rising interest rates.

Variable Tax-Deferred Annuities

These annuities have subaccounts that work like a series of mutual funds inside the annuity contract. You have your choice of subac-counts, and you are subject to the gains (or losses) on the principal you invest result from the investment choices you make.

When considering a variable annuity, make sure it offers a good choice of investment subaccounts. There may be limitations on how frequently you can switch among the subaccounts. Be sure to ask about the annual management fees charged on the individual sub-account mutual funds.

It is very important to consider the overall cost of the annuity as well as the annual surrender charges. Many annuities have huge expenses for certain promises they make. For example, "mortality charges" promise that if you die, your heirs get the entire amount you originally invested; but you'll pay for that promise. Remember also to consider the potential cost of surrender charges.

Don't be blinded by the promise of tax deferral. If the total annual-cost package adds up to more than 1.5 percent, you might be better off investing outside an annuity in a regular taxable mutual fund, unless you're getting income stream protection or death benefits. If you invest in a taxable account your gains will be taxed at capital gains rates, whereas gains withdrawn from an annuity are always taxed as ordinary income. And in ordinary mutual funds, you won't face steep surrender charges if you decide to take your money out and switch to something more conservative.

THE LATEST ANNUITY PRODUCTS

Insurance companies have recognized that investors are looking for security but don't want to lock themselves into fixed-rate annuities, so they developed new products that combine certain income guarantees, either now or at a future date, if your annuity investment account does not perform well. But you have a chance at larger streams of income if the market goes up—even after you start receiving income. Each of these products has its costs and limitations; but depending on your willingness to pay the price and give up some of the upside, they may appeal to investors nearing or in retirement and seeking tax-deferred growth as well as guaranteed current income.

Guaranteed Minimum Income Benefits

Annuities with guaranteed minimum income benefits (GMIB) are designed to grow your money on a tax-deferred basis with a guaranteed protected withdrawal value, from which you can take income regardless of the market performance of the funds inside your annuity. On the upside, you get the benefit of stock market gains, but your future income stream is protected if the stock market falls. The ultimate goal is to create a predictable lifetime stream of income along with growth of principal.

With these guaranteed minimum income benefits annuities, the insurance company offers a fixed, guaranteed rate of return (today around 5 percent) on the principal until you start taking a stream of income. The amount you can get in that monthly check is based on your age and the value of your account.

When you decide you want to "turn on" that lifetime income stream, the promised compounding stops. You will continue to get your monthly check, based on the greater of your initial investment, compounded at 5 percent a year, or the current cash value based on your investment growth—whichever is higher.

You'll get that same monthly check as long as you live, even if your investment account goes to zero. If the investment account were to increase because of a bull market, and your account grew more than the amount of your annual withdrawal, you might even get a larger check.

If you need more money than the monthly check, you can withdraw your cash value out, once you are beyond the surrender charges. But at some point, your protected withdrawal value (the initial deposit compounding at the promised rate) might be higher than the cash value (based on market performance). So you would think twice about withdrawing cash versus taking the monthly check based on the protected value.

When you die, your heirs will receive the amount you invested or current cash value, whichever is greater. However, you can purchase a rider that guarantees your heirs will receive the promised compounding as well as the initial investment at your death, regardless of how much you have withdrawn—unless the cash value goes to zero as a result of your withdrawals.

Consider this example: At age 60, you invest $100,000 into a 5 percent GMIB annuity, and also purchase a death benefit rider, also at 5 percent providing dollar-for-dollar withdrawal treatment. Here's what could happen 10 years from now:

- There's been a bull market and your investment account has grown by 10 percent annually and in 10 years is worth $269,000. At that point you could start to take 5 percent withdrawals, based on that $269,000 value.

- There's been a bear market, and your investment account has fallen to only $75,000. You need the income, so you start taking withdrawals based on your original investment of $100,000, which has been compounding at the promised rate of 5 percent per year; thus that "protected withdrawal value" is now $170,000. At age 70, you're going to get a check for about $8,500 a year. And you will never receive *less* than that amount as long as you live. (You could receive more if the market turns upward sharply, though.)
- Ten years from now, you might die without taking any withdrawals. If there has been a bull market, your heirs will receive the $269,000 cash value of your account (assuming a 10 percent annual rate of return). If there has been a bear market, your heirs will receive the initial $100,000 investment (if you did not purchase that death benefit rider). But if you *did* buy the death benefit rider, even with the bear market they will get the $170,000, which was the promised value based on the 5 percent compounding.
- Ten years from now you might need a hunk of cash. Since you are beyond the surrender charge period, you can take out the entire cash value. That cash value would be determined by the market value of your investment account.

When you buy one of these annuities, you should give careful thought to the costs of both the income and death benefit riders. The cost will be roughly 1 percent for the guaranteed withdrawal benefit, and half a percent for the death benefit rider—all taken out of the cash value of your investment account. Those seem a reasonable price to pay for the guarantees—but some annuities charge even more, so you must ask.

These annuities have another challenge. You must decide when to start making withdrawals. (Remember, your account stops compounding at the promised rate, when you start making withdrawals.) So you want to take them early enough to get the maximum value withdrawn before you die! Adding a death benefit rider can help you deal with that challenge.

In spite of this annual rate promise, this is really a variable annuity. You'll have a choice of mutual fund-type subaccounts that are invested in the stock market. If the market falls, the insurance company is promising that you'll at least get your principal, plus that 5 percent annual interest if you decide to take a check a month for life. If the market rises, of course, you'll have gains that you can withdraw at any time after the surrender period expires, paying ordinary income taxes on the gains. If your investments perform poorly, your monthly check will be based on the original investment plus the promised interest. And after you begin taking income, if your investment choices perform well, your monthly check could even increase. But it will never fall below that initial check amount.

As I noted at the start, annuities are a complicated investment, with many variables and costs that are not obvious. Please avoid seminars geared toward convincing novice investors that they can get higher returns and guarantees. Frequently they don't mention costs and inaccessibility of your money. For independent advice I trust, contact my expert, Jeffrey Oster at www.JeffreyOster.com. You do not have to mention my name, and I get nothing out of this but a confidence that you will be treated with intelligence and integrity.

Equity-Indexed Annuities: A Warning

Equity-indexed annuities offer tax deferral with features that take some of the attractiveness of fixed-rate annuities, which guarantee a certain amount of interest each year, and variable annuities, which have a return that depends on your investment decisions. In my opinion, equity-indexed annuities contain the worst features of both—typically at a high cost—and should usually be avoided.

Here's how they work. The interest you earn on the money you invest in this annuity is not fixed. Instead, it is based on the performance of some stock market index, typically the Standard & Poor's 500 Stock Index—without the dividends, which can provide as much as 40 percent of the total index return over the long run! So you have a guaranteed interest rate, combined with a chance to earn a bit extra based on the return of a stock market index. Sounds good if that's all you know, but in this case the devil is in the details.

On the downside, there is typically a floor. If the index falls, you don't lose principal. But, depending on the contract, you may not be credited with any interest. Or you may be guaranteed a floor of at least 90 percent of your original investment, along with a minimum guarantee of interest you will earn—a very low amount—even if the index falls. There is a variety of combinations, which makes it difficult to compare these products.

But it's not the downside protection that makes most of these annuities a bad deal. It's the restrictions on what you can earn on the upside to pay for that protection. You get some of the benefit of the stock market's gains, but definitely not all of the upside.

There are several ways the upside can be limited. The insurance company may set a *participation rate*, giving you perhaps only 70 percent (or even as low as 50 percent) of the total return of the index. That percentage factor might change every year, it might be guaranteed for as long as you keep your money in the annuity, or it might have a certain minimum. In any case, you're losing out on the upside potential of the stock market.

Other equity-indexed annuities provide for a *rate cap*, an upper limit on what you can earn. Even in a bull-market year, your return may be capped at 6 percent. That cap offsets the protection the insurance company offers in guaranteeing a floor—the promise that you won't earn a negative rate of interest even if the market falls. In my opinion, you're always paying too much for the protection. Of course, insurance salespeople will disagree.

The bottom line is that you might be better off with two separate annuities: (1) a fixed-rate annuity that will give you guaranteed positive interest, and (2) a variable annuity that lets you capture *all* the upside gains on your investment subaccounts. Remember, much of the stock market's historic long-term return of around 10 percent per year is made up of some very big years of gains that offset down years. Why limit your upside potential just because you're seeking security?

If that argument hasn't convinced you to stay away from equity-indexed annuities on principle (as well as principal), you'll want to consider the additional costs that can be packed into these products. For example, there may be an administrative fee, or margin, subtracted from your return. That could be 2 percent or more, again cutting into your upside potential. And the way the value of the index is calculated could, again, limit your participation.

Even worse, many of these contracts have extended periods for surrender charges with extremely high amounts, some as high as

20 percent, effectively locking your money up for an extended period of time. Others restrict you from withdrawal at any time, insisting you, or your heirs, "annuitize"—take a monthly check for life to get your money out with out a penalty.

TAX-DEFERRED ANNUITY WITHDRAWALS

After the surrender period (and the age 59½ federal tax period) have ended, you'll be faced at some point with deciding on withdrawals from your tax-deferred annuity. Your decisions can make a big difference in how you're taxed. As noted earlier, all annuity gains are taxed as ordinary income, even if the increases came from stock market gains in your mutual fund-like subaccounts. If you set up a systematic program for withdrawals, a portion will be taxable and a portion will be a tax-free return of your original investment. This doesn't reduce the ultimate taxes (unless tax rates fall during your withdrawal period), but it does spread out the payment of income taxes.

The other tax issue arises at the death of the tax-deferred annuity holder. Immediate annuities stop paying either at the death of the owner or the beneficiary or after a certain period of time that was guaranteed at purchase. But when the owner of a tax-deferred annuity dies, the balance in the account is part of the estate. Unlike most other investments, the gain inside an annuity does not get a step-up in basis at death. Instead, the beneficiary must pay income tax on the entire gain. However, there is the ability to stretch out the payments, and the taxes, over the lifetime of the beneficiary, much like an IRA, and this stretch provision is also applicable to annuities not held inside an IRA. You should review the rules with your CPA and estate planning attorney.

TAX-DEFERRED ANNUITY EXCHANGES

Before you're ready to withdraw money from your annuity, you might want to look for another annuity offering a better deal or higher rates. Once the surrender period has expired, you should look around to see what else is being offered. But don't just withdraw from one annuity, deposit the check, and buy another product. That will trigger taxes on the gains. Instead, the new insurance company will help you do a tax-free 1035 exchange or IRA transfer to move directly into the new product without paying taxes. The new annuity may create a new period of surrender charges.

Your IRA Inside an Annuity?

Your IRA is already tax sheltered. Why would you pay extra to purchase an annuity designed to offer tax shelter with your IRA money? There is only one reason: to use the income benefit and death benefit guarantees of an annuity. That guarantee means that whatever your investment choices are inside this annuity (which will rise or fall based on the performance of the subaccounts you've selected), your heirs cannot receive less than the amount you originally invested, and may offer your heirs the compounded value of interest on your original annuity investment. If you have added a Guaranteed Income Benefit rider, you'll be able to receive lifetime income from the rider's Protected Withdrawal Value while you are alive. Certain costs and restrictions apply when you invest your IRA inside an annuity product or when you roll over your IRA into one of these products. First, the annuity must be qualified to accept the IRA. Second, there is a cost to the death benefit. And third, the annuity itself will have surrender charges for a number of years and may limit the amount of withdrawals you can make in a single year. Consider these costs and restrictions carefully.

Remember, the death benefit insurance of an annuity is payable only at your death, not if your account declines because your investments declined in value. (You only get that guarantee against declining value if you purchase the GMWB rider.) So the death benefit guarantee is useless while you're alive. The industry sells lots of annuities to IRA holders who simply feel better knowing that they can't lose their retirement money. But they won't be around to see that happy ending because it will happen only after their death.

ANNUITIES: THE REAL RISK FACTOR

Annuities are products offered by insurance companies. Although fixed annuities may promise a fixed rate, they are not bank certificates of deposit. There is no federal insurance guarantee fund for money invested with an insurance company. Instead, there is a network of state funds that requires companies doing business in that state to ante up cash in case of the failure of an insurance company with policyholders in that state.

Funds held in the variable subaccounts of annuities are by law held separately from the insurer's General Account assets (this is why they are called Separate Account assets). These amounts are *not* subject to the claims of the insurer's creditors should the insurance company go into receivership or bankruptcy. This does not protect you from the impact of stock market declines on your separate account investments, but it does provide the ability for you to access your funds even if the insurer's general account assets are held in receivership.

The amount of coverage guaranteed by a guarantee association varies by state and by type of insurance. Here are the typical maximums: $300,000 in life insurance death benefits; $100,000 in cash surrender or withdrawal value for life insurance; $100,000 in withdrawal and cash values for annuities; $100,000 in health insurance policy benefits. That's why you'll want to make sure you're dealing with a highly rated insurance company. For insurance company safety ratings, go to www.weissratings.com, where you'll pay $15 for each company rating.

Now that you've seen the wrinkles involved in annuity contracts, you're probably hoping someone will come along to help you decide. And there are plenty of salespeople willing to do just that. Be sure you use trained agents who represent larger companies or use certified financial planners. Or go to financial services firms such as Vanguard, Fidelity, and USAA, which are noted for their low expense ratios. Annuities do have a place in your retirement portfolio, but you need to know their place.

Annuity Information and Pricing

- www.immediateannuities.com
- www.JeffreyOster.com
- www.annuityadvantage.com

Or for low-cost variable annuities go to major no-load mutual fund companies such as Vanguard, Fidelity, and TIAA-CREF.

Insurance Company Safety Ratings

A. M. Best Company
www.ambest.com
908-439-2200

Moody's Investors Service
www.moodys.com
800-811-6980

Standard & Poor's
www.standardandpoors.com/ratings
212-208-1199

Weiss Ratings
www.weissratings.com
800-289-9222

CHAPTER 13

SOCIAL SECURITY AND MEDICARE

If you're a baby boomer, Social Security can't possibly provide for you in the same way it provided for your parents. That's a simple statement of fact. Even though we of the boomer generation have paid into Social Security at high rates throughout our working lives, there are simply too many of us. The money we paid in has been used to pay our parents' current benefits, and there aren't enough younger people to take care of us in the same style. That fact is critical to your retirement planning.

SOCIAL IN-SECURITY

When I was asked to speak at a 2009 panel on The Future of Retirement Security for the Aspen Institute in Washington, D.C., I was astounded at the general belief that Social Security would provide any significant amount of retirement income, beyond mere subsistence. At the time I said: "If you believe in the Social Security Trust Fund, you must also believe in the tooth fairy!"

The future of Social Security is a hot button topic. But we can only begin to deal with the future when we face the current reality: There is no "trust fund"—only an accounting fiction. The "surpluses" in the fund that were supposed to accrue for the benefit of boomer retirement were long ago "consolidated" into the federal budget deficit. So when the government says it is running a trillion dollar deficit, that's *after* using up all the money that has been taken in through the Social Security payroll tax.

Don't be in denial about the severe problems facing Social Security, which have been exacerbated by high unemployment and recession. Here's a quote from the Social Security Trustees report: "Social Security has been changed over time to meet the needs of the American people. It will need to change again to meet future challenges." Now, what do you think that means for you?

Currently Social Security benefits provide 90 percent of their income for one-third of our seniors. It provides more than half of their income for 65 percent of today's seniors. It currently provides an average of 40 percent of the average worker's preretirement earnings. There is no way this program can do the same for the retiring baby boomers.

Will the next generation be willing to pay for boomer retirement? Or are we creating "generation warfare"? In 2008, 162 million workers paid into Social Security. But 51 million people were beneficiaries. You do the math. Do you know two or three members of the next generation who will be willing to pay for your retirement?

Some boomers may received promised benefits—but Social Security is likely to be transformed into a sort of welfare program for the needy elderly. If you have other income or savings, you'll find your benefit levels reduced or taxed away. It's unwise to base your retirement income strategy on any meaningful benefits from Social Security. That's something I've been saying for many years, amidst much consternation from officials. But there's been no denial from the actuaries!

In fact, they're saying quite the opposite. The 2009 Trustees Report reveals their forecast that in 2016, Social Security benefit payouts will be larger than payroll taxes collected. (That was moved up by one year from the previous report.) And they're predicting that the "trust fund" will be "exhausted" by 2037.

In fact, the actuaries predict that the fund would need an additional $5.3 trillion (in today's dollars) to pay all the promised benefits! And where will that come from? If the government merely "prints" the money, it will be worthless.

The facts are finally being publicly acknowledged and solutions debated. But solutions require political consensus, which is difficult to achieve. Even with promises to leave benefits unchanged for those presently over age 55, there is still a risk that inflation—and the basis on which it is calculated—will make that promised monthly check worth less to future retirees.

When it comes to planning your retirement income stream, you need to be a realist. So here's the most realistic approach you can take: Don't rely on Social Security for more than a minimal contribution to your retirement income. In the future, the need for benefits will be just as great and will last longer as boomers' life expectancy increases. In spite of increased payroll taxes on current workers, it's likely that future legislation will further delay the age at which you can collect full benefits, will reduce benefits, or will restrict Social Security payments to those of modest income and assets. And those promised retirement checks are likely to be an ever-smaller contributor to a reasonable retirement lifestyle.

How Much Can You Expect?

Every year, workers and former workers receive a statement from Social Security that details reported earnings and gives an estimate of benefits. It's important to check the reported earnings to make sure that your employers have the correct Social Security number and that you are being credited for all your wages. But unless you are planning to retire in the next few years, the statement of benefits has very little meaning, except as a reminder to save more.

If you haven't received a statement recently, you can use the calculator on the Social Security Administration's web site to get an estimate of your monthly benefit, based on your birth date and latest year's earnings. You'll need to have worked enough years to earn credits to get your Social Security benefit. Benefit calculations are based on an average of 35 years of earnings.

When you use the Retirement Estimator (www.socialsecurity .gov/estimator), it will securely request your personal information so it can create realistic scenarios based on your work history. You can check to see what your benefits are estimated to be if you retire at "full retirement age," or early at age 62, or even if you wait until the maximum age, 70. You can also do "what-if" scenarios to see the impact on your benefits if you should choose to stop work at an even earlier age, or if you received a big raise. This is especially useful for younger workers making career-changing decisions.

If you use the online calculator, you'll see that you have a choice of retirement years. Boomers may retire early at age 62 years and 1 month. Full retirement benefits no longer start at age 65, but at age 66, or even at 67, depending on your year of birth. Some people may decide to postpone taking benefits until age 70, at which point the benefit will be increased by about 8 percent per year you delay after full retirement age, up to age 70. Once you reach age 70, there is no additional financial benefit to waiting to collect your benefits. (There is a separate calculator for government employees whose retirement benefits are based on a different formula if they are eligible to receive a pension based on work not covered by Social Security.)

For example, a 62-year-old (in 2009) who had earned the maximum in Social Security covered earnings over the past 35 years might expect benefits (in 2009 dollars) like those listed in Table 13.1.

What's the best age to start taking benefits? If you were born between 1943 and 1954, and start taking benefits early—at age 62—your monthly check will be about 25 percent lower than at full retirement. For those born in 1960 and later, the reduction becomes greater for early retirees, rising to a maximum of 30 percent. Figure 13.1 shows the impact of your retirement date on a monthly check that would otherwise be $1,000 at full retirement age. This example assumes a benefit of $1,000 at a full retirement age of 66.

The other part of the answer to whether you should start taking your Social Security check at an earlier age depends on your longevity outlook. As Clint Eastwood asked, "Do you feel lucky?" If you think you'll live well into your eighties, it might pay to wait before

Table 13.1   Projected Monthly Social Security Benefits

Retirement Age	Monthly Benefit Amount*
62 years and 1 month in 2009	$1,769
66 years in 2013	$2,403
70 years in 2017	$3,223

*Assumes no future increases in prices or earnings.

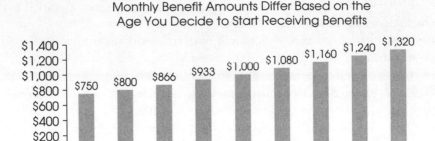

Figure 13.1   Monthly Benefit Amounts
Source: Social Security Administration.

you start collecting benefits. On the other hand, there's that old saying about a bird in the hand—not to mention that today's boomers might want to start collecting those promised checks while there's still money to fund them!

How Much Can You Earn?

This book is based on the premise that you'll probably have to continue working if you want to maintain your standard of living in retirement. There may be some advantage to continuing to work, because Social Security automatically uses the 35 highest earning years to compute your benefit. If you didn't start to work until later in life, or if you were out of the workforce for a number of years, these last, higher-income years could add substantially to your monthly check. (Retirees who return to work will have their benefit automatically recomputed if subsequent earnings are higher than a year previously counted.)

Those who take early benefits before full retirement age are penalized by reductions in their monthly check. If you start taking early benefits but continue to work, your check will be reduced by $1 for every $2 you earn above the annual limit (which is $14,160 in 2009). In the year you reach full retirement age, your check is reduced by $1 for every $3 you earn, above a higher limit ($37,680). That reduction occurs up until the month you reach full retirement age.

Once you reach full retirement age, there is no penalty for continuing to earn money. You can now earn as much as you want without losing any Social Security benefits, starting with the month you reach full retirement age. However, if you do work at a job that is covered by Social Security after you start receiving benefits, you and your employer must still make the appropriate contributions to Social Security and Medicare out of your earnings.

Your Social Security benefits may be subject to a very high income tax, depending on your total income and a calculation called *modified adjusted gross income* (MAGI). For a single person, your benefits will not be taxable unless the total of your MAGI plus one-half of your Social Security benefits exceeds $25,000. If you are married and file a joint return, your MAGI plus one-half of your Social Security benefits must exceed $32,000 before you are liable for taxes. (If you earn over $34,000 on an individual return, or $44,000 on a joint return, up to 85 percent of your benefits may be subject to income tax.) And don't think you can get around this issue by purchasing tax-free municipal bonds. For purposes of this calculation, income from tax-free bonds is included in determining modified adjusted gross income.

How to Apply for Benefits

Your monthly Social Security check will not start automatically. You must *apply* for Social Security benefits, and it's best to start the process at least three months before you plan to retire, whether at full retirement age or earlier, if you plan to access benefits at age 62.

As you start thinking about these questions, you'll find a wealth of information at www.socialsecurity.gov/retire2. That's a direct link to all the retirement planning information you need, including finding your own "full retirement age" as well as the current earnings limits, and the Retirement Estimator calculator. It's also the place to start your online application process and avoid the lines at your local Social Security office.

If you must speak to an individual to help you through this life-changing event, contact your local Social Security office at the beginning of the year in which you plan to retire. Then you can apply in person, online at www.socialsecurity.gov, or on the toll-free phone line at 800-772-1213, Monday through Friday between 7 A.M. and 7 P.M.

MEDICARE

This part of the book is about streams of *income*, but it's important to deal with one critical *outflow* in retirement: the cost of health care. Medicare will probably be your primary source of medical coverage once you reach age 65. (Note, Medicare currently starts at age 65, which is sooner than "full retirement age" for boomers.) Since health care will be one of the largest expenses in your retirement budget, it's important to get started in Medicare correctly. It's equally important to understand that the problems facing Medicare will dwarf the headlines about Social Security.

The Centers for Medicare and Medicaid Services project that over the next 75 years Medicare's unfunded liability will be nearly $46 *trillion* for Parts A, B, and D combined! This amount is more than eight times greater than Social Security's unfunded liability. At the current rate of promised benefits, the Medicare trustees estimate that the Medicare trust fund (Part A only) will be completely exhausted by 2017—absent some increase in taxes or cuts in benefits.

Medicare's financial woes present a different type of challenge to retirees. While you can save more and invest more aggressively to supplement declining Social Security benefits, it's almost impossible to plan enough funding for future health-care costs. Once again, living longer and having expensive treatments to prolong life can wreak havoc on the best retirement plans.

Medicare spending is projected to surpass Social Security spending in 2028 and to take a nearly 7 percent share of the federal budget by 2030—up from about 3.2 percent now. At some point, the nation will have to face up to the costs of health care and decide whether it must be rationed. In the meantime, if you're facing retirement, you must plan carefully to take advantage of the current benefits offered by Medicare.

Medicare Enrollment

Enrollment in Medicare for boomers, whose full retirement benefits from Social Security don't start until age 66 or 67, will require you to apply at your local Social Security office. Medicare still starts at age 65, even if you are not eligible for Social Security until age 66 or 67, and even if you decide to delay taking Social Security benefits until age 70. You should start the application process at least three months before reaching age 65, even if you are still working and covered by your employer's health insurance. Applying for Medicare in the very first month you are eligible has an impact on your eligibility for the best Medicare supplement policies.

If you retire before age 65, you may have a gap period in your health insurance. Ask your employer about continuing the company coverage through COBRA. You can search for temporary health coverage at www.ehealthinsurance.com.

How Medicare Works

Here's a quick look at just what Medicare covers and how it is designed. For more information, go to www.medicare.gov or call 800-MEDICARE, 24 hours a day, seven days a week, for personal assistance in English or Spanish. The examples below are for the original Medicare coverage, which gives freedom of choice in physicians and hospitals that accept Medicare. There is also a program called Medicare Advantage, which works like a preferred provider organization (PPO) for Medicare, somewhat limiting patient choice to a network of physicians but also eliminating the financial burden of most co-payments.

Medicare has Part A and Part B. Part A helps pay for necessary medical care and services given by Medicare-certified hospitals, skilled nursing facilities, skilled care provided by home health agencies, and hospices. It does not cover doctor visits or prescription drugs. (In spite of the reference to home health agencies, this coverage does not include custodial care, which is why Part 5 of this book, on long-term care insurance, is so important.)

Although there is no cost for Part A of Medicare, there is still a 20 percent copayment required for most services. For that reason, many people choose to buy a Medicare supplement, or Medigap, policy. Part B of Medicare helps pay for doctors, outpatient hospital care, ambulance transportation, and a variety of other tests and services, including some home health care when medically necessary. Part B pays 80 percent of most covered services. You are responsible for the other 20 percent. If you are treated by a doctor who bills for more than Medicare is willing to pay, you may have to pay the difference.

There is a monthly fee for Part B, adjusted upward each year. (In 2009, that premium starts at $96.40 per month, but based on income it could be more than $300 per month.) The monthly amount could be higher if you do not sign up for Part B when you become eligible. That amount is typically deducted from your Social Security check. However, if you are not yet receiving Social Security checks, you can arrange to be billed quarterly.

Medicare Supplement Policies

Medicare only covers services if you are sick or injured. As noted earlier, it does not cover all services in full. Most services require a 20 percent copayment, and there is a $135 annual deductible for services under Part B for 2009. There is also a limited number of hospitalization days paid under Part A. And although Medicare now covers many preventive services (mammograms, prostate cancer screening, bone density tests, etc.), it does not cover routine physical exams, dental care or dentures, cosmetic surgery, routine foot care, hearing aids, or glasses.

As generous as Medicare seems to be, it is worthwhile to purchase a supplemental policy to fill in the gaps. These are known as Medigap policies. Decades ago, the offerings from various insurers were so confusing that they were nearly impossible to compare. To simplify matters, the various supplemental policies were codified into 10 standard coverages ranging from option A to option J, each with incremental coverage and costs.

You should apply for a Medigap policy immediately after registering for Medicare Part B. (If you are 65 and still working and using your employer's health plan, you can apply for a Medigap policy when you apply for Part B during open enrollment.) During the six-month period after you enroll in Part B, you cannot be turned down for even the most generous policies because of previous medical conditions. If you don't buy this supplemental policy during your six-month open enrollment period, you may not be able to get the coverage you want later, or you may have to pay a higher price. Always make sure to pay the premiums on time, because you'll never get coverage this good at this price in the future!

If you are enrolled in the Medicare Advantage HMO, you won't need a supplemental policy because all charges are covered in this plan. If you think you might switch back to traditional Medicare, you'll want to maintain your Medigap coverage, even though there are special provisions for those who switch back.

Medicare Prescription Coverage—Part D

The Medicare prescription drug program is also called Medicare Part D. It is designed to cover the cost of prescription drugs that you currently take—or might take in the future. Like all insurance policies it must be purchased in advance of need, so even if you don't take prescription drugs you must sign up when you become eligible for Medicare, or face costly penalties in the form of higher monthly premiums if you wait.

The only exceptions to this requirement to buy Part D insurance are for those who can certify that their ongoing health insurance from work, or retiree health benefits, provide similar "creditable" prescription drug coverage, or VA drug coverage. Or, if you choose a Medicare HMO that provides drug benefits, you will not need to sign up for Part D.

The structure and cost of Part D defy description in one chapter. However, there is a simple way to deal with the pricing, deductibles, and the "donut hole"—the period when you must pay all the costs for your drugs, before a level called "catastrophic" costs, when the government takes over paying all drug costs.

To determine the least expensive plan, based on *the prescription meds that you are currently taking*, you should go to the Medicare Part D "plan finder" tool at www.Medicare.gov. You'll need to have all your prescriptions, and correct dosages, to enter them into the online tool. Then you'll be given a listing of plans that operate in your area, in order of the lowest monthly cost plans, using the pharmacies of your choice. You'll contact the plan directly to set up coverage.

Note: Even if you are not currently taking any prescription drugs you *must* sign up for Part D, unless you fit one of the exclusions above. Simply use the online "plan finder" tool, but skip the section that asks you to list the meds you are currently taking.

You should sign up at the same time you sign up for Medicare. You can change plans once a year during the open enrollment period from November 15 to December 31 of that year. One reason for changing might be that you have added some new, expensive drugs to your list and you want to switch to a plan that offers lower costs for those drugs, and thus an overall lower monthly payment.

A FINAL THOUGHT ABOUT SOCIAL SECURITY AND MEDICARE

It's a basic Savage Truth: The government has promised more benefits to more people than it can possibly provide, even by raising taxes. When making retirement plans, you must take these government promises with the proverbial grain of salt—or even a handful.

Social Security alone will not provide an adequate standard of living in retirement. You simply must save more. When it comes to health care, Medicare will remain the most important source of coverage. But the most important thing Medicare does *not* cover is long-term custodial care, and that is a cost that could devastate even the most-well-funded retirement plan. So I've devoted Part 5 of this book to the importance of understanding—and insuring against—the costs of long-term care.

GOVERNMENT BENEFIT RESOURCES

- **www.socialsecurity.gov**   800-772-1213 (also go directly to the section of the Social Security web site most important in retirement planning: www.socialsecurity.gov/retire2).
- **www.medicare.gov**   Complete and easy explanations of the Medicare program, eligibility, coverage, and answers to all questions. On the home page you'll find the instructions for the Medicare Part D "plan finder" tool.
- **www.medicarerights.org**   Independent advocacy and policy group offers up-to-the-minute information and answers to your questions in English and Spanish.

CHAPTER 14

HOW TO TURN YOUR HOME INTO YOUR PENSION

The credit crunch and real estate crisis have destroyed the myth that your home is an inexhaustible piggy bank. Suddenly there's a new awareness that home prices may actually decline for an extended period of time. That's a problem that may hit hardest for those in retirement, who had counted on selling their homes and downsizing to raise cash for their retirement years. The family home might represent a good portion of your retirement fund.

Even though current market values may have declined, strategies such as reverse mortgages, installment sales, and private annuity trusts can create a regular stream of income to support your lifestyle. You invested in your home over the years. Now it can pay you back. Or a reverse mortgage might be the answer to purchasing a new smaller home, freeing you from future mortgage payments.

REVERSE MORTGAGES

For many seniors, a reverse mortgage is the answer to a prayer. It allows you to withdraw money from your home equity, tax free, with no requirement that it be repaid until you die or move out of the home. *There is no way you can be forced out of your home as long as you keep paying your property taxes, insurance, and maintain the property.*

That promise is the key to making a reverse mortgage acceptable to seniors who worry about tapping into their home equity.

There are now two uses for a reverse mortgage. The first is for people who want to remain in their home for the foreseeable future. For them, a reverse mortgage offers a stream of cash to pay for their ongoing expenses. The second is for seniors who want to purchase a new, smaller home—but don't want to use all their cash from the sale of an existing home.

Reverse Mortgage for Income

First, let's look at the basic reverse mortgage that can be used by people age 62 or older who have paid off their mortgage completely or have only a small balance remaining. A participating lender, such as a bank or mortgage company, will process the paperwork and give you a choice of ways to receive the money from the reverse mortgage:

- You can take out one lump sum.
- You can get a fixed check a month for as long as you live in your home.
- You can opt for a fixed check for a set number of years, perhaps just long enough to pay off your vacation condo.
- You can get a line of credit against the equity in your home, which you can draw down as needed.

The Federal Housing Administration (FHA) insures these mortgages, which means your future stream of monthly checks or line of credit funds is guaranteed to continue as long as you live in the home. And again, a reminder that you can never "run out" of equity in your home and lose the house: It is yours, as is the income stream, or cash you've withdrawn in a lump sum—as long as you continue to live in the home. The basic fact bears repeating: *You can never be forced out of your home.*

The amount of your lump-sum distribution or lifetime monthly check is determined by three factors: the current appraised value of your home, your age, and the current level of interest rates. The maximum amount of home equity that can be tapped for a reverse mortgage is $625,500 (through 2009). That doesn't mean that you can't withdraw more than that amount over the years. It just means that even if your home is valued at $1 million or more, the maximum amount that can be "considered" in calculating your stream of income is $625,000 of the equity.

For many people, it's difficult to conceive of taking money *out* of your home without having a liability to make payments on that debt. And federal regulations require you to be counseled by an independent adviser so that you will understand how this product works. Here's an example of how a reverse mortgage might work, based on current interest rates.

A 65-year-old homeowner with a home appraised at $500,000 could receive either a lump sum of $238,139, net of all fees, or a line of credit for that amount. Or that 65-year-old homeowner could receive a monthly check of $1,546 for as long as he lives in the home.

The older you are when you set up a reverse mortgage, the more money you can withdraw. In the example above, a 75-year-old could receive a lump sum of $295,607 or a $2,135 monthly check. You can do anything you want with the money.

Interest is accruing on the amount that is withdrawn. That interest is a variable rate, determined by an index that will be explained when you take out the loan. But instead of paying interest on a monthly basis, it becomes part of the balance due when you leave the home, by choice or by death.

Remember, the total of your withdrawals and interest can never exceed the value of the home when it is sold. At that point, any remaining balance goes to you—or your heirs. Or your heirs can choose to keep the house and take out a new mortgage to repay the reverse mortgage loan balance.

If you move out of your home for longer than one year it can be sold, unless your spouse and co-owner is still living there. But if you just go to Florida for the winter, or spend time in a hospital, or have a short stay in a nursing home, you don't have to worry about your house being sold out from under you.

Fees on reverse mortgages can be substantial and mostly are determined by the FHA, but they are calculated into the amount you can receive in your monthly check or lump sum withdrawal. They include an origination fee, which depends on the value of the home, but cannot exceed $6,000. In addition, there is an FHA insurance fee of 2 percent of the total property value, which pays for the guarantee that the lender will be repaid if you outlive the value of your house. On top of that there are normal closing costs, such as appraisal fees, inspections, and title and recording fees.

The major fees are set by the FHA. But some high-volume lenders may charge less for the appraisals, title insurance, and recording fees. Be sure to ask not only about the amount of the monthly check, but also about the fees that go into establishing that check. You're required to be given an estimate of the fees before you sign up for the loan.

HUD requires anyone taking out a reverse mortgage to get independent counseling, typically provided by AARP or others on an approved list of counselors. Counseling can be done in person or over the phone; you'll have plenty of chances to ask these questions and more.

By this time you might be asking why it's not easier and less costly to simply take out a home equity loan. But as a senior, you may not qualify for a home equity loan based on your income in retirement, and seniors may not qualify for the lowest interest rates on a home equity loan. But most important, with a home equity loan, there will be some repayment required along the way. In the earlier example, the 75-year-old homeowner could withdraw $295,000 through a reverse mortgage, with no repayment required. But if he withdrew that amount in an interest-only (6 percent) home equity loan, he'd have to repay $1,475 per month. That doesn't solve the problem of seniors who need cash.

Reverse Mortgage for Purchase

As noted earlier, there is a new use for a reverse mortgage. As a result of changes in the law in early 2009, seniors can now use a reverse mortgage to help them purchase a home. This is particularly useful if seniors have only a small amount of savings, or don't want the burden of a monthly mortgage payment. And it's a process that can help a senior buy your existing home, as well as help seniors move into a new home.

These days, many seniors are having trouble selling their current home and downsizing to a smaller home. And others, just entering retirement, are having difficulty financing the purchase of a new home, since they no longer have an income and don't want to put all their savings into the purchase. But part of the purchase price can actually be financed by a reverse mortgage—meaning a senior comes up with less cash to buy the house, but you won't have a monthly payment!

Just go to www.reversemortgage.org and use the calculator there to see the dollar amount of the reverse mortgage you would qualify for, based on your age. For example, a 65-year-old could likely get about $240,000 on a reverse mortgage on a $500,000 home. That means a senior who wants to buy your existing $500,000 house needs to come up with only $260,000. The reverse mortgage would provide roughly $240,000 of the purchase price, with no monthly payments required. Now your old, larger home becomes more saleable to someone with cash from the sale of an existing home.

And once your home is sold, you can take part of the $500,000 sale proceeds, and use it—along with some of your cash and your own reverse mortgage—to buy your next, smaller retirement home. So, if you're age 75, and want to purchase a $350,000 condo, you could likely get a $230,000 reverse mortgage on that smaller condo. That means you'll only have to put down $120,000 in cash on your new condo, and you can put the remaining $380,000 from your home sale in the bank (or several banks)!

Using a reverse mortgage to *buy* a home opens an entirely new dimension to this fascinating product. Refer to the web sites listed at the end of this chapter to learn more about reverse mortgages and to use an online calculator to estimate your monthly check.

MORE INCOME FROM YOUR HOUSE USING TRUSTS

One of the first rules of investing is to diversify your assets, but it's hard to diversify your home without selling it. There are some perfectly legal techniques that allow you to sell your home and get it out of your taxable estate while deferring taxes on the sale.

Installment Sale

The installment sale is a real estate financing technique that has long been used for commercial properties. It also has real tax benefits for individual homeowners who want to lock in the sale at current high prices yet defer paying taxes on the gain. You can structure an installment sale with any buyer, assuming you are willing to take the risk of the buyer making regular payments. The advantage of an installment sale is that you don't pay taxes on the gains until you receive the payments.

You'll want to use an attorney who specializes in this kind of agreement, and you'll want to have a substantial down payment from the buyer—at least 20 percent—in case the buyer stops making payments and you have to foreclose. Although installment sales are frequently used for commercial property, they're not the kind of deal you're likely to make with the family home—with one huge exception. Suppose the buyer is your son or daughter, who agrees to purchase the property on an installment sale basis and rent it back to you at a fair market price while you continue to live there. Your child becomes the owner, and you receive the proceeds of the installment sale, which allows you to pay a fair rent. If you want to keep ownership of your home in the family, this is a strategy worth considering.

There are some conditions: If you sell your house on the installment plan, the buyer must begin payments to you immediately. The payments must be made in regular installments, with interest at a fair market rate. Since you are the seller, the contract means that the house is now out of your taxable estate and you've locked in the sales price. But you can stretch out payment of capital gains taxes, typically over a five-year period, as the payments come in.

An installment arrangement requires a great deal of trust between seller and buyer. In case of a family fight, the new owner— your adult child—might sell the property to someone else, repay the debt to you, and let the new buyer force you out of the home. Or your child could have financial problems and find it difficult to make payments on the installment sale or to maintain the house when repairs are needed.

Private Annuity Trust

If you're ready to sell your house (or other property) and move out, you still may have concerns about paying capital gains taxes in one lump sum. A private annuity trust can help you defer those taxes while creating a lifetime stream of income. This type of annuity has nothing to do with annuities issued by insurance companies. In this case, the homeowner creates a trust, with an independent trustee, and transfers title to the trust. The trust immediately sells the property and collects the proceeds of the sale. The trustee invests the cash from the sale of the house in safe money market investments.

The trust then pays the owner of the property not a single check for the full amount, but a stream of lifetime payments called a private annuity. The contract says that payments will go to the owner for the rest of her life on a regular basis, as determined by IRS life expectancy tables. When the individual dies, the payments stop, leaving nothing to the estate. Any balance in the private annuity trust goes directly to the beneficiaries, free of estate and gift taxes.

The amount of the distribution must be calculated based on the life expectancy of the seller as determined by IRS actuarial tables. The monthly check will be structured to include interest on the invested amount, at a rate determined by the IRS. The seller cannot get more than that annual amount, even if the investments in the trust increase the balance. The monthly or quarterly check is fixed at the time the trust is created. (If cash is desperately needed, it may be possible to borrow from the trust or from a bank by pledging the future stream of payments.)

The tax considerations are what make a private annuity trust so interesting. You've sold the house and locked in your profit, but you don't pay taxes until you start receiving a regular check. If you don't need the income immediately, the monthly payments from the trust can be deferred for years, as long as they start by age 70½. When you do get the check, a portion will be a tax-free return of capital.

There are three distinct taxable portions of that monthly or quarterly check the seller receives: (1) a return of capital—a proportionate share of the initial cost of the house on which no taxes are owed; (2) a proportionate distribution of capital gains from the sale of the house, which is taxed at then-current capital gains tax rates; (3) a much smaller portion that could be taxed at ordinary income tax rates because it results from interest earned by the trust on the invested capital.

With a private annuity trust, you've locked in your homeownership gains and moved that huge asset out of your estate. You've created a lifetime stream of income while ensuring the balance of the asset goes to your heirs at your death. And in the process, you've delayed payment of your capital gains taxes. Now the only issue that's still up in the air is the future capital gains tax rate.

REVERSE MORTGAGE RESOURCES

Not all banks and mortgage companies originate reverse mortgages. To find a lender in your area, go to www.reversemortgage .org. You can use the web site's online calculator to get an idea of the monthly amount you could receive from your home, based on your age, location, and the value of your home.

Other Sources for Reverse Mortgages

- www.goldengateway.com
- www.financialfreedom.com
- Major banks, including Bank of America and Wells Fargo, have committed to reverse mortgage originations.

PART

5

LONG-TERM CARE: THE GREATEST RISK OF ALL

LONG-TERM CARE INSURANCE: WHO NEEDS IT?

What's the greatest risk in your financial plan? We've seen how a stock market crash can devastate retirement plans. But the greatest risk is not the longevity of this bear market, or even another bear market. It's the devastating cost of long-term care (LTC). And just as many preretirees didn't take the possibility of declining stock prices into consideration when making their retirement plans, most people don't consider the costs of living longer and the health-care and lifestyle implications.

Living longer may bring with it challenges that we cannot handle on our own. We may need help with routine activities of daily living, our health may become impaired because of progressive diseases, or our cognitive ability may be limited by Alzheimer's disease or dementia. And as the boomers age, the demand for care will put a strain on the resources to deal with these issues—and on the price tag.

We baby boomers will eventually face these problems for ourselves, but right now many of us are confronting them for our parents. Do your parents and in-laws have enough money to pay for their own care for years to come, or will you be asked to supplement their long-term care needs just when your own children are in college and you are trying to save for your own retirement? I confronted this issue early, when it became my responsibility to arrange and pay for my grandmother's care. That's when I recognized the importance of long-term care insurance.

THE GOVERNMENT'S ROLE IN LONG-TERM CARE

As you can see in Figure 15.1, the big bulge in today's population is in the 35-to-55 age group. Right now, we are not only supporting ourselves and our children, but we are also paying taxes to support our parents, who are already receiving Social Security and Medicare benefits. Gone are the dreams of retiring "early." Still, in 20 years, we'll be the older, retired generation. The graph in Figure 15.1 becomes relatively top-heavy with seniors, and especially with older women.

Will government programs be able to care for baby boomers in their old age? Not if history is any example. Remember how

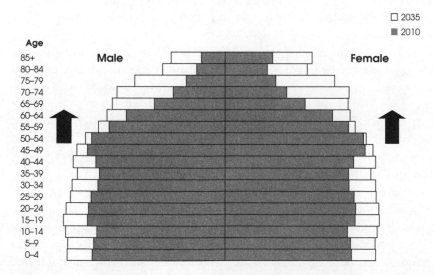

Figure 15.1   Aging Demographic: Population by Age and Sex, 2010 and 2035
Source: U.S. Census Bureau 2008, courtesy of Genworth Financial.

crowded the public schools were in the 1950s and 1960s? Remember the temporary classrooms in trailers? That's what state-provided nursing care for seniors could look like in 15 years—if state and federal budgets cannot provide any additional facilities.

By relying on government to pay for your long-term care, you give up the choice of having home health care for as long as possible. You'll probably be forced into a nursing home setting just when millions of other baby boomers find themselves in the same position.

Americans spent $131.3 billion for nursing home care in 2007, and that does not include the costs of assisted living or home health care. Of the amount spent to pay for care in nursing homes, 42 percent of the tab was picked up by Medicaid. How long do you think government can keep funding this growing expense?

If we depend on our savings to fund the possible need for long-term care, we court the risk of running out of money. If we depend on our families, we pass on an incredible burden to our children. If we're alone, as many women will be, what happens when we run out of money? And if we depend on the state, what kind of care can we expect to receive? You can plan ahead, or you can take your chances. Planning ahead involves purchasing insurance to cover the cost of long-term care.

It's a common misconception that Medicare, supplemental policies, or some other government program will pay for all the costs of care as we age. Medicare pays only for a limited number of days of skilled nursing care after hospitalization. It does not pay for long-term custodial care. Medicare supplement policies do not cover this type of custodial care at all. State Medicaid plans for the impoverished do cover custodial care, but only after most assets have been used up (unless you purchase Partnership), and primarily in facilities where you would least want to spend your last days or years.

Some seniors and their families mistakenly plan to become impoverished so that the state can take over their custodial care ("Medicaid planning") so their children receive their money. That's a tragic mistake. Relying on state Medicaid programs limits choice and practically guarantees that you'll be forced into a state-funded facility. As state budgets get squeezed, so do reimbursements to these nursing homes. State-funded facilities are already feeling the crunch—even before the boomer generation requires assistance. What kind of care can they provide without adequate financial resources from the state?

Since Medicaid reimbursement rates are low, many private nursing homes will not accept Medicaid patients, although they are required to allow a resident to remain if private funds run out and a state program takes over payment. Even then, the resident would have to move from a private room to a semiprivate or perhaps onto a floor with fewer services. Stop by for a visit, and I think you'll conclude that's not where you want to see your parents—or yourself.

Furthermore, because Medicaid is intended for people who are impoverished, the government has consistently adjusted the rules so that Medicaid planning does not work. For instance, between the first edition of this book and this second edition, the Deficit Reduction Act of 2005 invalidated the most common approaches, extending the "look-back" period for recapturing asset transfers. Although Medicaid currently exempts one home (with values ranging from $500,000 to $750,000, depending on the state), and one automobile of unlimited value, and several other types of assets, it's likely those exemptions will be revisited. It is quite possible that a "Medicaid plan" implemented today would not work when the time comes.

Your parents probably want to stay in their own home or apartment to receive care, but home health care costs money, and it is not covered by Medicare, Medicare supplements, or traditional health insurance. They might want to move to an assisted living facility instead of a traditional nursing home, but those facilities can be very expensive, and the costs are not covered by the federal programs or by health insurance.

Today, 80 percent of all long-term care is provided in the home by family members. Is someone in your family prepared to take on that responsibility? How much qualified home health care could you afford at today's average rate of $20 per hour (or higher in large cities) to provide additional help?

There are two reasons seniors find themselves in state-run nursing homes: Either they can't afford commercial home health care and have no family members to provide that care, or their caregivers simply burn out.

What will happen in *your* family? Will you be able to provide care for yourself—*and* your spouse? If you are alone, will an adult child or friend be able to sustain the kind of care you may eventually need? Will you have enough money to purchase care for an extended period of time? These are questions baby boomers should be asking for their parents and for themselves.

The answer to these concerns is long-term care insurance. It covers stuff we don't like to think about for our parents, much less ourselves: the need for assistance in managing the daily activities of living in our later years—bathing, dressing, or even feeding ourselves. That possibility seems so far away, and it may never happen. After all, our parents are still living vital, independent lives. That's exactly the time to make sure they have coverage. And it's the perfect time to buy coverage for yourself—while you're in your early fifties and in good health. If you can't stand the thought of ever needing this kind of care, take a different perspective. Tell yourself that you're buying long-term care insurance to give yourself peace of mind during your retirement years. You will never be any younger, healthier, or eligible for lower premiums than you are right now!

INSURANCE FOR YOUR RETIREMENT

When you own a long-term care insurance policy, you can live the retirement lifestyle you've planned without worrying about extended health-care expenses or caregiving being a burden on your spouse or your family. You can expect that your retirement withdrawal scenario won't be interrupted by ongoing and expensive custodial care costs. In short, you can enjoy your retirement years without worrying about depleting your assets.

It's human nature to look in the rearview mirror in order to predict the future. Indeed, history does repeat itself—as our recent stock market decline demonstrates. But when they focus on asset values, today's boomers are missing the oncoming disaster that is certainly facing an entire generation. It's the coming crisis in the cost of living longer—a cost that could devour our retirement assets. A lifetime of savings could be depleted in paying for just two or three years of nursing care.

We assess risk when we structure our investment portfolios to give us the best chance of having money to last a lifetime. It's a key ingredient in Monte Carlo modeling. We assess risk in everyday life when we buy homeowners or auto insurance to protect the assets we've worked so hard to accumulate. Yet relatively few people are insured against the more likely risk of needing long-term custodial care, although the odds are you'll need that kind of help if you live long enough.

Seven out of 10 people turning age 65 today will need some long-term care and one in five will need more than five years of care, according to the American Association for Long-Term Care Insurance (AALTCI), the industry association. Twenty percent will need care for between two and five years, and another 12 percent will need between one and two years of care.

Today, there are 1.8 million Americans residing in skilled nursing facilities, and 12 percent have been there for five years or more. But nursing home care shouldn't be your only option. You can have a range of choices if you have the money to pay for them. You might start with daily or twice-weekly visits from a home health-care aide. Or perhaps you want to move into an assisted living facility. Years later, you might require the 24-hour assistance that only a nursing facility can provide.

So don't make the mistake of calling long-term care insurance by its old name: nursing home insurance. Your long-term care insurance policy should be comprehensive, covering a range of options that keep you from being forced into a nursing home except as a last resort.

OUR PARENTS, OURSELVES

It's pretty obvious that you should buy a long-term care insurance policy for yourself to make sure you have a choice of care and to preserve your assets for a surviving spouse or your children. What may not be so obvious is the need for your aging parents to have a long-term care policy. Although it's better to purchase at a younger age, many policies may still be affordable for people in their seventies, as you'll see in the pricing examples in Chapter 17.

Bringing up the subject of long-term care insurance may reveal a huge generation gap in your family. It's possible that your parents don't know how long-term care insurance has changed since the old days. Originally, long-term care insurance only covered the cost of nursing home care. Today's policies pay for home health care and assisted living facilities, as needed. And if you are buying a policy for yourself, it may be helpful to explain to your children that you're making plans not to burden them.

When discussing LTC with your parents, it is usually best not to start with the idea of insurance. Rather, ask your parents what their plans are if one of them were to need LTC? What if their spouse had died? What would they like to experience? Would they like to remain in the family home? Then you could discuss with them how you and they can maximize the chances of such an alternative.

If your parents won't consider, or can't afford, such a policy, adult children in the family should think about joining together to make the cost of the annual premium a gift for their birthdays, Christmas, or Mother's and Father's Days. It helps assure that your parents will get quality care, while providing a hedge against the need to spend your own retirement dollars to care for the people who once cared for you.

LONG-TERM CARE INSURANCE: A WOMAN'S ISSUE

Long-term care insurance is a woman's issue for two reasons. First, women tend to live longer than men. In 1940, a 65-year-old woman could expect to live another 14.7 years. In 2000, that advanced to 19.5 years. And by 2040, a 65-year-old woman is expected to live another 22 years, according to the actuaries. Longevity increases the odds of needing some form of long-term care.

According to a Genworth Financial report, women are the fastest-growing segment of the older population, accounting for 70 percent of the population age 85 and older. And women have a 50 percent greater chance than men of entering a nursing home after age 65, according to AALTCI. Currently, 74 percent of nursing home residents are women, according to the 2009 Sourcebook of the American Association for Long Term Care Insurance (www.aaltci.org). Claims data from insurers reveal that increasing numbers of women have been using their policies for home health care and assisted living facilities. Those alternatives are not readily available to those who must rely on government Medicaid programs.

But there's another reason that long-term care insurance is a woman's issue: Women tend to be the caregivers for others in their lives, and that takes its toll, both physically and financially. Those who leave or scale back on their jobs to take on caregiving responsibilities can lose a small fortune in wages and forgo retirement plan contributions and potential Social Security benefits. Having insurance coverage lifts the financial burden of caregiving and permits caregivers to accumulate assets to provide for their own retirement.

Needing care when you're older is a nagging worry for women who don't have insurance to cover the costs. While 88 percent of men say their spouse will take care of them if they become ill or disabled, only 72 percent of women figure their spouse will be able to care for them.

Futurist Ken Dychtwald projects that today's American woman will spend more years caring for aging family members than she did caring for her own children! What—and who—will be left to care for the widow or single woman? The fear of becoming a bag lady is not unfounded. That's why long-term care insurance is a must for women. The cost of that policy is the price we pay for peace of mind.

And now to overcome your final objection: What if you don't use it?

WHAT IF YOU DON'T USE IT?

What if you never need help with the daily activities of living? I fervently wish that you—and I—never need custodial care! But we never complain that the money spent on homeowners or auto insurance is "wasted" because our house didn't burn down or we weren't in an auto accident. Why complain if you never use your long-term care policy? *Once you reach age 65, the chance that you'll need long-term care is 10 times greater than the chance that your house will burn down!*

We are living longer. In 15 years, there will be more than 250,000 Americans over the age of 100, triple the current number. Replacement parts—hips and knees—will allow more years for golf and fewer years with canes, walkers, and wheelchairs. Heart surgeries and angioplasty will prolong an active life and reduce sudden cardiac deaths.

Even so, at some point we're likely to need help with the basic activities of life. As reported in Kiplinger's Retirement Report, a 60-year-old woman has a 70 percent chance of living beyond age 85. After age 85, half of us will need help with the activities of daily living, and nearly half of us will experience Alzheimer's disease. While living longer is the best alternative, it is not without its own costs. Buying long-term care insurance is like betting on yourself to survive.

But just as you can't wait to buy fire insurance until you smell smoke, you can't wait to purchase long-term care insurance until you need the care. Not only do these policies cost exponentially more as you grow older, but at an older age you might not qualify for the coverage you want.

WHY YOU SHOULDN'T PROCRASTINATE!

The cost of procrastinating in the purchase of long-term care is not just money. It may mean the difference between being able to buy this insurance—or not being approved for coverage. Table 15.1 represents a survey of 250,000 applicants for long-term care insurance, which requires that individuals qualify based on health status.

Many employer-sponsored plans do not require an extensive health background check. So, if you have some existing health conditions, check to see if your employer offers long-term care insurance coverage. Many company plans also offer access to coverage to parents of employees and other extended family members, so ask your adult children if they have access to a company LTC insurance plan.

That said, it always pays to compare, especially if you are married and in good health. Most employer-sponsored plans do not offer spousal or partner discounts, or good health discounts. You may be able to obtain better coverage for less money with an individual policy.

The obvious conclusion is that the older you are, the more difficult it is to qualify for this coverage. That said, you should contact

Table 15.1   Percentage of Applicants Declined Long-Term Care Coverage

Age of Applicant	Average Declined
Under 50	7.3%
50 to 59	13.9%
60 to 69	22.9%
70 to 79	44.8%
80 and Over*	69.8%

Source: American Association for Long-Term Care Insurance (www.aaltci.org), June 2008 study of 250,000 individual policy applicants.

your LTC insurance sales agent to see whether any health issues you have will disqualify you, or just increase the premium cost. And let me emphasize that if one spouse does not qualify for health reasons, that makes it all the more important for the other spouse to have coverage. Consider the likelihood that you will use up your financial assets taking care of the spouse with health issues—leaving few resources for the remaining spouse.

LONG-TERM CARE— THE FACTS

- $77,380 = Average annual cost of nursing home care in a major city (2009).
- $212 = Average daily rate for a private room in a nursing home (2009).
- $191 = Average daily rate for a semiprivate room (2009).
- $20 = Average hourly rate for nonskilled home health aides provided by a home health-care agency.
- 2.4 years = Average length of stay in a nursing home. (But this average includes people who go into a nursing home temporarily for rehab and those who die soon after

entering. If you remove such people from the average, the average stay increases.)

- 4.5 years = Average need for LTC, after having needed care for at least one year, according to the Society of Actuaries.
- 8.25 million = Number of Americans who have long-term care insurance in 2008 (AALTCI).
- 180,000 claimants currently receiving benefits from their policy (AALTCI).
- 89 percent = Percentage of Americans between the ages of 45 and 64 who are uninsured for long-term care.
- 77 percent = Percentage of Americans over 65 who are uninsured for long-term care.
- 1 of 5 = Number of households providing care to an adult family member.
- 60 percent = Percentage of boomers who will need some form of long-term care after age 65.

CHAPTER 16

HOW TO UNDERSTAND LONG-TERM CARE COVERAGE

By now, I hope you're convinced that a long-term care insurance policy is an important part of your financial plan. But that still leaves some questions about the policy itself: What does it cover? How much coverage do you need? When should you buy it? What should it cost? These are issues you need to understand before you make your purchase.

This sector of the insurance industry is changing so quickly that I recommend you consult an agent who specializes in long-term care insurance. Some agents represent only one insurance company. Other independent agents can show you policies and prices from several different insurers. You can even get price quotations online, although you'll have to complete a detailed application, which typically requires working with an agent.

One thing is certain: You'll want to buy a policy from a large company that has shown its determination to be a force in the long-term care industry. You may need an agent different from the one you've worked with on homeowners or auto insurance, or you may find that the best long-term care policy does come from your current insurer. Comparisons are a must, but the project doesn't have to be complicated if you work with an agent you can trust.

Let's start with some perspective on the care costs you may need to cover—now and in the future.

RISING DEMAND, SOARING COSTS

More and more people are requiring long-term care—and the financial burden can be catastrophic. Despite an almost universal wish to stay *out* of traditional nursing homes, more and more people are requiring the care they provide. Others are forced into nursing homes when they could have received adequate care at home or in an assisted living facility. But if they don't have financial resources, and need to rely on state funding, they find that the vast majority of government-provided care is given only in nursing homes.

The average annual cost for a private room in a nursing home was about $77,000 in 2009, according to several studies. That works out to $212 a day. Semiprivate rooms save only about 10 percent of the cost. The range runs from $48,000 in the least expensive location to $194,000 in the most expensive. And although the average stay in a nursing home is less than three years, patients with dementia or Alzheimer's might need care for eight years or more.

Home health care can be even more expensive—an estimated $190 for a 10-hour shift. Purchased on an hourly basis, certified home health-care aides may charge more than $24 an hour in urban areas. The next step might be an assisted living facility, but that can be an equally expensive alternative and is available only to those who need limited care. A study published by the Urban Institute predicts that the cost of home care will soar because many more people will need care and there will be fewer caregivers available to take care of them.

The average cost of an assisted living facility (ALF) is only about half the cost of a nursing home, but ALFs charge more if their client has a cognitive impairment. But you won't have the choice of home health care or an assisted living facility unless you have personal funds to pay for then, *and*, if necessary, to care for a spouse remaining at home.

What if care is needed on a 24-hour basis? Dementia or multiple incapacities eventually wear down the most determined caregiver. A nursing home becomes the best alternative. Call a few facilities in your town, and ask about their rates. Then imagine yourself searching for care for your parents or spouse. It's a tough enough decision to make, without considering price. Insurance allows you to focus on which solution will work best for your loved one.

The cost of care will continue rising as boomers age, even if more nursing homes and other resources are added to the supply. And given the increasing demand for services, the price is likely to increase at a rate that is increasingly greater than the rate of consumer price inflation. Month over month, those rising costs can add up to a staggering sum. You must do something *now* to prepare for the future need for long-term care.

WHEN TO BUY? WHILE YOU CAN!

The need for long-term care immediately conjures up pictures of much older people, dependent on walkers and wheelchairs. Since that won't be you for a very long time, if ever, there's an inclination to put off buying insurance, to think about it tomorrow. That could be an expensive mistake.

Surprisingly, we may need long-term care even before we enter our retirement years. In fact, about 40 percent of the 13 million people currently receiving some form of long-term care are between the ages of 18 and 64, as a result of accidents, stroke, or disabling disease. That's one good reason to think about long-term care insurance now, as you reach age 50, or even earlier. Today you are healthy and independent. All that could change in a minute, and it's not just a question of aging. The idols of our youth are examples of that possibility.

Even Superman—Christopher Reeve, whose horseback riding accident left him a quadriplegic at age 43—needed years of expensive care before his death in 2004. Disney Mouseketeer Annette Funicello has been confined to a wheelchair with multiple sclerosis (MS) for years. (If Britney Spears is your Mouseketeer, then you should be telling your parents to buy a long-term care policy!) Michael J. Fox functions well, for now, with Parkinson's disease. Think of the costs of long-term care for President Reagan, who suffered from Alzheimer's for more than a decade. While we hope that research will restore spinal function, cure MS and Parkinson's, and delay Alzheimer's, we must insure against those possibilities.

Because the original purchase price of a policy rises exponentially with age, the younger you are when you purchase one, the less it will cost. Premium prices are typically projected to remain the same for the duration of the policy. But that has not been the experience of many policyholders.

Although insurance companies must certify to state insurance departments that they do not expect to have to increase premiums in the future, insurers reserve the right to increase premiums for a class of policies (e.g., all policies issued on the same policy form in a particular state) because the future cannot be predicted with certainty. Presumably, insurers now have a better forecasting ability for policy usage, and thus can price policies more realistically than in the past.

It's worth buying your policy while you're young (in your early fifties) and healthy because you never know when an accident or illness could require care or disqualify you from coverage or a change in health (osteoporosis, arthritis, adult-onset diabetes, for example) could cause the price for your insurance to be significantly higher.

Figure 16.1 shows the cost of procrastination. If you buy at age 40, your annual premium would be $2,244. At 50, your annual premium

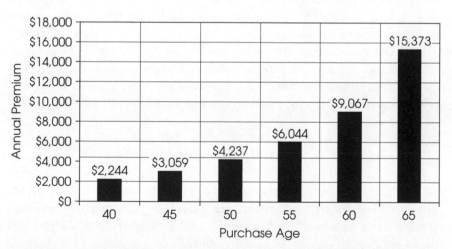

Figure 16.1   Cost of Waiting, Annual Premium for Long-Term Care Insurance
Source: Chart created by MAGA Limited based on hypothetical client information. Premiums vary based on benefits, age, health, and state of residence. Coverage illustrated is for a $6,000 monthly benefit with 5% compound inflation option, 90-day elimination period.

could be $4,237, and at age 60, the cost grows to $9,067 per year. The same policy coverage would cost more than $15,000 if you wait until age 65! But don't be overwhelmed by the costs, as this example is necessarily without credits for good health and discounts for spousal coverage.

According to the American Association for Long-Term Care Insurance's 2009 LTC Sourcebook, buyers between ages 50 and 54 paid as little as $989 per year to as much as $6,407 annually for coverage. For ages 60 to 64, the low amount was $1,125 and the highest premium paid was $7,413.

I also don't want to scare away buyers who are in their sixties—so it's important to point out that you could purchase a smaller amount of care, less than the four years in this illustration, or a lower dollar amount than the $6,000 per month in this illustration, in order to substantially lower the premium costs. Even a small amount of coverage might make the difference in getting access to a privately paid nursing facility.

The long-term care insurance market is changing quickly as insurance companies look at the aging population and analyze the increasing costs of extended care. Companies that were pioneers in selling long-term care insurance are redesigning their policies and offering new buyers limited benefits at higher premiums. Insurers are becoming more stringent in their health and cognitive examinations, and there is a growing list of medical conditions that limit an individual's ability to obtain long-term care insurance coverage at preferred prices or, in some cases, at any price. Don't procrastinate!

HOW DO I *USE* MY POLICY?

Before talking about the coverage you need, there's an important aspect of long-term care insurance policies you must understand. Unlike a life insurance policy that pays your beneficiaries when you die, a long-term care policy pays benefits you use while you're alive. But what triggers the benefits? What makes the insurance company *start* paying caregivers?

If you have a long-term care policy, the need for care must be certified by a health care practitioner who will state that you will need help with at least two of the six activities of daily living for at least 90 days. "Activities of daily living"(ADL) is not just a casual phrase. It refers to specific activities that are defined by insurance policies. They are *bathing, dressing, eating, toileting, continence,* and *transferring from bed to chair.* A policy can also be triggered by a physician's certification of cognitive impairment, ranging from the onset of Alzheimer's to dementia. Only then can you access the care at home or in a nursing home or assisted living facility after a specified elimination period (defined in the next section).

It's difficult to imagine that someday you might not be able to move from bed to chair or that you might need help in the bathroom. It's equally depressing to think that you could suffer from Alzheimer's and require extensive supervision. But what's hardest to accept is that you might have to pay someone $200 a day—or far more in 20 years—to assist you in basic daily living activities. That's why you own a long-term care insurance policy.

WHAT SHOULD MY LONG-TERM CARE POLICY COVER?

Long-term care insurance policies typically cover nonskilled, skilled, and custodial care in your own home or in an assisted living facility, adult day care center, or nursing home. All policies are not alike, so you will have to choose among certain features. Understanding the choices is essential to ensuring that you get the type of protection you'll need. Following are the most important options to look for in your long-term care policy.

Elimination Period

Just as you have a deductible on your car insurance, there will also be a deductible period—a waiting, or elimination, period—during which you must pay for services before the long-term care insurance policy kicks in. Typically this is a 90- or 100-day period. Choosing a longer elimination period would lower the premiums, while choosing a shorter elimination period would increase the monthly premiums. After paying for services for those first three months, you'll be glad you purchased a policy for yourself, your spouse, or your parents.

Daily or Monthly Benefit

Choosing a specific monthly benefit is the most common way to define the amount of coverage to buy. You'll want your policy to have at least $6,000 a month in coverage. But if that makes the policy too expensive, it's better to have a smaller amount of coverage than none at all. After all, you will still have some income and assets of your own to contribute to your care.

Make a few phone calls to check the costs of nursing homes and home health-care agencies in your area to make sure you are buying adequate coverage. A monthly benefit is superior to a daily benefit. For example, $6,000-per-month coverage could cover expensive rehab home health care a few days a week, costs that might exceed a daily benefit.

Most policies offer a pool of benefits. That means that although the maximum payout would be $6,000 a month, if you don't use that coverage in a particular month, the remainder stays in your pool of unused benefits and can extend the coverage period.

Length of Benefit

Your policy could offer benefits for a period of from two years to as long as you might need care ("lifetime benefit period"). (As noted earlier, a three-year policy could actually cover care for a longer period if the full daily benefit is not used in the early stages of care.) Lifetime coverage is very expensive, but it buys peace of mind in case of a lingering illness. Partnership policies (described below) can provide such peace of mind to the middle class, with a shorter benefit period.

Since the average stay in a nursing home is about three years, you might choose coverage for three-, five-, or ten-year periods. On the other hand, Alzheimer's patients and stroke victims may require assistance for a decade or more. Ask your agent to illustrate prices for a range of monthly benefits and lengths of benefits. Knowing what's affordable will help in your decision making. Remember, even if you can't afford extensive protection, a small amount is better than no coverage at all.

Inflation Protection

While a $6,000-per-month ($200 daily) benefit may be adequate today, inflation could make that amount inadequate in the future. Inflation protection is not built into your coverage, and it does cost extra; but make sure your policy has it.

Today, there are various forms of inflation protection offered by insurers. Some grow at a compounded rate; others offer a simple rate of growth. There are even formulas that keep pace with the Consumer Price Index. Compound inflation protection will increase more rapidly than the other formulas. But it is also the most expensive.

Adding this compound inflation protection could double or even triple the cost of your overall protection, depending on your age. If cost is a concern, consider buying a lower monthly benefit with compound inflation protection. Over the long run that should be more advantageous, especially for those in their fifties.

There is one additional type of inflation protection, but it can be even more expensive. Some policies allow you to increase the amount of your coverage from time to time without medical evidence of insurability. It's called a "guaranteed purchase option." If you plan to increase benefits when you're older, the cost will definitely be higher, reflecting your age at that time. As you age, adding benefits in that manner becomes prohibitively expensive.

Reimbursement Policy

There are three ways the insurance company pays out policy benefits once the need for care is triggered: (1) In a *reimbursement plan*, the insurance company reimburses actual costs to the care provider, typically not to exceed a monthly maximum. (2) In a *disability ("cash") plan*, the insurance company pays the full benefit regardless of what expenses are incurred. (3) In an *indemnity plan*, the insurance company pays the full benefit, but only on days when you incur a legitimate expense. Over 90 percent of newer policies are based on the reimbursement plan alternative.

With the daily, weekly, or monthly benefit reimbursement plan, you submit the nursing home, home health, or assisted living facility bills to the insurance company for payment. The insurance company reimburses the policyholder for the actual expenses, up to your maximum coverage. So if your monthly expense is $4,500 and your policy limit is $6,000, only the actual expenses are paid to you. If your policy limit is $4,500 per month and your expenses are higher, you must make up the difference. Be sure to look for a weekly or monthly reimbursement policy that allows the unused daily benefit to accumulate and be used later for approved services.

The other alternatives are similar. An *indemnity* policy pays you a fixed daily benefit specified in your policy, but you must submit bills from approved caregivers to justify the benefit for each day. A *cash benefit* policy simply gives you a monthly amount, to be used for any type of care or caregiver. (A health care professional must certify the need for care.) The flexibility of the cash benefit policy makes it much more costly.

Guarantee Period

Not long ago, people purchased long-term care policies and assumed that the prices would stay level for their lifetime. That was the implied promise, as insurance companies urged people to lock in lower prices by buying while they were young and healthy. But the fine print in many of those policies didn't actually guarantee that prices would be fixed for the buyer's lifetime.

In fact, in early 2000, insurers started taking a second look at the potential cost of the liabilities they had booked in selling their long-term care policies. They realized that unlike the previous generation of nursing home policies, which policyholders were reluctant to use, the promised benefits of assisted living and home care in the newer policies made usage especially attractive. The increased likelihood of usage meant that policies had been underpriced, so the insurers began applying to states for permission to raise rates as the guarantee periods expired. The resulting publicity put a dent in the sales of these policies. Who wants a policy that will cost more just when you are most likely to need it and least able to afford it?

Now that the long-term care industry has consolidated, there is less chance of substantial price increases. Still, when buying a long-term care insurance policy, look into the company's history of rate increases. Read the section in Chapter 17 on limited-pay options, which can create a "paid-up" policy in 10 years. Although these provisions make a policy far more expensive, they eliminate concern about future price increases after the policy is paid up.

Spousal Discounts

Some companies offer discounts ranging from 10 percent to 40 percent if both spouses purchase a policy. The definition of *spouse* can be very liberal, in some cases including domestic partners, so be sure to ask. Some companies have discounts if other family members buy.

If you're purchasing a long-term care policy with a spouse, ask about a *survivorship waiver of premium.* Some policies offer this plan, which promises that if one spouse dies after both have paid 10 years of premiums, without going on claim, the surviving spouse's policy will be considered fully paid.

Intergenerational Transfers

What happens if Mom doesn't use her long-term care policy, but her daughter or son needs it? We never know in advance who might be in an accident or suffer early onset of a disease that could trigger the need for long-term care.

John Hancock recognized that possibility in offering its FamilyCare policy. It allows an individual to add an adult child (or a child and his or her spouse) to the same policy at very little extra cost. Intergenerational policies typically offer a maximum of 10 years of care, which is available to either of the policyholders, up to the monthly limit of the policy.

If both of the policyholders need care at the same time, the monthly benefit is split between them. A younger insured, seeing that the parent is likely to consume the entire benefit, can purchase an individual policy while he or she is in good health. The intergenerational nature of this policy has some added benefits.

Consider the possibilities if the policy were purchased with a mother at age 67 and a daughter at age 45, for a $4,500 monthly benefit, with compound inflation protection. If the mother dies 20 years later without using any benefits, the daughter inherits the full coverage. But at this point, the monthly benefit could have grown to $10,080 per month because of the 5 percent automatic benefit increases. The premium drops to what she would have paid at her original issue age of 45 for $4,500-a-month coverage. The monthly premium she must now pay reflects her original underwriting class based on her health at the time the policy was purchased.

Care Coordinators

Make sure your long-term care policy offers the services of a professional care coordinator. These extraordinary individuals help the family identify sources of home care and nursing home care, and they are indispensable in coordinating and supervising care if the family member lives at a distance from the person needing care. The cost of this service should be included in the benefits, and you'll probably want the insurance company to contract with an independent organization to provide this service, giving you a choice of individual coordinators.

Not all policies provide the same definition of "caregiver" for coverage purposes. Certainly licensed individuals and certified home health care agencies will provide individuals who will be covered by your policy. But if you anticipate receiving care from a family member or neighbor or friend, you must tell your agent, and make sure the policy wording allows for reimbursement for this type of care.

Optional Riders

Waiver of Premium. Obviously, if you have enough health problems to trigger coverage, you don't want your spouse or your family to worry about continuing to pay your insurance premiums. Once you start accessing benefits, you can stop paying your annual premiums if your policy has a waiver of premium feature, which almost all policies have.

Nonforfeiture. If you purchase a nonforfeiture rider and pay premiums on your policy for at least three years, then stop paying, you're guaranteed enough future coverage to recover the premiums you paid, but not more. It's a costly rider.

Return of Premium. Some policies offer a return of premium option, which says that if you've paid for a number of years without making a claim, your premium will be returned to you or your beneficiary. If you've used some of the coverage, a portion of the premium may be returned. This coverage is costly, and your money might be better spent increasing your monthly benefit or taking a longer benefit period. Some policies return premiums at the time of death only if you die before age 65 or age 75; such features don't really address the concern that you might pay a lot of premiums and get nothing back.

Contingent Nonforfeiture. If the insurance company does raise premiums by a specified large amount and you choose to discontinue paying, the contingent nonforfeiture rider says you will continue to have benefits as though you had purchased a nonforfeiture rider.

Partnership Programs

Partnership programs are an effort by state governments to get their citizens to plan for future long-term care costs. California, Connecticut, Indiana, and New York have had Partnership programs for 15 or more years. Since the Deficit Reduction Act of 2005 permitted other states to have such programs, most states have developed such programs. Eventually all states will probably do so.

State legislatures and regulators know that people who have long-term care insurance are very unlikely to ever need to rely on Medicaid to pay for their long-term care. So the government saves a lot of Medicaid money when people buy long-term care insurance.

For that reason, state governments are willing to give middle-class people an incentive to purchase long-term care insurance. That incentive is a back-end safety net. It allows the insured person to protect $1 from Medicaid for every dollar of benefits received from their long-term care insurance policy.

For example, if a person received $400,000 from long-term care insurance and the policy then expired, that person could take $400,000 of assets "off the table" when applying for Medicaid coverage of their long-term care costs. In that way, they can preserve assets for their children to inherit—without doing "Medicaid planning" transfers of assets in order to qualify for coverage.

If people are affluent, taking $400,000 off the table may not do much good as they may have a lot of other assets they'd have to spend down before qualifying for Medicaid, and because their income would have to be contributed to the cost of their care. Thus, these Partnership programs are well-designed to benefit the middle class.

The government wants long-term care insurance policies to retain their purchasing power over time, to the degree possible. Therefore Partnership policies are required to have inflation protection, typically 5 percent compound inflation. To find out more about your state's "Partnership" long-term care insurance program, do an online search using the words "long-term care partnership" and add your state's name.

International Coverage

If you plan to retire in a foreign country, make sure your policy offers coverage for care given outside the United States. Remember, your Medicare health coverage does not typically provide for care outside the United States.

Now that you know what to look for in a long-term care policy, it's time to take action. Just think how terrible you would feel if you had all this information—but no policy—just when you or a loved one needed care. In the next chapter, you'll see how to go about buying your policy.

KEY ELEMENTS OF A LONG-TERM CARE INSURANCE POLICY

- Elimination period (deductible)
- Daily (or monthly) benefit amount
- Pool of benefits
- Length of benefit
- Inflation protection (simple or compound)
- Reimbursement policy
- Guarantee period
- Spousal discount
- Care coordinators
- Optional riders
- International coverage

CHAPTER 17

BUYING YOUR LONG-TERM CARE POLICY

Let's make this simple. You agree that you need to buy long-term care insurance to protect your financial future or that you need to let your parents and in-laws know about this type of coverage so they won't be dependent on you. You've read the previous chapter and decided on the most important issues: amount of monthly benefit, years of coverage, and inflation protection. You're now prepared to discuss those issues with an adviser who is knowledgeable about long-term care insurance.

WHICH INSURANCE COMPANY SHOULD YOU CHOOSE?

Now it's time to get price quotations and make the purchase. The most important consideration here is the strength of the insurance company that offers the policy. After all, you don't expect to use the benefits until many years down the road, and you want them to be around when you need them. In recent years, several major insurers have opted out of this fast-changing industry, while others have decided to make long-term care insurance a priority.

You want to be with a company that prices its policies with a long-term perspective. They won't necessarily be the cheapest policies, but you're less likely to face price increases in the future.

So which companies should you consider? In my opinion, you'll want to stick with the largest, best-known, and most committed insurers. These include MetLife, Genworth, John Hancock, Mass Mutual, New York Life, Prudential, State Farm, Transamerica, and Northwestern Mutual. Companies that have stopped actively selling *new* LTC policies continue to be responsible for existing policies or transfer the responsibility to another insurer to pay future claims.

WHAT SHOULD IT COST?

Policy premiums are based on your age, your location (which determines the cost of care in your area), any discounts for which you are eligible, your chosen policy design, and your health at the time you purchase the policy. Long-term care insurance companies try to hold their premiums level for as long as you have the policy, but there are few guarantees.

The insurance company has the right to increase the price, but only for all holders within that class of policy. Insurance companies must obtain approval from the state's department of insurance before any premium increases can be put into effect, and the insurance company must give appropriate notification to the affected policyholders.

One of the most important and often overlooked aspects of a policy is the inflation protection offered in the benefits. After all, you don't expect to use the policy for many years. And while $5,000 a month could buy excellent care today, it might not cover one week in a nursing home in years ahead. Although inflation protection, simple or compound, adds substantially to the annual premium cost, it is a good idea. Consider buying a lower monthly benefit with such increases rather than a higher benefit without such increases. Table 17.1 shows the cost impact of buying inflation protection.

Table 17.1   Sample Prices of Long-Term Care Insurance

Age	No Inflation	5% Simple Inflation	5% Compound Inflation
40	$714.00	$1,326.00	$2,244.00
50	$1,020.00	$1,785.00	$2,601.20
60	$1,581.00	$2,805.00	$3,417.00
70	$3,723.00	$5,814.00	$6,579.00

$6,000/month, 90-day elimination, 4-year benefit period, preferred rate, no spousal or group discount included.
Source: Chart created by MAGA Limited based on hypothetical client information. Premiums vary based on benefits, age, health, and state of residence.

1 0-PAY: CONTROLLING
PRICE RISK

There's always the risk that the annual premium on your long-term care insurance policy will rise. That's been happening in recent years, as insurance companies have learned that the earlier policies were underpriced. Some policy premiums have remained level for years and then suddenly increased substantially.

Based on their experience with the earlier policies, insurers now charge higher prices when you buy long-term care insurance. With today's higher prices, the chances of a price increase have reduced substantially, but the premiums are not guaranteed to remain at their current level.

One way to limit the risk of price increases in future years is to purchase a limited-pay policy—one with payments lasting only 10 or 15 years. Although premiums may rise during that limited period, at least you know your coverage will be fully paid up at the end of that time. Limited-pay policies are generally much more expensive. Still, you can arrange to pay the premiums now, while you're working and can afford the cost. Then you won't have to worry about price increases in your later years when you are less able to afford them. Most companies offer these limited-pay policies.

LONG-TERM CARE POLICIES AND INCOME TAXES

Almost every policy sold today is considered tax qualified. That means that the policy meets basic federal requirements, so any payout of benefits will be tax free to the recipient. (Some cash indemnity policies can be taxable if you receive a significant amount in excess of your daily long-term care expenses.)

Depending on your age, if your premium is not paid by a business or a Health Savings Account, you may be able to deduct a portion of long-term care insurance premiums. (Hopefully, Congress will make the entire long-term care insurance premium deductible in the future.) Those premiums are considered medical costs, which are tax deductible to the extent that they are greater than 7.5 percent of adjusted gross income. In 2009, if you are between ages 61 and 70, $3,180 of your long-term care insurance premium counts as a medical expense in determining the 7.5 percent of adjusted gross income that creates a tax deduction. Over age 71, $3,980 of premium is considered a medical expense.

This web of tax provisions allows for some creative ways to reduce the after-tax cost of long-term care insurance premiums. For example, instead of paying for your parents' long-term care insurance policy, you might want to gift them an amount equal to the annual premium. If *they* pay the premium, a portion may be tax deductible for them.

The best tax deals are reserved for companies that pay income taxes directly to the federal government (such as C Corporations) and purchase long-term care insurance for their employees. When such a corporation pays for long-term care insurance for employees, the premium cost is fully deductible to the corporation, and the premium paid is not considered to be income to the employee. As with all long-term care insurance, when the employee actually uses the policy and starts receiving benefits, those payments are not considered taxable.

Partnerships, limited liability corporations (LLC), Subchapter S corporations, and other entities that report earnings to their owners (on which earnings their owners pay income taxes) can fully deduct the premiums for long-term care insurance for nonowner employees.

Employees who are partners or owners, however, have to take the amount of the premium as income, subject to some exclusions based on age. So they get a significant tax break. This interesting tax provision, while it lasts, is an opportunity to provide benefits to owners of small businesses. Unlike most other employee benefits, there is no requirement that this benefit be available to all employees.

Most states also have tax deductions or credits for long-term care insurance. Refer to your state tax return instructions or ask your accountant or financial adviser for information regarding state tax breaks. For the most current federal and state tax deduction limits and rules, visit the American Association for Long-Term Care Insurance's website: www.aaltci.org/tax.

As explained in Chapter 16, the government recognizes that it cannot afford to provide long-term care for everyone. Medicaid is a valuable but expensive welfare program. So the government is trying to encourage people to buy long-term care insurance. These tax breaks and the Partnership program mentioned in Chapter 16 are two financial incentives that the government is using.

In addition, the governors in 22 states have sent out letters to 45-year-old to 65-year-old citizens (age range varies by state) informing them that they are responsible for their long-term care costs and should plan ahead, specifically encouraging them to consider long-term care insurance. You can obtain the free CD and booklet by going to the following web site: www.longtermcare.gov. If you enter "Own Your Future" and the name of your state into an Internet search engine, you'll find a specific site for your state, if there is one.

PAYING FOR LONG-TERM CARE WITH LIFE INSURANCE AND ANNUITIES

The insurance companies have come up with answers for those who worry that they won't ever use the long-term care insurance before they die. Chapter 16 discussed return of premium riders and intergenerational policies. In addition, insurance companies offer blended life insurance and annuities and accelerated death benefit riders and blended policies, to address the "use it or lose it" concern. Using these types of combination policies tends to be costly and may not be necessary if you have a complete financial plan.

Acceleration Riders

As a part of or an addition to life insurance policies, these acceleration options pay benefits if the insured needs long-term care due to chronic illness or other circumstances that qualify for long-term care.

The concept allows a percentage (which varies by company and product) of the death benefit from the life insurance policy to be paid out to the policy owner for long-term care needs. Payout periods range from 24 to 48 months, with the monthly payment generally being larger with shorter payout periods. In some policies, a terminal illness can trigger a lump-sum acceleration of benefit.

Accelerated death benefit riders provide significant flexibility in the use of the life insurance policy's ultimate benefit, but there are limitations as well. First, the monthly benefit for long-term care expenses may be less than what you would find in a separate long-term care policy, and the rider might not include home health care options. In addition, loan interest rates could be applied once part of the death benefit is converted to paying long-term care costs. You have to carefully evaluate the limitations of the riders in order to determine if this life insurance option is right for you and your potential need for long-term care.

Blended Life Insurance Policies

Blended policies offer a combination of life insurance and long-term care insurance. If you don't ever access the long-term care, your heirs receive the life insurance benefit when you die. The policy also allows you to take a portion of the death benefit each month to fund long-term care needs, using the same types of definitions that apply in standalone long-term care insurance policies (e.g., needing help with two of the six activities of daily living or being cognitively impaired).

Any unused death benefit is paid to your heirs. You can pay an additional premium so that the insurance company will continue to pay your long-term care insurance benefit even after you've used up your death benefit. Often these policies also grant you the right to cancel your policy and get your premium back at any time.

The coverage is similar to other long-term care policies, covering home care, assisted living, nursing homes, adult day care, hospice care, and respite care. However, many of these policies do not offer inflation protection. When blended policies offer inflation protection, this feature may be limited and is rarely purchased because it significantly reduces the death benefit. Check the policy details carefully and get expert advice to understand the trade-offs. These policies typically offer a wider range of long-term care options, including home health care, than the accelerated benefit riders.

Lincoln National invented this type of policy. Their MoneyGuard policy is completely guaranteed. At any time, you can get your money back or wait to get your death benefit or long-term care benefits. Your death benefit can be spread over 24 or 36 months, and you can extend the coverage up to 4 to 7 years. Genworth, John Hancock, New York Life, and many other insurers offer similar combination policies.

Some life policies and blended policies offer a return-of-premium option, which gives policyholders a chance to recapture the premiums paid on the policy or to pass those premiums on to their beneficiaries if the benefit is not used.

Blended policies, accelerated death benefits, and other options increase the price of the underlying policy. Be sure you understand their advantages and limitations so that you can determine if they are worth the price.

Blended Annuities

Blended annuities are similar to blended life insurance policies. Instead of using your death benefit to fund your long-term care expenses, you use your annuity values to do so. If you qualify as needing long-term care (definitions may be the same as mentioned above, but may be more restrictive), some annuities augment each month's payment while others extend the period during which you can obtain the monthly payment beyond the time when your annuity proceeds are entirely drained.

EMPLOYEE GROUP LONG-TERM
CARE POLICIES

If your employer doesn't offer a group long-term care policy, the company is missing a terrific opportunity to include a benefit that is valuable to employees and doesn't have to cost the company a penny.

A group policy allows employees to purchase LTC insurance for themselves or for a related family member at a discounted price and with a limited medical evaluation. Sometimes coverage is guaranteed for any actively-at-work employee, regardless of health. Family members can also purchase at the discounted price, but generally have to provide full medical evidence.

The insurance is portable; if the employee leaves the company, the policy can be continued through individual payments. And the company can choose to make the payments for certain executives as part of a benefits plan, while other employees deduct the premiums from their paycheck. Or the company could pay a portion of the cost for everyone, with the balance being deducted from the employee's paycheck.

If your company needs convincing, just ask the boss or owner to consider the cost of losing a valuable employee such as his or her administrative assistant if that person has to quit or work part-time to care for an aging parent. According to one MetLife study, more than 17 percent of upper-level managerial workers who were employed while caregiving had to quit their jobs or take early retirement because of their caregiving responsibilities. A Conference Board survey indicates that the cost of replacing them amounts to about 75 percent of the annual salary costs for employees who quit.

The MetLife Mature Market study estimates that U.S. companies incur $11.4 billion to $29 billion in lost productivity annually because workers are distracted by caregiving duties. That includes costs related to workday interruptions, partial absenteeism, and elder care crises. That's why the number of employers offering some form of long-term care coverage is growing rapidly.

You've probably had a co-worker in this situation. AARP estimates that nearly one-quarter of U.S. households—22.4 million—contain a family caregiver for someone age 50 or older. Nearly two-thirds of family caregivers work full- or part-time, and more than half of them have had to make some kind of workplace accommodation. The MetLife study shows that nearly half those workers reported coming in late or leaving early. Many others took leaves of absence or turned down promotions. Clearly, from both the employer's and the employee's point of view, providing long-term care insurance as an optional benefit is simply good business.

It should be noted that premiums for group policies factor in expected average costs. If you're young and very healthy and have a spouse or domestic partner, you might find lower premiums and more choices of benefits in an individual policy. It makes sense to compare; but if your employer is offering a group plan, be sure to act within the initial enrollment period, which might have more flexible underwriting standards, in order to be able to take advantage of the reduced health questions.

THE FEDERAL LONG-TERM CARE INSURANCE PROGRAM

The country's largest employer, the federal government, is setting a good example by offering its own voluntary, long-term care insurance program to employees at a reduced group premium. The federal program, launched in 2002, was widely hailed as an acknowledgment that individuals need to prepare for the possibility that they will require custodial care. The government cannot provide that care for its own employees, much less the average U.S. citizen.

The Federal Long-Term Care Insurance Program (FLTCIP) is underwritten by John Hancock. It is open to current and retired employees of the federal government, the postal service, the military, and their families. For information, go to www.opm.gov to reach the web site of the federal Office of Personnel Management. Then click on Benefits. Or, go to www.ltcfeds.com.

LONG-TERM CARE INSURANCE FROM AFFINITY PROGRAMS

AARP (formerly the American Association of Retired Persons) is one of the largest affinity programs offering long-term care policies at group rates to members and their families. The AARP policy, underwritten by Genworth, is available to all AARP members and their families who qualify.

The AARP long-term care insurance program has several plans. One, called My Choice, is based on an interesting concept. Instead of a daily benefit amount or coverage for a fixed number of years, this policy offers a total pool of assets or cash benefit, as opposed to a reimbursement plan. Coverage can be purchased up to $600,000, with a maximum payout of $6,000 per month. When the need for coverage arises and is certified by a physician, the money can be spent for any purpose, not necessarily medical costs. This approach trusts the individual not to waste the benefits on unnecessary expenses.

The AARP plan offers a variety of optional benefits, depending on your state of residence, and its offerings continue to change. For information, go to www.aarp.org or to www.genworth.com/aarp.

Many other affinity programs also offer long-term care insurance so you can check with your professional association, Chamber of Commerce, American Automobile Association, or other affinity groups to find out whether they have a long-term care insurance program or to encourage them to initiate such a program.

A FINAL ARGUMENT: THE COST OF NOT HAVING LONG-TERM CARE INSURANCE

Long-term care insurance is expensive, but *not* having it can be much more expensive. Figure 17.1 shows the number of days a policy would have to pay benefits for a nursing home stay in order for you to have recovered the premiums you paid on a traditional long-term care policy, assuming no premium increases in the interim. If you buy a policy as a 50-year-old, it would take you only about 12 weeks in a nursing home to recover 10 years of premiums paid. Obviously, if you wait until your sixties, the higher premiums will take longer to recoup; but it still looks like a good deal if you need the services of a nursing home. If you bought at age 60, it would take about four months in a facility or of full-time home care to recoup your 10 years of premiums paid.

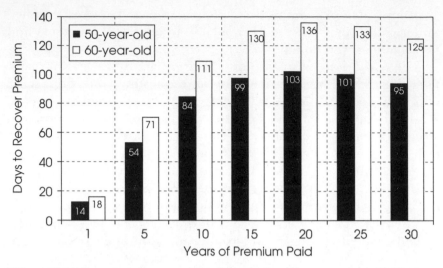

Figure 17.1 Premium Recovery, Traditional Pay (Number of days policy will have to pay benefits to equal premium paid)
Source: Chart created by MAGA Limited based on hypothetical client information. Premiums vary based on benefits, age, health, and state of residence.

Now that you know the facts about long-term care insurance, it's time to make the purchase. If you procrastinate, you're tempting fate and increasing your costs. That's a Savage Truth.

RESOURCES FOR PURCHASING LONG-TERM CARE INSURANCE

To find qualified agents, check the web sites of major insurance company providers, searching under the topic of long-term care insurance. Several of these companies, and state and federal government agencies, have web sites that include long-term care insurance education and planning tools:

- www.longtermcare.gov (federal government)
- www.aaltci.org (The American Association of Long-Term Care Insurance)
- www.researchltc.com
- www.maturemarketinstitute.com (MetLife)
- www.financiallearning.com (Genworth)
- www.gltc.jhancock.com (John Hancock)

To get price quotations, and product comparisons, I am listing my two independent expert agents, whom I trust to give you good advice. (I receive absolutely *no* personal benefit from this, and you may feel free to use my name, or not.)

- www.compareltc.com   (800-999-3026—Claude Thau)
- www.magaltc.com   (800-533-6242—Brian Gordon)

To find independent agents:

- www. www.aaltci.org/findagent
- www.nahu.org.consumer/findagent
- www.ltcconsultants.com
- www.ltc-cltc.com

To learn more about policies regarding long-term care insurance:

- www.centerltc.com (a private institute dedicated to "ensuring quality long-term care for all Americans")

To learn more about the federal government employee long-term care plan, go to:

- www.ltcfeds.com

To make sure that a senior is not being pressured into unwisely transferring assets to qualify for Medicaid, find an elder law specialist in your area through:

- www.elderlawanswers.com

PART 6

ESTATE PLANNING: THE PRICE OF SUCCESS

CHAPTER

18

WHAT'S LEFT?

ongratulations! It looks as though your money will outlive you and you'll have some to pass on to family and friends. That's the result of smart planning. And it's the reason for this last chapter—to make sure those extra assets wind up in the hands of your loved ones, instead of in the government's pocket. If you have used up all your money in your lifetime, you still might want to leave something for your heirs, so this chapter also deals with life insurance.

Estate tax law is uncertain and confusing. Estate tax reductions are scheduled to take effect yearly, but the planned repeal of the estate tax in 2010 might not occur. In 2011, under current legislation, we could be back to the laws of a decade ago. Additionally, states searching for revenues are imposing their own estate taxes. The solution is to base your estate plan on existing law, make it as flexible as possible, and review it with your estate planning attorney at least every two years, or when you see headlines about tax changes.

As of right now, it would be best to die in 2010, because that is the year the estate tax is scheduled to go away! However, under current law, the heirs of those who die in 2010 will lose the "step-up" in cost basis for long-held assets. It will be replaced by a complicated system that will, after a certain threshold is reached, tax gains on assets such as stocks and your home, which previously would have been valued as of the date of your death. For those who didn't keep good records, this new system could be more challenging than the old estate tax.

Even more dramatic, the entire estate tax law will unravel in 2011, when the estate tax is scheduled to return to the original pre-2001 format, with the exemption level moving back down to $1 million and a top rate of 55 percent! You can be sure this scheduled "sunset" to the 2001 estate tax revision will open the door to an entirely new piece of estate tax legislation.

Since you can't predict the date of your death, you need to structure your finances in a way that ensures your wishes will be carried out and that a minimum of taxes will be paid, no matter when you die. Just because you don't have—or don't expect to have—a lot of assets, don't make the mistake of thinking that you don't need to plan. If you expect to leave an "estate" of over $1 million—and remember, that could include your home, retirement plan assets, and even life insurance, unless ownership is structured properly—you'll need to stay in close touch with your financial advisers.

WHAT COULD HAPPEN?

The death of Michael Jackson focused attention on the issue of "estate planning." Yes, he had a fortune in assets—and a matching fortune in debt! Media speculation revolved around the fact that his father was not mentioned in the five-page will that was made public. But it was clear that Jackson had some great estate-planning advice. His short, public will covered only the basics—naming of executors, his wishes for his mother to take custody of his minor children, and the existence of the Jackson Family Trust. And it specifically noted that he declined to provide for his ex-wife, Deborah Rowe, a clause included in an effort to preclude a claim against the estate.

But the will revealed nothing specific about his money. All of Michael Jackson's financial assets and distributions were kept inside that trust—a revocable living trust, which became irrevocable upon his death. And the will left instructions for any assets not owned by the trust to be given to the trust. Inside that trust document were all the instructions about distribution of his wealth.

So it's likely we'll never know whether Jackson's father, or siblings, received *any* money or other assets. The courts upheld his choice of executors of the will. And they were also the likely successor trustees of that financial asset trust. They went right to work, both on defending his assets and on distributing them according to his written wishes, as written in the Jackson Family trust—not the will!

The trust also may have provided some protection against creditors for assets owned by the trust—unless they had previously been pledged against his debt. That will be for the attorneys to sort out, and so some details may come out in open court. But the public will likely never know the specifics of his bequests.

The benefits of good estate planning using a revocable living trust include privacy, swift distribution of assets, and some degree of creditor protection. Good estate planning may also be used to minimize estate taxes—or to provide liquidity so assets don't have to be sold to pay the taxes. It all sounds very complicated, which is why there are estate planning attorneys to advise you on the latest rules and regulations.

Just don't make the mistake of thinking that estate planning is a topic only for the wealthy.

In my speeches, I talk about a young couple who had no children and few assets beyond their home, which was titled in joint name. They named each other as beneficiaries of their retirement accounts at work. They had a small balance in their checking account, and a joint savings account. So they thought they didn't need a will or estate plan.

Sadly, they were in a terrible auto accident. She died at the scene, and he died in a hospital a few weeks later. Since everything was titled jointly, at the woman's death her husband became the heir. When he died, everything went to her mother-in-law. (I'll let you think about that for a moment!)

If there are minor children, the situation becomes even more complicated. Without written direction, the court will be left to make the decision about who should care for them. Think you've solved the problem by leaving life insurance or other assets to them? Think again. Minors cannot be beneficiaries of insurance policies or your other properties. The court will assign a financial guardian, who may take a dim view of summer camp or a car at age 16.

If you're single, depending on state laws, your parents will become your heirs. If they die soon after, your assets will be added to theirs, and much of the money you saved may go in taxes on their estate. Your brothers, sisters, nieces, nephews, and friends could have received that money if you had taken the initiative to leave written directions.

If you're living with someone but are not married, the complications can be a nightmare. You may have told everyone that your friend or partner should receive all your personal effects, but the law says otherwise. If you care, you should plan. Make it official, and make it legal.

You need to create an estate plan.

WHAT IS YOUR ESTATE?

Your estate is everything you own. It's your share of your family home, if it's owned in joint name. It's your retirement plan at work. It's your car, your sports equipment, your clothing, and your jewelry. It's also your life insurance, if you are listed as the owner, even though someone else is the beneficiary.

When you add it all up, your estate might be larger than you think. Whether you've left your assets in joint tenancy or made someone the beneficiary of your IRA or 401(k), it's still your estate, and you have to deal with it while you're alive and well.

This is not a do-it-yourself project. Even the most basic estate planning requires professional help from someone who knows the laws of your state. Even so, there are a few estate planning issues you will have to address on your own before you meet with your attorney. You will want to think carefully about the important choices you'll have to make—how your assets will be distributed and whom you will entrust with that responsibility.

It's tempting to close the book right here, without taking action. But if you don't take steps to organize your estate properly, it will be laid out in full view in probate court, subject to delays and expenses, before it gets to your intended heirs. In fact, before it is given to the people you care about, it could even be subject to estate taxes.

WHAT ARE ESTATE TAXES?

You may think that estate taxes are something rich people pay at death; but when you add up your house, retirement fund, and other assets, you might very well fall into that category. The federal estate

Table 18.1   Federal Exemptions and Maximum Tax Rates

Year	Estate Tax Exemption	Highest Rate
2005	$1.5 million	47%
2006	$2.0 million	46%
2007	$2.0 million	45%
2008	$2.0 million	45%
2009	$3.5 million	45%
2010	N/A (taxes eliminated, replaced by complicated asset-appreciation taxes	0%
2011	$1.0 million	55%

tax kicks in after the *exemption level*, which includes the value of your estate at death, plus all the gifts you've made above the allowable $13,000 annual exclusion per person per year. (See Table 18.1.) In case you don't remember, estate tax rates were substantially higher in previous years, and are scheduled to revert to the highest previous rate (55 percent) and lowest exemption ($1 million) in 2011— absent any action from Congress. (Note: Table 18.1 does not include state death taxes, which can add substantially to the total.)

You may remember the old truism that there are two things you can't escape: death and taxes. But there may be some ways you can avoid estate taxes through careful planning. This is where the use of trusts, including "generation-skipping" trusts, and charitable gifting may come into play. In addition, the use of life insurance (discussed later in this chapter) can mitigate the bite of estate taxes.

As long as there is an estate tax, there will be a need for attorneys who specialize in allowing you, and your heirs, to keep as much of your hard-earned wealth as possible. But you can't leave estate planning to chance, and you *must* keep updating your plans as the laws change.

WHAT IS PROBATE?

Probate is the very public process by which the court changes title to your assets. Attorneys charge substantial fees for handling the probate of your estate. You can avoid probate by creating a revocable living trust and titling your assets in the trust. Then no judicial proceeding is required to distribute them. Titling assets in joint name, with rights of survivorship, will cause these assets to pass directly to the survivor at your death, without going through probate. But it does not solve the problem of giving power to another person to deal with the assets in case you are incapacitated. That's another advantage of a revocable living trust.

Some assets pass directly to your heirs anyway without going through probate or distribution from your revocable living trust. Those assets, such as retirement plans and life insurance policies, have specifically named beneficiaries. As you'll see in this chapter, choosing the appropriate beneficiary is very important.

It's also very important to give serious thought to the person you will name to be the executor of your will, and "successor trustee" of the revocable living trust you will create, as described next. You will invest these people with the power to carry out your wishes, hopefully many years from now. While it's tempting to name the attorney who is guiding you through the estate planning process, you should consider whether he/she will be in a position to handle this matter in the future. Similarly, you may automatically consider a surviving spouse, but think carefully about whether she could overcome the grief of loss to handle this task. The choice may be to name co-executors, or co-trustees—though that could lead to conflicts.

Of course, you can always change your will—and the names of your executor(s) or trustee(s) at a later date. But this is a costly process, and one you're not likely to revisit for a while. So think as carefully about the people you entrust as you do about the future distribution of your assets.

WHAT IS A REVOCABLE LIVING TRUST?

A *revocable living trust* is a trust that you create while you are alive. You are the trustee, or you and your spouse can be co-trustees. You retitle all of your major assets—your house, investment accounts, and other properties—in the name of the trust. There is no tax consequence for this action. Your title or mortgage simply reflects that the Smith Family Trust, with John and Mary Smith as co-trustees, owns the house, instead of John and Mary Smith as Joint Tenants. You can buy or sell real property, mutual funds, or stocks in the name of the trust very easily. Any taxes on capital gains or interest are reported on your own tax return.

The revocable living trust is really useful if you become incapacitated or die. Then the successor trustee you named takes over and deals with the trust assets as you instructed. No court approval is required. So if you want your engagement ring to go to your daughter at your death, just put that in your trust instructions along with other assets to be distributed.

Some things you own, such as your car or your everyday checking account, you wouldn't bother to retitle. For these items, you'll need a *pour-over will*, which simply states that all remaining assets you own at the time of your death will pour over into your revocable living trust, to be distributed according to the instructions in the trust. Just remember to retitle the large, important assets into the trust name, or else they'll have to go through the probate court process when you die or if you become incapacitated.

But you're not finished yet. There are three more key documents you should discuss with your estate planner.

HEALTH-CARE POWER OF ATTORNEY

A *health-care power of attorney* names someone to act in matters of health-care treatment in case you are unable to make decisions for yourself. This person will authorize hospital treatment and tests, and will sign waivers for surgery. Given stringent rules about disclosure of health-care records, your health-care power of attorney should specifically release providers from the obligation to keep this information confidential. A copy of this document should be in your physician's files so there is no debate about who has power in these matters.

LIVING WILL

A *living will* is what I call the "pull the plug" document. It states your wishes that treatment not be prolonged in the event that there is no chance of recovery. It's something to talk about with your family. The decision may haunt the person who has to make this call, so give careful consideration to your choice. Give your physician a copy of your living will to put in your medical file. If you've signed an organ donor card, this should also be made known to your family, and a copy should be given to your physician.

DURABLE POWER OF ATTORNEY

A revocable living trust is the preferred way to title assets, so a successor trustee whom you have named can take over in case of your death, or if you are incapacitated. But there is another way to cover the aspect of business and financial management if you are unable to act on your own behalf. A *durable property power of attorney* names someone to act in matters concerning your property, such as paying bills, selling assets, filing tax returns, and making certain elections concerning your retirement plans that may impact taxes *if you cannot act on your own behalf.*

This authority can be made effective immediately or it can be made effective only if you have become incapacitated. You never want to give a blanket power of attorney for business and financial decisions to anyone—whether an attorney, financial adviser, or broker. But this type of power can "spring" into action only when you cannot act for yourself.

This power governs all of your assets that have not been retitled in your revocable living trust, and it may be used in certain instances to avoid the necessity of obtaining court approval should you become incapacitated.

Just remember that a springing business power of attorney does not solve all issues that a revocable living trust would cover. After all, the successor trustee of your living trust is bound to carry out *your* wishes, while the person holding your power of attorney makes decisions based on his own best judgment.

NAMING RETIREMENT PLAN BENEFICIARIES

You can name beneficiaries of your retirement plans just by signing a form with the custodian of your plan. There's no cost if you do it correctly, but it could be very costly if you make a mistake.

Your 401(k) Plan Beneficiary

Back in the days when retirees received a monthly pension check, the decisions were simple. You elected either a lifetime pension or a pension that included the life of your spouse. (Today's pension plans are required to include a spousal distribution unless the non-working spouse signs away his or her rights.) But your pension plan has probably been replaced by a 401(k) plan, and that can create problems.

You'll be asked to name a beneficiary for your 401(k) account. Get legal advice from your estate planner before doing so. Most company 401(k) or nonprofit 403(b) defined contribution plans require an immediate distribution of assets at the death of the plan participant. Since all distributions from these plans are taxed as ordinary income, an immediate distribution can trigger a huge tax bill for the beneficiary. If you had elected to roll over your 401(k) or 403(b) plan into an IRA at a mutual fund company, bank, or brokerage firm while you were still alive, there would be several options for distribution after your death—choices that could allow the assets to continue growing tax deferred, while minimizing the impact of income taxes.

Beginning in 2010, if a nonspouse inherits a company plan (like a 401(k) plan), the plan must allow the nonspouse beneficiary to do a direct transfer (a trustee-to-trustee transfer) to an inherited IRA (*not* his own IRA) or convert the inherited plan funds to an inherited Roth IRA (*not* his own Roth IRA) (which also must be done as a trustee-to-trustee transfer).

If the beneficiary chooses to convert the plan funds to an inherited Roth IRA, the beneficiary would owe income tax on the amount converted (just like anyone else who converts funds to a Roth IRA). Once the funds are transferred either to an inherited IRA or an inherited Roth IRA, the beneficiary is subject to taking required minimum distributions beginning in the year after death. The distributions can be stretched over the beneficiary's lifetime, which is a much better deal than being forced to pay tax on all the funds at once, when inherited from the plan. If the beneficiary converts the plan funds to an inherited Roth IRA, then the mandatory distributions are tax-free to the beneficiary.

Your IRA Beneficiary

If you die without naming a beneficiary for your IRA, you may limit the opportunity to extend the life of your IRA and keep the money growing tax-free for your heirs. The rules state that if the IRA owner dies before the required beginning withdrawal date at age 70½, the money must be paid out by the end of the fifth year following the year of the IRA owner's death (the five-year rule). If the IRA owner dies *after* the required beginning date, then distributions will be calculated over the remaining life expectancy of the IRA owner, had she lived. That's why it's so important to check your various retirement plans to make sure you've named a beneficiary—and that it is the most appropriate beneficiary.

Spousal Beneficiaries. If the IRA beneficiary is a spouse, he has two options that are not available to other beneficiaries: (1) roll over the assets into an IRA in his own name, or (2) leave the assets in the deceased spouse's account. These options can stretch out the tax-deferred growth of the account.

Rolling over the assets allows them to continue to grow. If the surviving spouse is younger, distributions need not begin until she reaches age 70½. And that survivor's beneficiaries can later extend the period of growth of any remaining assets over their own life expectancies, after the death of the surviving spouse. A spousal beneficiary may roll over inherited assets into her own IRA at any time following the death, as long as the deceased spouse's required minimum distribution obligations have been met.

A surviving spouse might elect to leave some or all of the assets in the deceased owner's account if the surviving spouse is under age 59½ and wants to take distributions prior to that age, but avoid the 10 percent federal early withdrawal penalty. Distributions from her own IRA would be subject to the penalty, but distributions from a deceased spouse's IRA would not be penalized.

Leaving assets in the deceased owner's account, however, limits the ability to stretch out the tax-deferred growth.

Nonspouse Individual Beneficiaries. Recent changes in the law now permit an individual other than a surviving spouse, under certain circumstances, to roll over amounts that would otherwise be received from the deceased participant into an inherited IRA.

Unlike a surviving spouse, who may use the joint life expectancies of the surviving spouse and a hypothetical 10-year-younger beneficiary, the nonspouse beneficiary must use her single life expectancy to calculate the minimum required distribution, so the ability to stretch out the tax-deferred growth is not as good as for the surviving spouse. Still, this enables each of the children to control his inherited IRA.

Trusts as Beneficiaries. It's generally unwise to name a trust as beneficiary of your retirement plan because it complicates the distribution process. The recipient trust must be specifically designed to handle the receipt of retirement benefits in order to qualify to distribute payments over the life expectancy of each beneficiary.

However, the trust's beneficiaries can be treated as if they were named individually and not through the trust—if the trust meets several requirements. To meet these requirements, all of the beneficiaries must be individuals. If there are several beneficiaries, they must use the age of the oldest so that postdeath distributions on the inherited IRA can only be stretched over the life of the oldest. If you're going to name a trust as beneficiary, inform your estate planning attorney of that fact, and make sure the trust meets the distribution rules, which are very complicated.

Minor Child as Beneficiary. You may want to name a minor as beneficiary in order to stretch out the future growth of your IRA assets as long as possible. But be sure your estate plan has named a guardian for that child while the child is a minor. The guardian will start taking required distributions for the minor in the year following your death, and those required distributions will be calculated based on the age of the minor. At the age of majority, the assets belong to the child—unless you have set up a restrictive trust to handle future distributions.

Nonaccepting Beneficiary. Some beneficiaries may choose to disclaim, or refuse to accept, the proceeds from a retirement account. That must be done within nine months of the death of the account owner. If a beneficiary disclaims, she is not permitted to name a replacement beneficiary. This decision becomes very complicated and generally requires the advice of an attorney.

WHAT ELSE SHOULD YOU CONSIDER?

There are a few more issues to think about before you meet with your estate planning attorney.

Guardianship of Children

If you're married and have young children, this is the time to sit down with your spouse and consider the possibility that both of you could die in an accident together. Who would raise your children? It's not just a question of choosing one family over the other. You need to ask now, to make sure your brother, or your husband's sister, or either set of parents would take responsibility for your children, whether or not you left enough life insurance to cover the cost.

Bequests to Minor Children

As noted, you can't just leave an inheritance or life insurance benefits outright to a minor child. You will have to set up some sort of trust arrangement to make sure the child receives the benefits, and you will have to decide at what age the principal of the trust is to be given to your child. It could be at age 18, if that's legal in your state, or age 21, or even older. The trust can even be designed for creditor protection and, for very large estates, to take advantage of generation-skipping tax planning opportunities.

You'll wield control from the grave as long as the assets remain in trust, but does that create a more responsible young adult? Should you keep these provisions hidden—or discuss them with your responsible children, so they will understand your wishes, and the reasons for any restrictions? These are discussions to have with your spouse—and with guidance from your attorney.

Trusts for Disabled Adult Children

If you have a child with special needs, it is particularly important to get competent advice on structuring a trust that will allow the money to be used for the child's benefit as he becomes an adult, but does not disqualify him from helpful state and federal programs. It's not a question of gaming the system. Even if you have plenty of money, there are some programs you simply cannot buy into; they are restricted by law to disabled people who qualify for Medicaid. Group homes, which are a good solution for handicapped adults, often fall into this category.

Two types of trusts are appropriate in planning for disabled adult children:

1. The *special needs trust* is sometimes called a 15.1 trust after that section of the Trust and Trustees Act. Money in this type of trust can be used over and above government funding, but not for basic support. Uses could include special clothes, entertainment such as movies or bowling, or other personal needs. A special needs trust must be funded with third-party money. That means it cannot be money that is the property of the child.

2. A *payback special needs trust* is also known as a (d)(4)(A) trust. It can be set up only by parents, grandparents, guardians, or the court. It is for money in the name of the person with the disability, from sources such as earnings, gifts, inheritances, or accident settlements. It can be used to support additional needs above government benefits; but when the disabled person dies, Medicaid is reimbursed out of the balance.

Division of a Business

Many books have been written on this topic because it can be so contentious. One child may have worked in your business; but if it is a major part of the estate, and you don't want your children to be forced into a sale, you'll need to consider replacing the value of the business by purchasing an appropriate amount of life insurance. That's where you'll need real expertise. The situation requires even more advance planning if you have a business partner.

MOVING ASSETS OUT OF YOUR ESTATE

If you've really been successful at accumulating assets and living within your means, you might have enough money left over to worry about getting money out of your estate before it is subject to estate taxes. Even though the exempt limits have risen every year, there is now the likelihood that this trend will be reversed. You'll want to develop an estate plan that can be revised later if necessary. After all, no one informs you of your end date in advance. Estate planning attorneys specialize in coming up with ways to keep your estate from being taxed. That's why you need professional advice. But here are two simple strategies that you can employ on your own.

529 College Savings Plans to Avoid Estate Taxes

These popular plans offered by every state allow money to grow tax-free for college expenses. Many families use them to save as much as they can to meet future college expenses. But 529 plans also have great estate planning applications. As noted earlier, each spouse can give $13,000 per year to any number of people without impacting the combined estate and gift tax. But the 529 plan law allows each parent or grandparent to aggregate five years of that $13,000 annual gift—$65,000 in total—and place the money in a 529 college savings plan for each child or grandchild. If one child or grandchild doesn't use the money, another child can use it for college expenses.

Very wealthy families can get a lot of cash out of their estates without creating an expensive legal trust by using a 529 plan. (Go to www.savingforcollege.com for information on 529 plans and your state plan.) Of course, when grandparents consider transferring large amounts of money before their death, they may worry about needing the cash in the future. If the need arises, they can withdraw the money by paying a 10 percent penalty and ordinary income taxes on any gains, much as early withdrawals on a retirement plan are treated. It's a stiff price to pay, but the money is not completely out of reach; it is, however, out of the estate.

Reverse Mortgage to Fund Life Insurance Outside the Estate

Many people have a lot of their wealth tied up in the family home—a home they don't want to sell. As explained fully in Chapter 14, they can use a reverse mortgage to withdraw equity from the home that reduces the value of their estate as they spend the money, and they can gift some of the cash to their children each year.

They can also use some of the proceeds from the reverse mortgage to fund an irrevocable insurance trust that pays for insurance on their lives. When they die, the trust keeps the life insurance proceeds out of their estate. Their children receive the life insurance proceeds tax-free. The heirs can pay off the reverse mortgage and keep the house. Or they can keep the life insurance proceeds and whatever equity is left after the house is sold and the reverse mortgage is repaid. Either way, the couple will have used the equity in their home to maximize the transfer of assets to their heirs, free from estate taxes.

LIFE INSURANCE AND YOUR ESTATE

Life insurance is a complicated subject, and I'll assume that you met with your insurance agent or financial planner long ago to determine the appropriate amount and type of life insurance. As you get older you may have more—or less—need for life insurance. It's best to plan in advance, while you are younger and insurance costs less, and while you are healthy enough to qualify.

Your original reasons for owning life insurance may disappear as your children mature and your fortune grows. But a growing retirement fortune creates its own new need for life insurance—to liquefy your estate so a family home or closely held business does not need to be sold to pay estate taxes. As the prospect of rising estate taxes on the wealthy becomes a greater probability, it means you might need to re-evaluate how much life insurance you have—and *where the ownership of that life insurance resides.*

What Kind of Life Insurance Do You Need?

Young families are usually best off buying inexpensive term life insurance, which can guarantee a low, level premium for at least 20 years or as long as 30 years. To get price quotations, go online to services like www.accuquote.com. Calculators at the web site will help you determine how much coverage you need. Term life insurance is a commodity business, with fairly standard attributes that allow easy online price comparisons. Simply choose term life that is annually renewable and convertible into a permanent life policy, without providing evidence of insurability.

A young couple typically buys term insurance in their twenties to cover the possibility of loss of income and create funds to pay off a mortgage, or pay for college education. But 30 years later, when that term policy expires, it may be difficult to arrange new insurance to cover estate planning needs. That's why you should always buy term that is convertible into cash value life.

Cash value policies become more complicated. Some policy designs allow you to change the amount of coverage or annual premium, depending on your financial circumstances. Other cash value policies project that by paying larger premiums in the early years, the interest or investment buildup within the policy will cover premiums when you are older. But many of those projections were made when interest rates were at far higher levels. These days, some insurance policy owners are suddenly finding out that, because of years of lower interest rates credited to their policies, they'll owe huge additional annual premiums to keep their insurance in force.

If you have a cash value policy, immediately contact your insurance company for a current projection of cash values, called an *inforce ledger*, to see how long you must keep paying premiums and how large those payments are now projected to be. You don't want to be hit with huge premium increases just when you're planning to retire and might not qualify for a different policy.

Keep Life Insurance Outside Your Estate

In estate planning, the *ownership* of the insurance counts as much as the beneficiary designation. If you purchased—and own—the life insurance policy, then the proceeds are considered part of your estate even though your named beneficiary receives the payout tax-free. That value of your life insurance could increase your estate into the realm of estate taxes.

The answer, in many cases, is to have the insurance policy owned by an *irrevocable life insurance trust*, where it will be considered outside of your estate. Then you can gift money to the trust each year, allowing the independent trustees to use the cash to pay the premiums on the insurance. Remember, you can gift $13,000 a year (and your spouse can gift an additional $13,000) to the trust or to anyone else, outside the combined estate and gift tax calculations. That will allow for the purchase of a sizeable policy, yet keep the ultimate proceeds out of your taxable estate. The one drawback is that you can't personally access any cash that builds inside the policy owned by the trust; so it's important to consult a professional for the appropriate insurance policy design.

If you're not sure who owns your life insurance policy, contact your insurance agent before meeting with your estate planner. You can't just transfer your existing policy into an irrevocable trust. If you die within three years of the transfer, it will be considered part of your estate. But if you don't qualify for a new policy, the transfer might be something you'd rather do now than later. Again, you need professional advice. Just be sure to bring up this topic.

Changing Policies

You may have purchased your life insurance policy years ago. If so, now is the time to check on its current cash value, as well as the ownership and beneficiary. As the owner of the policy, you can change the beneficiary. (That's why I recommend that all divorced spouses who have a court order requiring life insurance to be purchased become the *owner* of the policy on their ex-spouse's life. Then he or she cannot change the beneficiary!) Make sure the beneficiary is appropriately named as part of your new estate plan, and never name a minor child as the beneficiary of a life insurance policy.

It's possible that your existing life insurance policy has not kept pace in design or returns with currently offered policies. But you'll need an independent appraisal to make sure there are better policies available and that you'll still qualify for preferred rates. If you decide to switch, you can move the cash value from one policy into another by doing a *1035 exchange*—a tax-free transfer of funds between policies. There may be a period of one or two years in which the new policy is contestable by the insurance company should you die suddenly. Never switch from an existing policy to a new one without double-checking prices, terms, and tax consequences.

SPOUSES AND ESTATE PLANNING

My favorite form of estate planning is just to leave everything to your spouse. It's the one simple thing in the very complicated estate tax code: *Assets left to a spouse at death are not subject to estate taxes.* That would be a perfect solution—except that when the surviving spouse dies, the entire remaining estate is subject to taxes. And by that time the estate may be large enough to take a big tax hit.

Estate planners have devised some interesting ways to take advantage of the estate tax exemption listed in Table 18.1 earlier in this chapter. They usually create two trusts. One, often known as the credit shelter trust, is funded by an amount equal to the estate tax exemption in the year of death. Since that exemption amount will change over time, planners are careful not to list a specific amount, but only "the amount of the exemption." Now, with the changes in state death taxes, the amount of the exemption may need to be reduced to avoid triggering a state death tax.

If you live in a community property state, more than two trusts may be created, and if you have a very large estate and wish to do generation-skipping tax planning, still more trusts may be created. This is yet another reason to consult an attorney in your state of residence.

The surviving spouse can be a trustee of the credit shelter trust, and he or she can obtain income from it and, if necessary, can dig into the principal of the trust. If the surviving spouse doesn't use those assets, at his or her death they will pass directly to the children or other heirs that were specified when the trust was created. The remaining assets will pass to those heirs free of all estate taxes, regardless of the future value of the credit shelter trust at the time of the surviving spouse's death.

The second trust, set up for the balance of the estate, is typically left to the surviving spouse, who will not be required to pay estate taxes. There is actually no requirement that these assets be placed in trust for the surviving spouse and no tax benefit to doing so. They could easily be given outright. But that would make the assets vulnerable in case a surviving spouse remarries or is a spendthrift. Upon the death of the surviving spouse, the assets left in this second trust will be considered part of the surviving spouse's estate and so may be subject to estate tax at that time if the surviving spouse's estate is large enough.

Spouses should read carefully the restrictions placed on the assets left to them in this second trust, often called the "marital trust." They may be unable to make withdrawals over a certain amount, unable to change investment managers, or unable to change the terms of what happens to the money after the surviving spouse dies. While these provisions may be helpful in second marriages to ensure that children from a first marriage are protected, they can be very limiting. That's why both spouses need to participate in the planning process. Ask a lot of what-if questions along the way, and keep asking until you understand the answers.

CHOOSING AN ESTATE PLANNER

After considering the basic planning issues outlined in this chapter, you are ready to meet with an estate planner. If you've moved to another state since you created your plan, you should have it revised to meet the laws of your new state of residence. You'll need a specialist—an attorney who may be part of a large law firm or a sole practitioner. You can consult your state bar association, but it's usually better to get a personal reference. Sometimes the trust department of a local bank will be willing to give you a list of estate attorneys. Or you can ask business associates or friends. Set up a meeting, and come prepared to ask and to answer questions.

If you don't feel comfortable with a particular attorney, back out and start over with someone else. You're dealing with your most personal issues—not only assets, but also emotional issues that have to do with trusting your spouse, your children, and your attorney—so you want to choose an estate planner whose advice you can trust. Your attorney will help you decide how to carry out your wishes within the law. She will have experience with the future impact of decisions rendered today.

By the way, you might be tempted by estate planning "kits" or do-it-yourself estate planning programs. While that might be fine for a simple health-care power of attorney, it is not recommended for your will, or trust. If you make a mistake, you won't be around to fix it when it is finally discovered! Seek legal counsel from a specialist.

Don't let the expense deter you. Depending on where you live, you'll probably get the basic estate planning documents for about $1,500. But if your situation is complicated, with significant assets and complex distribution plans, you may spend many thousands dollars. Whatever the price, it's worth it, not only in the taxes you'll avoid, but also in peace of mind. It's worth it to create a plan that keeps your family intact and well cared for, while avoiding family fights that mar your legacy.

So, no matter what your age or financial situation, I ask you to start considering these issues now. It pays to plan while you can! And once you've made your plan, tell your family members that it exists. That could open the door for a discussion with your parents about their own plans. They may not know how to broach the subject with you—their adult children—so you can take the first step. You also owe it to your children to let them know that your affairs are in order and to tell them where you have left instructions in the event of your death.

ESTATE PLANNING CHECKLIST

- Find a qualified attorney. Ask your bank trust department, wealthy friends, and the state bar association for referrals.
- Decide who will be your co-trustee or successor trustee for your revocable living trust.
- Decide who will act as guardian for your minor children if you and your spouse die together in an accident.
- Decide who will act for you in the health-care and durable property powers of attorney.
- Decide who will make the decision to enact your living will (pull the plug).
- Contact each IRA, 401(k), or 403(b) plan provider and ask to check the name of the beneficiary you have designated. (Hint: Do this *after* your estate planning session, which might lead you to reconsider who gets what.)
- Evaluate the ownership and the beneficiaries of your life insurance policies. If you have minor children, make sure

you have established the proper trust relationship if they are life insurance beneficiaries.

- Consider carefully the issue of who gets what. Remember, dividing an estate equally might not be "fair," but dividing an estate unequally is asking for discord.

- Make a list of where all important documents can be found, in case of emergency. List the name and phone number of your professional advisers: attorney, physicians, accountant, insurance agent, and financial planner. Give the location of your cemetery deed and funeral instructions. Be sure to include the name and number of the estate planning attorney who has a copy of your Revocable Living Trust. Then leave this basic information—not necessarily the details of your assets or bequests—in a location where your spouse, child, or successor trustee could easily access it if you are incapacitated.

Resources

Terry Savage's Personal Financial Organizer form is available free online. Just print it out and fill in the blanks—everything from your vital statistics to the location of your bank and brokerage accounts, as well as insurance policy numbers and safe deposit box, and more. Then leave it in a safe, accessible place, telling your trusted family member where it could be found in an emergency.

To get the organizer, go to www.TerrySavage.com and fill in the pop-up box, with your name and e-mail address. Then, you'll receive a return e-mail containing the link to the organizer form. Feel free to print out copies for yourself and others. It's only four pages. You'll also be added to my private mailing list, to receive updates on my market and economic commentaries.

To understand more about the emotional consequences of your estate plan, as well as the legal implications, I highly recommend *The Family Fight: Planning to Avoid It*, by Les Kotzer and Barry Fish (Continental Atlantic, 2002), www.familyfight.com.

CONCLUSION

Those are the Savage Numbers. They take you from starting your first job to midlife crisis through the reading of your will. You *can* plan ahead if you refuse to be intimidated by the unknown.

You *can* know with reasonable certainty how much you need to save for the retirement you want and how much you'll need to continue earning in retirement to supplement those savings. You can know with reasonable certainty how to invest your savings—ranging from immediate lifetime annuities to income funds to conservative and aggressive stock funds. And you can know with reasonable certainty how much you can withdraw every year without running out of money in your lifetime.

Notice the words *reasonable certainty.* That's not the kind of absolute certainty you'd need to convict someone of a crime. But it is far better than the guesswork you get from pencil-and-paper calculations or even from the myriad of online calculators at financial services web sites. This reasonable certainty derives from projections that are based on historic data, with the same modeling techniques statisticians and scientists use to do everything from sending a spaceship to Mars to decoding the human genome. The calculations are not always perfect, but they're far better than closing your eyes and making a wish.

These calculations are not disrupted by market crashes or economic crises—if you believe in the future. Extreme and extraordinary events such as a financial collapse cannot be predicted—but the possibility should be incorporated into your planning. Similarly, extraordinary bull markets or valuation bubbles should not be taken as a basis for planning, but recognized as an extreme that must eventually revert to the mean. The pendulum swings in opposite and equal directions. It is the job of financial planning to keep you within the wide middle ground, while protecting you from the extremes.

It's up to us as individuals to face the challenge of planning for our own new world of retirement. If you're a baby boomer, don't be afraid. We in the baby boomer generation have always refused to be intimidated, and we have changed the world to acknowledge our massive presence. We've explored space and expanded medicine. We embraced computer technology and physical fitness as symbols of our dominance. And now we will conquer the challenges of living longer and living well.

If you're in the generation that must live in the wake of boomers, learn the lessons of your parents and grandparents. Start saving sooner. Don't live in fear—and don't fear to live. But take advantage of the time that is ahead of you to make your money work for you, as hard as you work for it.

Boomers should see retirement planning is just one more opportunity to leave our mark on history. But we must *all* take action now. If too many of us fail to plan, our children will carry the tax burden and the social costs of our huge, aging generation. That's not a legacy I want to leave, and I hope you share my views.

Economic growth is the answer to our financial demands. Only a growing economy can provide the jobs, and the opportunities, and the wealth needed to keep our promises to all generations. So we have two responsibilities. The first is to think of our precious, unique free-enterprise system—and consider how our demands on our leaders will impact not only the present, but the future of our economy. The second is a personal responsibility to look around the corner and to take advantage of the simple and inexpensive planning techniques that can help us grow our money and make it last as long as we do.

We can reach the Savage Number. And that's The Savage Truth!

ACKNOWLEDGMENTS

Years of experience have brought me to the point where I could write this book—not only my *own* experiences, but also the generously shared knowledge of true experts in their own fields. In this era of instant access, I urge you to visit their web sites to learn more about their concepts and services.

This book relies heavily on the Monte Carlo analysis tools that Dr. Sam Savage of Stanford University made understandable for me. What a surprise to find we shared not only the same last name but also the same fascination with the possibilities of numbers. I highly recommend his web site (www.drsamsavage.com), which will walk you through the concept. And I hereby predict he will follow Dr. William Sharpe in receiving a Nobel Prize one day for his work in this field.

And speaking of Dr. Sharpe, my sincere thanks to him for allowing my readers a free, one-year trial to FinancialEngines.com, the web site he created to offer Monte Carlo analysis to individual investors through corporate retirement plans. (The free access comes through the special link on the home page of www.TerrySavage .com.) And special thanks to Asma Emneina at Financial Engines, for being so helpful in facilitating the connection.

Communicating the importance of long-term care insurance has become my passion, as I hope to save my girlfriends from being bag ladies in our old age. (And men, too.) Sincere thanks to Murray and Brian Gordon of MAGA Ltd. (www.magaltc.com), who have been my constant guides through the complexity of policy issues—especially when I purchased my own and my parents' policies. (And to Elaine Polisky of MAGA, who organized all the graphics!) Industry expert Claude Thau (www.targetins.com) has for years been more than generous with his perspective, comments, and contacts. I do not hesitate to recommend any of them to help you with your LTC insurance needs, and you may feel free to use my name, or not, because I receive absolutely nothing in return.

When it comes to historical information on the stock market, Ibbotson Associates, now a part of Morningstar.com, is the acknowledged leader, and for years I've called upon Alexa Auerbach there to create (and recreate) graphic market pictures that are worth a thousand words. Also at Morningstar, my appreciation to Paul Kaplan, Eric Jacobson, Scott Burns, and Courtney Dubrow for their help in organizing the wealth of knowledge on Morningstar.com for various parts of this book.

Dallas Salisbury of the Employee Benefit Research Institute (www .ebri.org) was a great source for information gleaned from a decade of surveys about retirement confidence. He continues to provide the best planning tools at the EBRI web site, www.choosetosave.org. Finance professor Moshe Milevsky of York University in Toronto and Anna Rappaport of Mercer Consulting turned mathematical formulas into English for me.

The mutual fund industry is a driving force in investor education, dedicated to providing resources to help baby boomers build a realistic retirement plan. Special thanks go to Steve Norwitz and Heather Mcdonold of T. Rowe Price, John Woerth of Vanguard, and Steve Austin of Fidelity—all of whom where generous with their time and expertise in helping me update this edition.

Peter Gottlieb is always ready with wise stock market investment advice (pgottlieb@nsimc.com). And IRA expert Ed Slott (www .irahelp.com) has been another generous adviser with his vast knowledge of current regulations, tax laws, and strategies for making the best use of your retirement plans.

Over the years, I have continued to rely on advice from experts who always are willing to take my column deadline calls: Jack Fischer of GallagherRetirement and Byron Udell (www.accuquote.com) for life insurance; Michael Hartz (www.kmzr.com) and Janna Dutton (www

.duttonelderlaw.com) in the field of estate planning. As well, attorney Mark Bischoff and financial planner Allan Kaplan (www.newcentury planners.com) have added their expertise to the revised edition.

Jeffrey Oster (jeffrey.oster@raymondjames.com)is a true, honest voice in the world of annuities and I rely on him frequently to answer my questions, and those of my readers—as well as for my own annuity investments. Peter Bell, president of the National Reverse Mortgage Lenders Association (www.reversemortgage.org) has helped me expand my contacts in this growing industry, and I urge you to visit their nonprofit web site if you or your parents are considering tapping your home equity.

Bill Brodsky, chairman and CEO of the Chicago Board Options Exchange (www.cboe.com), and Mark Wolfinger, author of several books on the subject, brought my early experiences as a floor trader on the CBOE into focus for current options opportunities.

Over the past few years, technology has given individuals incredible new powers to control their financial destiny. Special thanks to Chris Repetto of Intuit, parent company of Quicken, who has been my contact and support there for many years, as well as Chelsea Marti, who helped with the updated information for this edition. Judy Wicks at Checkfree became a friend as well as expert adviser on the subject of online bill payments.

I thank the readers of my *Chicago Sun-Times* personal finance column (and Creators Syndicate) as well as theStreet.com, and Moneyshow.com for their thought-provoking questions, which have frequently turned into column ideas and fodder for this book. And I thank my former *Sun-Times* editor, Dan Miller, and current editor, Polly Smith, as well as Howard Gold at Moneyshow.com for making sure those columns are tightly focused.

My colleagues at the Chicago Mercantile Exchange (where I was once a trader and am now a member of the board of directors) have ensured that I am focused on the futures. Special appreciation to Leo Melamed.

My thanks to the editorial staff at John Wiley & Sons, and especially for the support of Adrianna Johnson in creating this extensively revised edition, who got far more than she bargained for when she took the job. Joan O'Neil has been both patient and generous, as well as persistent—for which I am so grateful.

I now know why every author thanks family and friends. It's supposed to make up for the time and attention given to the manuscript and research. They accept without question the fact that they'll hear the click of the keyboard while they try to stay in touch by phone!

I have always understood the value of long-term investing, but only more recently have I learned the importance of long-term friends, especially Harry. I point with special pride, once again, to my son, Rex Savage, whose financial expertise is acknowledged by his peers and who is my greatest source of satisfaction. And I am beyond grateful that I am blessed to have both my mother and father here to read this new edition.

A final note: Because tax laws and financial products are constantly changing, I invite you to visit my web site, www.TerrySavage .com, where you can read my latest columns, post questions on my blog, and where I make every effort to answer e-mails sent to terry@ TerrySavage.com.

INDEX